CCNA Routing and Switching

Matthew J. Rees

Jeffrey T. C.

D1445011

CORIOLIS

CCNA Routing and Switching Exam Cram

Limits Of Liability And Disclaimer Of Warranty

Trademarks

The Coriolis Group, LLC
14455 N. Hayden Road, Suite 220
Scottsdale, Arizona 85260

480/483-0192
FAX 480/483-0193
http://www.coriolis.com

Library of Congress Cataloging-in-Publication Data
Coe, Jeffrey.
    CCNA routing and switching exam cram / by Jeffrey Coe and Matt Rees.
        p.   cm.
    Includes index.
    ISBN 1-57610-434-6
    1. Electronic data processing personnel--Certification.   2.Telecommunications--Switching systems--Examination Study guides.   I. Rees, Matt.   II. Title.
QA76.3.C64   1999
004.6'6--dc21
                                                    99-26452
                                                    CIP

Printed in the United States of America
10 9 8 7 6 5 4 3 2 1

Publisher
Keith Weiskamp

Acquisitions Editor
Shari Jo Hehr

Marketing Specialist
Cynthia Caldwell

Project Editor
Dan Young

Technical Reviewer
Jerry Anderson

Production Coordinator
Meg E. Turecek

Cover Design
Jody Winkler
Jesse Dunn

Layout Design
April Nielsen

Coriolis: The Training And Certification Destination™

Thank you for purchasing one of our innovative certification study guides, just one of the many members of the Coriolis family of certification products.

Certification Insider Press™ has long believed that achieving your IT certification is more of a road trip than anything else. This is why most of our readers consider us their *Training And Certification Destination*. By providing a one-stop shop for the most innovative and unique training materials, our readers know we are the first place to look when it comes to achieving their certification. As one reader put it, "I plan on using your books for all of the exams I take."

To help you reach your goals, we've listened to others like you, and we've designed our entire product line around you and the way you like to study, learn, and master challenging subjects. Our approach is *The Smartest Way To Get Certified*™.

In addition to our highly popular *Exam Cram* and *Exam Prep* guides, we have a number of new products. We recently launched Exam Cram Live!, two-day seminars based on *Exam Cram* material. We've also developed a new series of books and study aides—*Practice Tests Exam Crams* and *Exam Cram Flash Cards*—designed to make your studying fun as well as productive.

Our commitment to being the *Training And Certification Destination* does not stop there. We just introduced *Exam Cram Insider*, a biweekly newsletter containing the latest in certification news, study tips, and announcements from Certification Insider Press. (To subscribe, send an email to **eci@coriolis.com** and type "subscribe insider" in the body of the email.) We also recently announced the launch of the Certified Crammer Society and the Coriolis Help Center—two new additions to the Certification Insider Press family.

We'd like to hear from you. Help us continue to provide the very best certification study materials possible. Write us or email us at **cipq@coriolis.com** and let us know how our books have helped you study, or tell us about new features that you'd like us to add. If you send us a story about how we've helped you, and we use it in one of our books, we'll send you an official Coriolis shirt for your efforts.

Good luck with your certification exam and your career. Thank you for allowing us to help you achieve your goals.

Keith Weiskamp
Keith Weiskamp
Publisher, Certification Insider Press

This book is dedicated to my family, Christine, and Luke. You are the most special people in the world.
—Matthew J. Rees

This book is dedicated to Brenda, Daniel, Jackee, Jessica, my family and friends. I will always remember your love and support for me.
—Jeffrey T. Coe

About The Authors

Matthew J. Rees is a consultant with the Forté Consulting Group L.L.C. in Tempe, Arizona. He has worked in a diverse set of technical environments ranging from software development and testing to Wide Area Network design and implementation. Matthew has expertise in network planning, international network design, internetworking technologies, year 2000 network requirements, voice and data network integration, network modeling, campus design, and local and wide area network installation and testing. He has worked with a diverse set of Fortune 100 clients; however, Matthew's primary clientele has been telecommunications companies. Matthew currently holds a Cisco Certified Networking Associate (CCNA) certification. He is also pursuing other Cisco internetworking certifications.

Jeffrey T. Coe is an internetworking consultant with the Forté Consulting Group L.L.C. in Tempe, Arizona. He has over ten years of experience in various information technologies including applications development and support, database and distributed systems architecture design, and enterprise-wide application security. His internetwork experience includes designing and implementing computer networks for Fortune 500 companies using network protocols such as Frame-Relay, SMDS, IP, IPX, STUN, and SNA. In addition, Jeffrey has designed and implemented fault tolerant LAN architectures for call centers, Web complexes, and third-party connectivity. Jeffrey currently holds a Cisco Certified Networking Associate (CCNA) certification. He is also pursuing other Cisco internetworking certifications.

Acknowledgments

To begin, I would like to thank Jeff Kellum for presenting me with the opportunity to write this book. This book could not have been possible without the fantastic forum for obtaining knowledge created by the Forté Consulting Group. For everyone at Forté, thanks for your consistent perseverance to achieve excellence. I have grown and gained tremendous personal and technical benefits from having you as colleagues and friends.

This book would have never of reached fruition without the commitment to closing the contract demonstrated by Shari Jo Hehr of The Coriolis Group. We will all benefit from your efforts. To the maestro of this book, Dan Young, thanks for hounding me to write, write, and write some more. Your professionalism during the entire process did not go unnoticed. Also, thank you to Keith Weiskamp for publishing this book, and many thanks to the rest of the team for their excellent work, including Production Coordinator, Meg Turecek; Marketing Specialist, Cynthia Caldwell; Cover Designers, Jody Winkler and Jesse Dunn; and the Layout Designer, April Nielsen. All of your work should be commended. Special accolades go to Jerry Anderson (of Sprint Paranet) and Ellen Strader for providing relentless technical and editorial advice.

Most importantly, I want to thank my Mom and Dad for always believing in me no matter what walk of life I chose. Words cannot express the confidence you have instilled in me by always being there. To my brother, Dave, I would have always thought that you would have been the first to publish a book. I never owned a Commodore 64 nor a chemistry set, however, it was your love of computers that drew me to this profession. Most of all, though, thanks for never judging me on anything but being a good brother. You're the best, Dave.

Special thanks to my co-author, Jeff Coe, for his tremendous dedication and his technical contributions in helping to write this book.

I could not finish these acknowledgments without identifying those people that sacrificed the most while I was helping to write this book. To my girlfriend, Christine, thank you for being so understanding during this trying experience. Your support and love are the cornerstone of my strength to complete this book. Finally, to my best friend, Luke, thanks for spending time with Geti during my late-nights writing.

—*Matthew J. Rees*

Acknowledgments

This is the only part of the book remaining for me to write. I saved it until last because there were so many people involved in this adventure that I just wanted to savor it a little bit more....

Thanks to the entire team at The Coriolis Group! You've been incredibly professional and patient with me. Thanks Shari Jo Hehr for getting us through the toughest part of the book so that we could start writing. To Dan Young, you've been great! You've pushed and encouraged me to write when I didn't think I could. Your supervision and people skills kept all of us on track – you were truly the cornerstone of this book. Ellen Strader, I'm appreciative of your sharp eye in editing the book. Thanks for catching my late-night typos. Jerry Anderson, thanks for the terrific technical editing. I knew that if I missed anything, you'd be on top of it. The editing and comments were always sharp and crisp! I'm grateful to have worked with such a terrific team including Keith Weiskamp for publishing our book, Meg Turecek for production coordination, Cynthia Caldwell for marketing (I've already been watching **amazon.com.**), Jody Winkler and Jesse Dunn for the cover design, and April Nielsen for the layout design. You may have only been doing your job, but I really appreciate the effort you put into this book! I also need to acknowledge Jeff Kellum for his contribution in shuttling different parts of the book back and forth. We would have been in sad shape without you on our team.

Thanks to everyone at Forté! The environment we have is something special. I continue to learn so much from each of you about networking, teamwork and fun, and about doing the job well. I owe a deep heartfelt thanks to my friends at SSCC and those on the block who patiently waited and prayed for me while I worked on this book. I won't forget how you forced me to take a break when you saw I needed one. It encouraged me tremendously since I knew people were vicariously writing through me.

Thanks Mom, Dad, Pam and Cindy! I'm thankful for your input early in the process and for calling me to make sure everything was okay. To Matt Rees, my co-author, thanks for asking me to be involved in this adventure. I owe you big time for challenging me! Without your initiative, this book would still be just a cool idea!

Finally, I want to acknowledge my wife Brenda, and my kids, Daniel, Jackee, and Jessica. You've really been an inspiration during this entire process. You knew precisely when to let me concentrate and when to distract me. I'll always be grateful for your patience, support, and love—it means the world to me.

—*Jeffrey T. Coe*

Contents At A Glance

Table Of Contents

Introduction

Welcome to *CCNA Routing and Switching Exam Cram*! This book aims to help you get ready to take—and pass—the Cisco Certification Exam 640-407, titled "Cisco Certified Network Associate." This Introduction explains Cisco's certification programs in general and talks about how the *Exam Cram* series can help you prepare for Cisco's certification exams.

Exam Cram books help you understand and appreciate the subjects and materials you need to pass Cisco certification exams. *Exam Cram* books are aimed strictly at test preparation and review. They do not teach you everything you need to know about a topic (such as the ins and outs of configuring ISDN services, or all the nitty-gritty details involved in using routing protocols). Instead, we (the authors) present and dissect the questions and problems we've found that you're likely to encounter on a test. We've worked from Cisco's own training materials, preparation guides, and tests, and from a battery of third-party test preparation tools. Our aim is to bring together as much information as possible about Cisco's certification exams.

Nevertheless, to completely prepare yourself for any Cisco test, we recommend that you begin by taking the self-assessment included in this book immediately following this introduction. This tool will help you evaluate your knowledge base against the requirements for a CCNA under both ideal and real circumstances.

Based on what you learn from that exercise, you might decide to begin your studies with some classroom training or some background reading. On the other hand, you might decide to pick up and read one of the many study guides available from Cisco or third-party vendors on certain topics.

We also strongly recommend that you install, configure, and fool around with the software and hardware that you'll be tested on, because nothing beats hands-on experience and familiarity when it comes to understanding the questions you're likely to encounter on a certification test. Book learning is essential, but hands-on experience is the best teacher of all.

The Cisco Certification Program

It is important that when you start the Cisco Career Certification process, first determine the technological career path you wish to master. Cisco offers wide variety of certifications; however, they are designed to follow two distinct career paths with multiple tracks along each path. In an effort to summarize the material, this book presents each career path and the tests required for proceeding along each path. Cisco Systems Inc. offers a wide variety of training courses that are designed to facilitate the certification process. Of course you have to pay for these training courses. You can find the recommended training courses and a more in-depth analysis of each test on Cisco's Web page at www.cisco.com/warp/customer/10/wwtraining/certprog/index2.html.

Career Path 1: Routing And Switching

The Routing and Switching Career Path is shown in Table 1.

Track 1: Network Support

The Routing and Switching Network Support Certification Career Path is focused for professionals supporting networks with Cisco LAN and WAN routers and switches. This path has three core certifications.

CCNA - Cisco Certified Network Associate (CCNA Exam 640-407)

The skills expected of a CCNA are the ability to install, configure, and operate simple-routed LAN, routed WAN, and switched LAN networks.

CCNP - Cisco Certified Network Professional

The skills expected of a CCNP are the ability to install, configure, operate, and troubleshoot complex routed LAN, routed WAN, switched LAN networks, and Dial Access Services. Two different test options are available for achieving the CCNP.

Test Option 1:

➤ CCNA Certification (CCNA Exam 640-407)

➤ Foundation R/S Exam (Exam 640-409)

➤ Cisco Internetworking Troubleshooting (CIT Exam 640-406)

Test Option 2:

➤ CCNA Certification (CCNA Exam 640-407)

Table 1   Cisco CCNA, CCNP, And CCIE Requirements*

CCNA

Only 1 Exam Required	
Exam 640-407	CCNA (Cisco Certified Network Associate)

CCNP

All 5 of these are required	
Exam 640-407	CCNA (Cisco Certified Network Associate)
Exam 640-403	ACRC 11.3 (Advanced Cisco Router Configuration)
Exam 640-404	CLSC (Cisco LAN Switch Configuration)
Exam 640-405	CMTD (Configuring, Monitoring, and Troubleshooting Dial-up Services)
Exam 640-406	CIT (Cisco Internetwork Troubleshooting)

CCIE

1 Written Exam and 1 Lab Exam Required	
Exam 350-001	CCIE Routing and Switching Qualification
Lab Exam	CCIE Routing and Switching Laboratory

* This is not a complete listing. We have included only those tests needed for the Routing and Switching track.

➤   Advanced Cisco Router Configuration (ACRC Exam 640-403)

➤   Cisco LAN Switch Configuration (CLSC Exam 640-404)

➤   Configuring, Monitoring, and Troubleshooting Dialup Services (CMTD Exam 640-405)

➤   Cisco Internetworking Troubleshooting (CIT Exam 640-406)

The only difference between test option 1 and 2 is the second set of tests required for test option 2. These tests are designed to cover the same material as the Foundation R/S Exam in test option 1, but they are broken up to reduce the test time and make the certification process more manageable.

In addition, Cisco offers specialization exams for people who have achieved the CCNP certification. These tests are designed for professionals to demonstrate superior knowledge in specific technical disciplines. These tests include the following specialization:

Security Specialization:

➤   Managing Cisco Network Security (MCNS Exam 640-442)

➤   Network Management Specialization

➤ Managing Cisco Routed Internetworks (MCRI Exam 640-443)

➤ Managing Switched Internetworks (MCSI Exam 640-444)

LAN ATM:

➤ Cisco Campus ATM Solutions (CATM 640-446)

Voice Access:

➤ Cisco Voice (CVOICE Exam 640-447)

SNA Solutions:

➤ SNA Configuration for Multiprotocol Administrators (SNAM Exam 640-445)

➤ Cisco Data Link Switching Plus (DLSWP Exam 640-450)

CCIE - Routing And Switching

The CCIE is the pinnacle of career certifications in the Cisco certification process. The skills expected of a CCIE are the ability to install, configure, operate, and troubleshoot complex routed LAN, routed WAN, switched LAN and ATM LANE network, and Dial Access Services. Also, you are expected to diagnose and resolve network faults, use packet/frame analysis and Cisco debugging tools document and report the problem-solving processes used. The CCIE is split up into a written test and a grueling laboratory test:

➤ Routing and Switching CCIE Written Exam

➤ Routing and Switching CCIE Lab Test

For more information on the CCIE Routing and Switching certification please visit Cisco's CCIE Routing and Switching Web page at **www.cisco.com/warp/customer/10/wwtraining/certprog/lan/programs/ccie.html**.

Career Path 2: Network Design

The Routing and Switching Network Design Certification Career Path is focused for professionals who want to design Cisco-based networks that predominantly include routed LAN, routed WAN, and switched LAN networks. This career path has two core certifications.

CCDA - Cisco Certified Design Associate

The skills expected of a CCDA are the ability to design simple routed LAN, routed WAN, and switched LAN networks. The test required to achieve the CCDA certification is as follows:

➤ Design Cisco Networks Exam 640-441

CCDP - Cisco Certified Design Professional

The skills expected of a CCDP are to design complex routed LAN, routed WAN, and switched LAN networks. The test assumes prerequisite knowledge and skills to install, configure, and operate these networks. Two different test options are available for achieving the CCDP:

➤ CCDP - Cisco Certified Design Professional.

Test Option 1:

➤ CCNA Certification (CCNA Exam 640-407)

➤ CCDA Certification (CCDA Exam 640-441)

➤ Foundation R/S Exam (Exam 640-409)

➤ Cisco Internetworking Design (CIT Exam 640-425)

Test Option 2:

➤ CCNA Certification (CCNA Exam 640-407)

➤ CCDA Certification (CCDA Exam 640-441)

➤ Advanced Cisco Router Configuration (ACRC Exam 640-403)

➤ Cisco LAN Switch Configuration (CLSC Exam 640-404)

➤ Configuring, Monitoring, and Troubleshooting Dialup Services (CMTD Exam 640-405)

➤ Cisco Internetworking Design (CIT Exam 640-425)

The only difference between test option 1 and 2 is the third set of tests required for test option 2. These tests are designed to cover the same material as the Foundation R/S Exam in test option, 1 but they are broken up to reduce the test time and make the certification process more digestible.

Career Path 3: WAN Switching Network Design And Support

The WAN Switching Network Design and Support Career Path is designed for professionals who focus on WAN switching, such as ISPs and carriers. Two tracks are available in the WAN Switching Network Design and Support Career Path.

Track 1: Network Support

The Routing and Switching Network Support Certification Career Path is focused for professionals who configure, operate, troubleshoot, and manage

WAN switched networks. The exams are designed to test required skills in the following areas:

➤ Media and telephony transmission techniques, error detection, and Time Division Multiplexing (TDM).

➤ Knowledge of frame relay and ATM.

➤ Knowledge of Cisco-specific technologies, including WAN switch platforms, applications, architectures, and interfaces.

➤ Knowledge of service provider technology, including packet encapsulation and network-to-network interconnections.

CCNA (WAN Switching)
The skills expected of a CCNA (WAN switching) are the ability to install WAN switches: IPX, IGX, BPX, AXIS, Shelf, and modems. The test required to achieve the CCNA-WAN switching certification is:

➤ (CCNA WAN Exam 640-10)

CCNP - Cisco Certified Network Professional (WAN Switching)
The skills expected of a CCNP (WAN switching) are the ability to configure, operate, troubleshoot, and manage WAN switched networks. Three different test tracks are available for achieving the CCNP (WAN switching).

Test Track 1:

➤ CCNA-WAN Switching Certification (CCNA Exam 640-410)

➤ BPX Switch and Service Configuration (BSSC Exam 640-425)

➤ MGX ATM Concentrator Configuration (MACC Exam 640-411)

➤ Multiband Switch and Service Configuration (MSSC Exam 640-419)

➤ Cisco StrataView Plus (CSVP Exam 640-422)

Test Track 2:

➤ CCNA-WAN Switching Certification (CCNA Exam 640-410)

➤ Cisco WAN Switch Service Networking (CWSSN Exam 640-424)

➤ Cisco WAN Switch Configuration (CWSC Exam640-423)

➤ Cisco StrataView Plus (CSVP Exam 640-422)

Test Track 3:

➤ CCNA-WAN Switching Certification (CCNA Exam 640-410)

➤ Network Operations for BPX/AXIS Products (BNOC Exam 640-414)

➤ Network Operations for IGX Products (NNOC Exam 640-415)

➤ Cisco StrataView Plus (CSVP Exam 640-422)

Track 2: Network Design

The skills expected of the Network Design track are the ability to design and implement ATM and frame networks, troubleshoot existing WAN switched networks, and manage traffic and voice technologies.

CCDP - Cisco Certified Design Professional (WAN Switching)

The skills expected of a CCDP (WAN switching) are the ability to design and implement an ATM network (with CBR, ABR, and VBR traffic) and a frame relay network (using CIR and MIR traffic parameters), troubleshoot an existing WAN switched network, and manage traffic and voice technologies. The test required to achieve the CCDP certification is as follows:

➤ Designing Switched WAN Voice Solutions (DSWVS Exam 640-413)

CCIE - WAN Switching

The CCIE is the pinnacle of career certifications in the Cisco certification process. The skills expected of a CCIE are the ability to implement an ATM network (with CBR, ABR, and VBR traffic) and a frame relay network (using CIR and MIR traffic parameters), troubleshoot an existing WAN switched network, and manage traffic and voice technologies. The CCIE is split up into a written test and a grueling laboratory test:

➤ WAN Switching CCIE Written Exam

➤ WAN Switching CCIE Lab Test

For more information on the CCIE WAN switching certification, visit Cisco's CCIE WAN switching Web page at **www.cisco.com/warp/customer/10/ wwtraining/certprog/wan/programs/ccie.html**.

The many different career tracks in the certification process are designed to meet the requirements of a variety of career fields. Most of you will want to proceed down the Routing and Switching Network Support or Network Design career tracks; these are the most mainstream certifications. Those of you who need to proceed down the WAN switching career path will be working in that type of environment. The ultimate goal of any one of these tracks is to achieve the CCIE certification. This is a noble achievement and the marketplace recognizes the value of CCIEs.

Taking A Certification Exam

The CCNA exam can be registered for on Cisco's Web page at **www.cisco.com/ warp/customer/10/wwtraining/certprog/testing/register.html.**

You can also call 1-800-829-NETS, and choose option 3, then 2 to register for the exam. We strongly recommend that you take the time to learn Cisco's Exam Web sites that have been mentioned previously. The cost of the exam is $100 that can be paid by credit card, personal check, or money order.

You will be taking the test at Sylvan Prometric Testing Center at the location you choose. The first thing to do when you arrive at the testing location is to sign in with the test coordinator. You will need to have two forms of identification, one of which needs to be a photo ID. The test coordinator will give you a set of rules for you read and abide by during the test. You will also receive some scratch paper and a pencil or a dry-erase board and marker. The amount of scratch paper required to take the test will vary by each individual, but we recommend that you get as much as possible to be safe. If you are given a dry-erase board, ask for two of them so you don't have to erase previously written material to make extra room for notes or calculations during the test. The test coordinator will then take you to a room with a number of computer stations divided by walls. You will have the option of taking a tutorial on the exam before the time starts for the test. If this is your first Cisco test, we recommend that you review this material.

A Cram Sheet has been provided at the beginning of the text with material that most often appears on the test. If it helps you, write down as much as you can remember on your scratch paper before taking the test. You can use the time provided to take the tutorial to take down these notes. The test will consist of 70 questions and you will be given 90 minutes to complete the exam. Strategies for time management are provided in the next section. Just remember to take a deep breath and have confidence in yourself. If you have spent the time studying the material in this book, you will be well equipped to tackle the test head on.

After you have completed the test, you will be given the results of your test immediately online. After you have received your passing score, you will be prompted to print your results. *Do print your results.* Don't go any further until you have seen a printed copy of your results, because this is your only true verification that you have passed the exam. After you have seen this printout, conclude the exam and see the test coordinator.

CCNA Exam Test Format

The CCNA exam uses the typical certification test format of asking multiple choice questions with either one or more answers per question. What makes some of questions more difficult on the exam is that more than five answer choices are listed on many different questions. This reduces the power of eliminating answers and choosing from the remaining answers. However, the nice part is that the number of required answers is given for each question.

The test consists of 70 questions and requires a 70 percent score to pass, meaning you need to get 49 questions correct to pass. The test questions can be grouped into nine topics, all of which are covered in this book. We have attempted to estimate the number of questions that are taken from each subject area to give you an idea at where to focus the majority of your time. The percentage of questions you get for any topic will most certainly vary. We have developed this list from taking the test and talking with several other people who have passed the exam.

As you can see, the OSI model, router configuration basics, TCP/IP, and WAN protocols make up 65 percent of the test. Make sure you spend extra time learning these concepts. Especially concentrate on the OSI model. Without a thorough understanding of the it, you will have difficulty passing the test. Also, to develop a foundation for obtaining further internetworking skills, you need to master these topics.

Tracking Cisco Certification Status

As soon as you pass any Cisco certification, you'll attain Cisco certification status. Cisco also generates transcripts that indicate which exams you have passed and your corresponding test scores. Cisco will send these transcripts to you. In additional, you will receive a login ID and password that will allow you to track your status on Cisco's Web page.

How To Prepare For An Exam

The CCNA exam requires test-taking skills that many of us learned in high school or college. This section will be a refresher for many and important for all.

The first thing to focus on is time management during the test. The CCNA exam allows 90 minutes to complete the test. This gives you 1 minute and 17 seconds per question. Don't worry about how long it takes you to finish an individual question, but divide the test into three checkpoints to monitor your progress during the test. You should have finished approximately 18 questions after 23 minutes of the test. When you begin the test write down the 23, 46, and 69 minutes on the supplied scratch pad. Next to these time amounts write down 18, 36, and 54 to represent the number of test questions you should have completed by this time. If you reach the first checkpoint and you are following behind, don't panic. However, you need to proceed more quickly through the remainder of the test. A good suggestion to increase your pace is to mark the more difficult questions and come back to them later. Some of questions relating to TCP/IP require calculating numbers and deriving an answer. These are the best questions to mark and come back to at the end of the exam.

If you get to the point that you only have five minutes left in the exam and you have not answered all of the questions, it is now time to just fill in the answers and live with the result. Remember that a wrong answer incurs no penalty, so answer all the questions. No correct way exists for filling in the remaining answers; you can select all answers as "c" or just randomly choose. Your odds of getting a correct answer are the same either way.

Another advantage of marking difficult questions and returning to them at the end is that often the answer for a previously asked question will be in a later question. I have also found that at times when I can't remember an answer that I should know, later my mind is refreshed by another question. So, remember to just mark questions that you cannot answer and come back to them at the end. The test is not designed to test an individual's ability to crank out answers, so most of you will not have a problem completing the exam. However, for those of you that tend to be slower at taking exams, employ some of the strategies just mentioned and your chances of success will increase.

Another very important item to remember is to read every question and answer it carefully. The CCNA exam has many questions that are not designed to be trick questions; however, they require careful examination of the test question's syntax. Many of the questions refer to exact commands required to implement a function on a router. It is important to know the different syntax and to recognize small differences in commands. This book will highlight areas that might be tricky on the exam.

Make sure to read every answer before choosing one. Often one answer might sound great; however, another answer will be more correct than the first. How an answer can be more correct than another is another argument, but just remember to read all the answers before choosing the best one. In addition, saying questions out loud often makes them easier to understand and thus easier to answer.

About This Book

Each topical *Exam Cram* chapter follows a regular structure, along with graphical cues about important or useful information. Here's the structure of a typical chapter:

➤ **Opening Hotlists** Each chapter begins with a list of the terms and techniques that you must learn and understand before you can be fully conversant with that chapter's subject matter. We follow the hotlists with one or two introductory paragraphs to set the stage for the rest of the chapter.

➤ **Topical Coverage** After the opening hotlists, each chapter covers a series of topics related to the chapter's subject title. Throughout this section, we highlight topics or concepts likely to appear on a test using a special Exam Alert layout, like this:

This is what an Exam Alert looks like. Normally, an Exam Alert stresses concepts, terms, software, or activities that are likely to relate to one or more certification test questions. For that reason, we think any information found offset in Exam Alert format is worthy of unusual attentiveness on your part. Indeed, most of the information that appears on the Cram Sheet appears as Exam Alerts within the text.

Pay close attention to material flagged as an Exam Alert; although all the information in this book pertains to what you need to know to pass the exam, we flag certain items that are really important. You'll find what appears in the meat of each chapter to be worth knowing, too, when preparing for the test. Because this book's material is very condensed, we recommend that you use this book along with other resources to achieve the maximum benefit.

In addition to the Exam Alerts, we have provided tips that will help you build a better foundation for CCNA knowledge. Although the information may not be on the exam, it is certainly related and will help you become a better test taker.

This is how tips are formatted. Keep your eyes open for these, and you'll become a networking guru in no time.

➤ **Practice Questions** Although we talk about test questions and topics throughout each chapter, this section presents a series of mock test questions and explanations of both correct and incorrect answers. We also try to point out especially tricky questions by using a special icon, like this:

➤ **Trick Questions** Ordinarily, this icon flags the presence of a particularly devious inquiry, if not an outright trick question. Trick questions are calculated to be answered incorrectly if not read more than once, and carefully, at that. Although they're not ubiquitous, such questions make regular appearances on the Cisco exams. That's why we say exam questions are as much about reading comprehension as they are about knowing your material inside out and backwards.

➤ **Details And Resources** Every chapter ends with a section titled "Need To Know More?" This section provides direct pointers to Cisco and third-party resources offering more details on the chapter's subject. In addition, this section tries to rank or at least rate the quality and thoroughness of the topic's coverage by each resource. If you find a resource you like in this collection, use it, but don't feel compelled to use all the resources. On the other hand, we recommend only resources we use on a regular basis, so none of our recommendations will be a waste of your time or money (but purchasing them all at once probably represents an expense that many network administrators and would-be CCNAs, CCNPs, and CCIEs might find hard to justify).

The bulk of the book follows this chapter structure slavishly, but we'd like to point out a few other elements. Chapter 14 includes a sample test that provides a good review of the material presented throughout the book to ensure you're ready for the exam. Chapter 15 provides an answer key to the sample test that appears in Chapter 14. Additionally, you'll find the glossary, which explains terms, and an index that you can use to track down terms as they appear in the text.

Finally, the tear-out Cram Sheet attached next to the inside front cover of this *Exam Cram* book represents a condensed and compiled collection of facts and tips that we think you should memorize before taking the test. Because you can dump this information out of your head onto a piece of paper before taking the exam, you can master this information by brute force—you need to remember it only long enough to write it down when you walk into the test room. You might even want to look at it in the car or in the lobby of the testing center just before you walk in to take the test.

How To Use This Book

If you're prepping for a first-time test, we've structured the topics in this book to build on one another. Therefore, some topics in later chapters make more sense after you've read earlier chapters. That's why we suggest you read this book from front to back for your initial test preparation. If you need to brush up on a topic or you have to bone up for a second try, use the index or table of contents to go straight to the topics and questions that you need to study. Beyond helping you prepare for the test, we think you'll find this book useful as a tightly focused reference to some of the most important aspects of routing and switching.

Given all the book's elements and its specialized focus, we've tried to create a tool that will help you prepare for—and pass—Cisco Exam 640-407, "Cisco Certified Network Associate". Please share your feedback on the book with us, especially if you have ideas about how we can improve it for future test takers. We'll consider everything you say carefully, and we'll respond to all suggestions.

Send your questions or comments to us at **cipq@coriolis.com**. Please remember to include the title of the book in your message; otherwise, we'll be forced to guess which book you're writing about. And we don't like to guess—we want to *know*! Also, be sure to check out the Web page at **www.certificationinsider.com**, where you'll find information updates, commentary, and certification information.

Thanks, and enjoy the book!

Self-Assessment

The self-assessment in this *Exam Cram* book will help you evaluate your readiness to tackle Cisco Certified Network Associate (CCNA) certification. It should also help you understand what you need know to master the topic of this book—namely CCNA Exam 640-407. But before you tackle this assessment, let's talk about the IT networking profession and understand the opportunity Cisco certifications can create for you.

IT Networking Opportunities

The demand for experienced and skilled IT networking professionals is forecast to grow tremendously over the next decade. In addition, the supply of skilled IT networking professionals does not meet the current demand, thus requiring IT organizations to pay a premium for these skills. The demand for IT networking professionals at all levels is increasing, and it's creating an opportunity for both the novice and the expert to increase their personal net worth to corporate America.

The beauty of IT networking is that it is in an industry that builds upon a core set of technical skills into a wide variety of diverse and highly challenging technical focuses. The mastery of the foundation IT networking skills enables an individual to learn more complex subjects at a more rapid pace. Many professionals attempt or are forced to learn the more complex subjects of IT networking before they truly understand the basic networking skills. These people often become frustrated and their ability to learn new skills is drastically reduced, because they never took the time to master the foundation skills.

The CCNA exam is an excellent starting point or checkpoint for determining if you have mastered the basic skills in IT networking. We cannot emphasize enough the advantages you will realize by mastering these skills before attempting to understand the more complex subjects of IT networking.

Mastering the basic skills before attempting to understand the more difficult technologies is critical to your success. Now for the good news: The CCNA exam is designed for IT networking professionals of all levels. It tests the basic foundations skills required to be successful in the profession.

If you are a novice IT networking professional, this book is focused on assisting you to obtain possibly your first IT certification. If you are an experienced IT professional, this book gives you the opportunity to go back and master the basic skills and substantially increase your ability to learn more complex technologies quickly.

Choosing Cisco Systems Inc. Career Certifications as a starting point for your career certification process is the right step. Cisco Systems Inc. currently owns 80 percent of the internetworking arena. Cisco is the dominant player in corporate network infrastructures and the Internet. Individuals that have Cisco Certifications find jobs, period.

CCNAs In The Real World

In the next section, we describe an ideal CCNA candidate, knowing full well that only a few real candidates will meet this ideal. In fact, our description of that ideal candidate might seem downright scary. But take heart: Although the requirements to obtain CCNA certification may seem pretty formidable, they are by no means impossible to meet. However, you should be keenly aware that it does take time, requires some expense, and consumes substantial effort to get through the process.

You can get all the real-world motivation you need from knowing that many others have gone before, so you will be able to follow in their footsteps. If you're willing to tackle the process seriously and do what it takes to obtain the necessary experience and knowledge, you can take—and pass—all the certification tests involved in obtaining an CCNA. In fact, we've designed this *Exam Cram* to make it as easy on you as possible to prepare for these exams. But prepare you must!

The Ideal CCNA Candidate

Just to give you some idea of what an ideal CCNA candidate is like, here are some relevant statistics about the background and experience such an individual might have. Don't worry if you don't meet these qualifications, or don't come that close—this is a far from ideal world, and where you fall short is simply where you'll have more work to do.

➤ Academic or professional training in network theory, concepts, and operations.

➤ Two-plus years of professional networking experience in a LAN environment, including experience with Ethernet, token ring, modems, switches, and other networking media. This must include installation, configuration, upgrade, and troubleshooting experience.

➤ Two-plus years in a WAN environment that includes hands-on experience with frame relay, HDLC, or ISDN architecture, installation, configuration, maintenance, and troubleshooting is also essential.

➤ A thorough understanding of key networking protocols, routing protocols, and addressing, including TCP/IP, IPX/SPX, RIP, and IGRP.

Fundamentally, this boils down to a bachelor's degree in computer science, plus three years of work experience in a technical position involving network design, installation, configuration, and maintenance. We believe that well under half of all certification candidates meet these requirements, and that, in fact, most meet less than half of these requirements—at least, when they begin the certification process. But because all who already have been certified have survived this ordeal, you can survive it too—especially if you heed what our self-assessment can tell you about what you already know and what you need to learn.

Put Yourself To The Test

The following series of questions and observations is designed to help you figure out how much work you must do to pursue CCNA certification and what kinds of resources you can consult on your quest. Be absolutely honest in your answers, or you'll end up wasting money on exams you're not yet ready to take. You'll not find right or wrong answers, only steps along the path to certification. Only you can decide where you really belong in the broad spectrum of aspiring candidates.

Two things should be clear from the outset, however:

➤ Even a modest background in computer science will be helpful.

➤ Hands-on experience with Cisco products and technologies is an essential ingredient to certification success.

Educational Background

1. Have you ever taken any computer-related classes? [Yes or No]

    ➤ If Yes, proceed to Question 2.

    ➤ If No, proceed to Question 3.

2. Have you taken any networking concepts or technologies classes? [Yes or No]

    ➤ If Yes, you will probably be able to handle networking terminology, concepts, and technologies. If you're rusty, brush up on basic networking concepts and terminology, especially the OSI model, TCP/IP, IPX/SPX, and networking technologies such as Ethernet, token ring, FDDI, and WAN links.

➤ If No, you might want to read one or two books in this topic area. The two best books that we know of are *Computer Networks, 3rd Edition*, by Andrew S. Tanenbaum (Prentice-Hall, 1996, ISBN 0-13-349945-6) and *Computer Networks and Internets*, by Douglas E. Comer (Prentice-Hall, 1997, ISBN 0-13-239070-1).

➤ Skip to the next section, "Hands-On Experience."

3. Have you done any reading on networks? [Yes or No]

➤ If Yes, review the requirements stated in the first paragraphs after Question 2. If you meet those requirements, move on to the next section, "Hands-On Experience."

➤ If No, consult the recommended reading. A strong background will help you prepare for the CCNA exam better than just about anything else.

Hands-On Experience

The most important key to success on all of the Cisco tests is hands-on experience, especially with Cisco routers. If we leave you with only one realization after taking this self-assessment, it should be that you can't find any substitute for time spent installing, configuring, and using the various Cisco equipment upon which you'll be tested repeatedly and in depth.

4. Have you installed, configured, and worked with Cisco routers? [Yes or No]

➤ If Yes, make sure you understand addressing, TCP/IP, IPX/SPX, and routing protocols. Be sure to study WAN services like frame relay and ISDN.

➤ If you haven't worked with Cisco routers, we recommend that you obtain access to at least two routers, so you can exercise the concepts you will be learning.

5. Have you installed, configured, and worked with Cisco switches? [Yes or No]

➤ If Yes, make sure you understand the concepts and benefits of network segmentation and the types of LAN switching.

➤ If No, you will need to obtain access to a switch.

Before you even think about taking any Cisco exam, make sure you've spent enough time with the related equipment and software to understand how to install, configure, monitor, and troubleshoot it. This will help you during the exam, and in real life.

Testing Your Exam-Readiness

Whether you attend a formal class on a specific topic to get ready for an exam or use written materials to study on your own, some preparation for the CCNA certification exam is essential. At $100 a try, pass or fail, you want to do everything you can to pass on your first try. That's where studying comes in.

For any given subject, consider taking a class if you've tackled self-study materials, taken the test, and failed anyway. The opportunity to interact with an instructor and fellow students can make all the difference in the world, if you can afford that privilege. For information about Cisco classes, visit the Training and Certification page at **www.cisco.com**.

If you can't afford to take a class, visit the Training and Certification page anyway, because it also includes pointers to free practice exams other self-study tools. And even if you can't afford to spend much at all, you should still invest in some low-cost practice exams from commercial vendors, because they can help you assess your readiness to pass a test better than any other tool. All of the following Web sites offer practice exams online:

➤ Beachfront Quizzer at **www.bfq.com/**

➤ CramSession at **www.cramsession.com/**

➤ MeasureUp at **www.measureup.com/**

7. Have you taken a practice exam on your chosen test subject? [Yes or No]

   ➤ If Yes, and you scored 70 percent or better, you're probably ready to tackle the real thing. If your score isn't above that crucial threshold, keep at it until you break that barrier.

   ➤ If No, obtain all the free and low-budget practice tests you can find (see the list above) and get to work. Keep at it until you can break the passing threshold comfortably.

When it comes to assessing your test readiness, no better way exists than to take a good-quality practice exam and pass with a score of 70 percent or better. When we're preparing ourselves, we shoot for 80-plus percent, just to leave room for the "weirdness factor" that sometimes shows up on Cisco exams.

Assessing Readiness For Exam 640-407

In addition to the general exam-readiness information in the previous section, you can do several things to prepare for the CCNA exam. As you're getting ready for Exam 640-407, visit the Cisco Web site at **www.cisco.com**. Its open forum or technical tips sections are great places to ask questions and get good answers, or simply to watch the questions that others ask (along with the answers, of course).

You should also cruise the Web looking for "braindumps" (recollections of test topics and experiences recorded by others) to help you anticipate topics you're likely to encounter on the test.

When using any braindump, it's okay to pay attention to information about questions. But you can't always be sure that a braindump's author will also be able to provide correct answers. Thus, use the questions to guide your studies, but don't rely on the answers in a braindump to lead you to the truth. Double-check everything you find in any braindump.

For OSI model, TCP/IP, and basic router configuration preparation in particular, we'd also like to recommend that you check out one or more of these resources as you prepare to take Exam 640-407:

➤ Chappell, Laura: *Introduction to Cisco Router Configuration*. Cisco Systems Inc., MacMillan Publishing Company, 1998. ISBN 0-76453-186-7.

➤ Douglas Comer: *Internetworking with TCP/IP: Principles, Protocols, and Architecture, Vol. 1*. Prentice Hall, Englewood Cliffs, NJ, 1995. ISBN 0-13216-987-8.

➤ Stallings, William: *Handbook of Computer Communications Standards: The Open Systems Interconnection (OSI Model and OSI-Related Standards) Vol. 1*, Prentice-Hall, 1990. ISBN 0-02415-521-7.

Stop by your favorite bookstore or online bookseller to check out one or more of these resources.

One last note: Hopefully, it makes sense to stress the importance of hands-on experience in the context of the CCNA exam. As you review the material for that exam, you'll realize that hands-on experience with the various router configuration and monitoring commands is invaluable.

Onward, Through The Fog

Once you've assessed your readiness, undertaken the right background studies, obtained the hands-on experience that will help you understand the products and technologies at work, and reviewed the many sources of information to help you prepare for a test, you'll be ready to take a round of practice tests. When your scores come back positive enough to get you through the exam, you're ready to go after the real thing. If you follow our assessment regime, you'll not only know what you need to study, but when you're ready to make a test date. Good luck!

Cisco Career Certification Exams

Terms you'll need to understand:

√ Radio button

√ Checkbox

√ Exhibit

√ Multiple-choice question formats

√ Careful reading

√ Process of elimination

Techniques you'll need to master:

√ Preparing to take a certification exam

√ Practicing (to make perfect)

√ Making the best use of the testing software

√ Budgeting your time

√ Saving the hardest questions until last

√ Guessing (as a last resort)

√ Breathing deeply to calm frustration

Exam taking is not something that most people anticipate eagerly, no matter how well prepared they may be. In most cases, familiarity helps ameliorate test anxiety. In plain English, this means you probably will not be as nervous when you take your fourth or fifth Cisco certification exam as you will be when you take your first one.

Whether it is your first exam or your tenth, understanding the details of exam taking (how much time to spend on questions, the environment you will be in, and so on) and the exam software will help you concentrate on the material, rather than on the setting. Likewise, mastering a few basic exam-taking skills should help you recognize—and perhaps even outfox—some of the tricks and gotchas you are bound to find in some of the exam questions.

This chapter, besides explaining the exam environment and software, describes some proven exam-taking strategies that you should be able to use to your advantage.

The Exam Situation

When you arrive at the exam testing center, you will need to sign in with an exam coordinator who will ask you to show two forms of identification, one of which must be a photo ID. After you have signed in and your time slot arrives, you will be asked to deposit any books, bags, or other items you brought with you. Then, you will be escorted into a closed room. Typically, the room will be furnished with anywhere from one to half a dozen computers, and each workstation will be separated from the others by dividers designed to keep you from seeing what is happening on someone else's computer.

You will be furnished with a pen or pencil and a blank sheet of paper, or, in some cases, an erasable plastic sheet and an erasable felt-tip pen. You are allowed to write down any information you want on both sides of this sheet. Before the exam, you should memorize as much of the material that appears on The Cram Sheet (inside the front cover of this book) as you can so that you can write that information on the blank sheet as soon as you are seated in front of the computer. You can refer to your rendition of The Cram Sheet anytime you like during the test, but you will have to surrender the sheet when you leave the room.

Most test rooms feature a wall with a large picture window. This permits the exam coordinator standing behind it to monitor the room, to prevent exam takers from talking to one another, and to observe anything out of the ordinary that might go on. The exam coordinator will have preloaded the appropriate Cisco certification exam—for this book, that's Exam 640-407—and you will be permitted to start as soon as you are seated in front of the computer.

All Cisco certification exams allow a certain maximum amount of time in which to complete your work (this time is indicated on the exam by an on-screen counter/clock, so you can check the time remaining whenever you like). Exam 640-407 consists of 70 randomly selected questions. You may take up to 90 minutes to complete the exam with a score of 70 percent to pass.

All Cisco certification exams are computer generated and use a multiple-choice format. From time to time you may be prompted to enter actual configuration commands as if you were at the command line interface. It is important not to abbreviate the commands in any way when this type of question is posed. Although this may sound quite simple, the questions are constructed not only to check your mastery of basic facts and figures about Cisco router configuration, but also to require you to evaluate one or more sets of circumstances or requirements. Often, you will be asked to give more than one answer to a question. Likewise, you might be asked to select the best or most effective solution to a problem from a range of choices, all of which technically are correct. Taking the exam is quite an adventure, and it involves real thinking. This book shows you what to expect and how to deal with the potential problems, puzzles, and predicaments.

Exam Layout And Design

Some exam questions require you to select a single answer, whereas others ask you to select multiple correct answers. The following multiple-choice question requires you to select a single correct answer. Following the question is a brief summary of each potential answer and why it is either right or wrong.

Question 1

> What is the key piece of information on which routing decisions are based?
>
> ○ a. Source network-layer address
>
> ○ b. Destination network-layer address
>
> ○ c. Source MAC address
>
> ○ d. Destination MAC address

Answer b is correct. The destination network-layer, or layer 3, address is the protocol-specific address to which this piece of data is to be delivered. The source network-layer address is the originating host and plays no role in getting the information to the destination. Therefore, answer a is incorrect. The source and destination MAC addresses are necessary for getting the data to the router or to the next hop address. However, they are not used in pathing decisions. Therefore, answers c and d are incorrect.

This sample question format corresponds closely to the Cisco certification exam format—the only difference on the exam is that answer keys do not follow questions. To select an answer, position the cursor over the radio button next to the answer. Then, click the mouse button to select the answer.

Let's examine a question that requires choosing multiple answers. This type of question provides checkboxes rather than radio buttons for marking all appropriate selections.

Question 2

Which of the following services exist at the application layer of the TCP/IP model? [Choose the three best answers]

❑ a. SMTP

❑ b. FTP

❑ c. ICMP

❑ d. ARP

❑ e. TFTP

Answers a, b, and e are correct. SMTP, FTP, and TFTP all exist at the application layer of the TCP/IP model. Answer c is incorrect because ICMP exists at the Internet layer of the TCP/IP model. Answer d is incorrect because ARP exists at the network interface layer of the TCP/IP model.

For this type of question, more than one answer is required. As far as the authors can tell, such questions are scored as wrong unless all the required selections are chosen. In other words, a partially correct answer does not result in partial credit when the test is scored. For Question 2, you have to check the boxes next to items a, b, and e to obtain credit for a correct answer. Notice that picking the right answers also means knowing why the other answers are wrong!

These two basic types of questions can appear in many forms, they constitute the foundation on which all the Cisco certification exam questions rest. More complex questions include so-called *exhibits*, which are usually network scenarios, screen shots of output from the router, or even pictures from the course materials. For some of these questions, you will be asked to make a selection by clicking on a checkbox or radio button on the screenshot itself. For others, you will be expected to use the information displayed therein to guide your answer to the question. Familiarity with the underlying utility is your key to choosing the correct answer(s).

Other questions involving exhibits use charts or network diagrams to help document a workplace scenario that you will be asked to troubleshoot or configure. Careful attention to such exhibits is the key to success. Be prepared to toggle frequently between the exhibit and the question as you work.

Using Cisco's Exam Software Effectively

A well known principle when taking exams is to first read over the entire exam from start to finish while answering only those questions you feel absolutely sure of. On subsequent passes, you can dive into more complex questions more deeply, knowing how many such questions you have left.

Fortunately, Cisco exam software makes this approach easy to implement. At the top-left corner of each question is a checkbox that permits you to mark that question for a later visit.

Marking questions makes review easier, but you can return to any question if you are willing to click on the Forward or Back button repeatedly.

As you read each question, if you answer only those you are sure of and mark for review those that you are not sure of, you can keep working through a decreasing list of questions as you answer the trickier ones in order.

You will find at least one potential benefit to reading the exam over completely before answering the trickier questions: Sometimes, information supplied in later questions will shed more light on earlier questions. Other times, information you read in later questions might jog your memory about router configuration facts, figures, or behavior that also will help with earlier questions. Either way, you will come out ahead if you defer those questions about which you are not absolutely sure.

Keep working on the questions until you are certain of all your answers or until you know you will run out of time. If questions remain unanswered, you will want to zip through them and guess. Not answering a question guarantees you will not receive credit for it, and a guess has at least a chance of being correct.

At the very end of your exam period, you are better off guessing than leaving questions unanswered.

Exam-Taking Basics

The most important advice about taking any exam is this: Read each question carefully. Some questions are deliberately ambiguous, some use double negatives, and others use terminology in incredibly precise ways. The authors have taken numerous exams—both practice and live—and in nearly every one have missed at least one question because they did not read it closely or carefully enough.

Here are some suggestions on how to deal with the tendency to jump to an answer too quickly:

➤ Make sure you read every word in the question. If you find yourself jumping ahead impatiently, go back and start over.

➤ As you read, try to restate the question in your own terms. If you can do this, you should be able to pick the correct answer(s) much more easily.

➤ When returning to a question after your initial read-through, read every word again—otherwise, your mind can fall quickly into a rut. Sometimes, revisiting a question after turning your attention elsewhere lets you see something you missed, but the strong tendency is to see what you have seen before. Try to avoid that tendency at all costs.

➤ If you return to a question more than twice, try to articulate to yourself what you do not understand about the question, why the answers do not appear to make sense, or what appears to be missing. If you "chew" on the subject for a while, your subconscious might provide the details that are lacking or you might notice a "trick" that will point to the right answer.

➤ Breathe. Deep rhythmic breathing is a stress reliever. Breathe in for a count of four, hold it for two, then, exhale for a count of four. You will be surprised how this can clear your mind of the frustration that clouds it and allow you to regain focus.

Above all, try to deal with each question by thinking through what you know about Cisco routers and their configuration—the characteristics, behaviors, facts, and figures involved. By reviewing what you know (and what you have written down on your information sheet), you will often recall or understand things sufficiently to determine the answer to the question.

Question-Handling Strategies

Based on exams the authors have taken, some interesting trends have become apparent. For those questions that take only a single answer, usually two or three of the answers will be obviously incorrect, and two of the answers will be plausible—of course, only one can be correct. Unless the answer leaps out at you (if it does, reread the question to look for a trick; sometimes those are the ones you are most likely to get wrong), begin the process of answering by eliminating those answers that are most obviously wrong.

Things to look for in obviously wrong answers include spurious menu choices or utility names, nonexistent software options, and terminology you have never seen. If you have done your homework for an exam, no valid information should be completely new to you. In that case, unfamiliar or bizarre terminology probably indicates a totally bogus answer.

Numerous questions assume that the default behavior of a particular utility is in effect. If you know the defaults and understand what they mean, this knowledge will help you cut through many Gordian knots.

As you work your way through the exam, another counter that Cisco thankfully provides will come in handy—the number of questions completed and questions outstanding. Budget your time by making sure that you have completed one-quarter of the questions one-quarter of the way through the exam period (or the first 18 questions in the first 22 minutes) and three-quarters of them three-quarters of the way through (53 questions in the first 66 minutes).

If you are not finished when 85 minutes have elapsed, use the last 5 minutes to guess your way through the remaining questions. Remember, guessing is potentially more valuable than not answering, because blank answers are always wrong, but a guess may turn out to be right. If you do not have a clue about any of the remaining questions, pick answers at random, or choose all a's, b's, and so on. The important thing is to submit an exam for scoring that has an answer for every question.

Mastering The Inner Game

In the final analysis, knowledge breeds confidence, and confidence breeds success. If you study the materials in this book carefully and review all the exam prep questions at the end of each chapter, you should become aware of those areas where additional learning and study are required.

Next, follow up by reading some or all of the materials recommended in the "Need To Know More?" section at the end of each chapter. The idea is to become familiar enough with the concepts and situations you find in the sample questions that you can reason your way through similar situations on a real exam. If you know the material, you have every right to be confident that you can pass the exam.

After you have worked your way through the book, take the practice exam in Chapter 14. This will provide a reality check and help you identify areas you need to study further. Make sure you follow up and review materials related to the questions you miss on the practice exam before scheduling a real exam. Only when you have covered all the ground and feel comfortable with the whole scope of the practice exam should you take a real one.

 If you take the practice exam and do not score at least 75 percent correct, you need additional practice.

Armed with the information in this book and with the determination to augment your knowledge, you should be able to pass the certification exam. However, you need to work at it, or you will spend the exam fee more than once before you finally pass. If you prepare seriously, you should do well. Good luck!

Additional Resources

A good source of information about Cisco certification exams comes from Cisco itself. Because its products and technologies—and the exams that go with them—change frequently, the best place to go for exam-related information is online.

If you haven't already visited the Cisco Certified Professional site, do so right now. The Cisco Connection Online home page resides at **www.cisco.com/warp/public/10/wwtraining/certprog/index.html**, as shown in Figure 1.1.

Note: This page might not be there by the time you read this, or it might have been replaced by something new and different, because things change regularly on the Cisco site. Should this happen, please read the sidebar titled "Coping With Change On The Web."

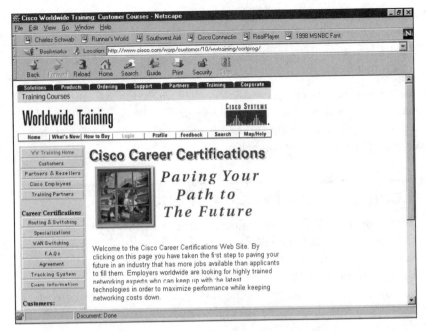

Figure 1.1 The Cisco Career Certifications home page.

The menu options in the left column of the home page point to the most important sources of information in the Career Certification pages. Here's what to check out:

➤ **Routing and Switching** Use this entry to explore the CCIE certification track for routing and switching.

➤ **Specializations** Use this entry to explore different CCNP specialization options.

➤ **WAN Switching** Use this entry to explore the CCIE certification track for WAN Switching.

➤ **FAQs** Use this entry to access the most commonly asked questions regarding any Cisco Career Certification.

➤ **Agreement** Prior to certification, all candidates must complete the certification agreement or Cisco will not recognize them as certified professionals.

➤ **Tracking System** Once you have registered with Sylvan Prometric and taken any Cisco exam, you will automatically be added to a living certification tracking system so that you can keep up with your progress.

➤ **Exam Information** This entry actually points to a class locator. It should be noted that no book is an adequate replacement for instructor-led, Cisco authorized training. This entry will assist your efforts to find a class that meets your scheduling needs.

These are just the high points of what's available in the Cisco Certified Professional pages. As you browse through them—and we strongly recommend that you do—you will probably find other informational tidbits mentioned that are every bit as interesting and compelling.

Coping With Change On The Web

Sooner or later, all the information we have shared with you about the Cisco Certified Professional pages and the other Web-based resources mentioned throughout the rest of this book will go stale or be replaced by newer information. In some cases, the URLs you find here might lead you to their replacements; in other cases, the URLs will go nowhere, leaving you with the dreaded "404 File not found" error message. When that happens, do not give up.

There's always a way to find what you want on the Web if you are willing to invest some time and energy. Most large or complex Web sites—and Cisco's qualifies on both counts—offer a search engine. Looking back at Figure 1.1, you can see that a Search field appears along the top edge of the page. As long as you can get to Cisco's site (it should stay at **www.cisco.com** for a long while yet), you can use this tool to help you find what you need.

The more focused you can make a search request, the more likely the results will include information you can use. For example, you can search for the string "training and certification" to produce a lot of data about the subject in general, but if you are looking for the preparation guide for Exam 640-407, "Introduction to Cisco Router Configuration," you will be more likely to get there quickly if you use a search string similar to the following:

```
"Exam 640-407" AND "preparation guide"
```

Finally, feel free to use general search tools—such as **www.search.com**, **www.altavista.com**, and **www.excite.com**—to search for related information. The bottom line is this: If you can't find something where the book says it lives, intensify your search.

The OSI Model

Terms you'll need to understand:

- √ OSI model
- √ Protocol
- √ Protocol data unit
- √ Peer-to-peer communication
- √ Encapsulation
- √ De-encapsulation
- √ Session
- √ Handshake
- √ Congestion
- √ Flow control
- √ Buffering
- √ Multiplexing
- √ Parallelization

Techniques you'll need to master:

- √ Identifying and describing the functions of each of the seven layers of the OSI model
- √ Identifying at least three reasons why the industry uses a layered model
- √ Describing peer-to-peer communication
- √ Contrasting data encapsulation and data de-encapsulation
- √ Explaining the five conversion steps of data encapsulation
- √ Describing the different types of flow control

11

This chapter provides an overview of the *Open Systems Interconnect (OSI) model*. It also highlights the layers within the OSI model and provides detailed information regarding the "upper" layers of the OSI model, application, presentation, session, and transport.

The OSI Model

Computers and programs that share and move data must use common protocols to communicate effectively. A *protocol* is simply a formal description of a set of rules and conventions that defines how devices on a network must exchange information. If a wide variety of protocols for data communication exists, linking computers into networks becomes extremely difficult. As a result, computer vendors began developing their own protocols. Because protocols were being developed rapidly and for different computer platforms, some vendors developed more than one.

This situation led to the creation of standards for the various computer platforms and systems. In 1984, the International Organization for Standardization (ISO) released the OSI reference model to help computer vendors create interoperable network equipment. (See the following note.) Since then, the OSI reference model has become the primary architectural model for inter-computer communication. Most network vendors now relate their products to the OSI reference model in order to educate customers about the product's features and capabilities. Each technology addressed in this book can be mapped to one of the layers in the OSI model. As a result, the OSI model is the best and most valuable tool available for people needing to learn about network technologies.

> *Note: ISO does not stand for International Standards Organization. ISO is not an acronym for anything. The International Organization for Standardization borrowed its name from the Greek word isos, which means equal. Creating an acronym for the organizations three official languages (English, French, and Russian) would be incredibly difficult.*

A Layered Network Model

The problem of moving data among different computer systems over a network is significant. Using a "divide and conquer" approach, the OSI reference model addresses this problem by dividing one large problem into seven smaller and more self-contained problems. The solution to each of the seven problems comes in the form of a layer within the OSI model. This layered approach does not constrain or define how a vendor's implementation should be; it simply provides a framework in which vendors can build their specific products. In other words, a network implementation or product does not conform to the OSI model, but it conforms to the standards and protocols developed from the OSI model.

Each of the seven layers within the OSI model represents a specific and separate network function. Standards and protocols have been defined for each layer. These protocols sit one atop the other and, as a whole, can be considered a protocol stack. Communication is achieved as information flows down the stack when a system sends information and flows up the stack when a system receives information. This division of separate network functions in a stack provides the following benefits:

➤ The interrelated aspects of network operations are divided into simpler components.

➤ Complex internetworking components can be divided into discrete subsets.

➤ Hardware and software engineers can focus their designs and development efforts in a modular fashion.

➤ Enhancements to one area are isolated from another area.

➤ Standard interfaces for plug-and-play compatibility between vendors can be defined.

The OSI model details how, for example, data should be communicated from a word processing application residing on one computer, through a network medium (like a copper wire) to a word processing application residing on another computer. The specific network layers and functions within the OSI model are described in Table 2.1.

 Another way to remember layers 1 through 7 is with the phrase: "**P**lease **D**o **N**ot **T**hrow **S**ausage **P**izza **A**way."

Note: *Layers 1 and 2 of the OSI model are implemented using hardware and software; layers 3 through 7 are implemented in software.*

Peer-To-Peer Communication

Each layer in a single system uses its own layer protocols to communicate with its peer layer in another system. The peer layers between systems communicate

Layer Number	Layer Name	Layer Function
Table 2.1	**The OSI model.**	
7	Application layer	This highest layer in the model is the closest to the user. It provides network services to a user application program.
6	Presentation layer	This layer provides data representation, data encryption, and data compression. It ensures that data sent from and arriving to the applications layer is readable.
5	Session layer	This layer establishes, maintains, and terminates sessions between applications.
4	Transport layer	This layer segments and reassembles data into a data stream.
3	Network layer	This layer determines the optimal way to move data from one place to another within the network.
2	Data Link layer	This layer (also called the link layer) provides physical transmission across the network medium.
1	Physical layer	This layer provides the electrical, mechanical, procedural, and functional means for establishing and maintaining the physical link among systems.

by exchanging *protocol data units (PDUs)*, that is, *peer-to-peer communication*. Figure 2.1 illustrates peer-to-peer communication between two systems.

 Layers within the OSI model exchange different types of PDUs. The transport layers in different systems exchange segments, network layers exchange packets, data link layers exchange frames, and physical layers exchange bits. All PDUs exchanged between the other layers are generally referred to as data.

In Figure 2.1, the dashed horizontal lines with arrows illustrate the peer-to-peer communication between systems. Layers within different systems must interact and communicate with their peer layers. For example, the network layer within System A must communicate with the network layer within System B. However, the OSI model's layering precludes direct communication between peers. Even the physical layers cannot communicate directly and must communicate over the network.

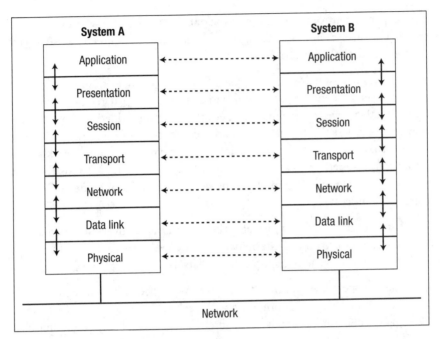

Figure 2.1   Peer-to-peer communication.

As a result, each layer in the OSI model must provide services to the layer directly above it and receive services from the layer directly beneath it. In other words, the layers within a system interact and communicate hiearchically. In Figure 2.1, the vertical lines with arrows illustrate this type of communication. For example, the network layer within System A must rely upon the data link layer within System A to accomplish this task.

Encapsulation And De-Encapsulation

For the peer-to-peer communication to occur, the data must move through the layers within a single system before traversing the network to another system. For example, the application layer must send its PDUs to the presentation layer. The presentation layer then sends its PDUs to the session layer, and so on down the protocol stack until the physical layer sends bits across the network.

However, each layer (source layer) includes control information with its PDUs that informs its peer layer (destination layer) what should be done with the PDU. This control information is included in a PDU by the source layer through a process known as *encapsulation*. The control information is read and processed by the destination layer through a process know as *de-encapsulation*. During the encapsulation process, a layer prepends control information in a header block to the data it received from the layer directly above it. When a layer appends control information to the data it receives, the layer has added a trailer. The layer then passes the header block and the original data it received to the layer directly beneath it, as shown in Figure 2.2.

During the encapsulation process, the information changes from layer to layer as each layer prepends header information to the PDU it receives from the layer directly above it. Although header information is added as the information moves down the protocol stack, the contents or original data does not change. In other words, the original data continues to be "wrapped" and header information added as is sent from layer to layer. Figure 2.2 illustrates an internetwork example (beginning at the session layer) that includes a five-step conversion process:

1. A user creates an email message; the upper layers convert and format the message for use on the internetwork. The message is sent from the session layer to the transport layer as data.

2. The transport layer receives the data, converts the data into segments, and includes header information with each segment to ensure that the email systems at both ends of the internetwork can reliably communicate. The transport layer sends the segments (segment header and data) to the network layer.

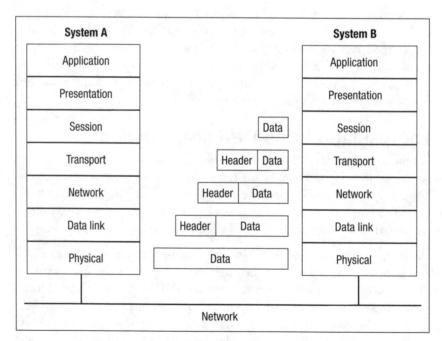

Figure 2.2   The encapsulation process.

3. The network layer receives the segments from the transport layer, converts the segments into packets, and prepends its header information, that is, logical source and destination addresses, to each packet. The network layer then sends the packets (packet header and segments) to the data link layer.

4. The data link layer receives the packets from the network layer, converts the packets into frames, and prepends its header information, that is, physical source and destination addresses, to each frame. The data link layer then sends the frames (frame header and packets) to the physical layer.

5. The physical layer receives the frames from the data link layer and converts the frames into a pattern of electrical voltages that represent 0s and 1s. The 0s and 1s (or bits) can then be transmitted on the network medium.

The de-encapsulation process takes place whenever a system receives bits on the network. De-encapsulation is simply the reverse of encapsulation: A layer reads its corresponding header information, processes the header, removes the header information, and, if necessary, sends the PDU to the layer directly above it for further processing. The encapsulation and de-encapsulation processes can occur several times on a single data stream during its transmission across an internetwork to its final destination.

 It is important to understand all functions of a given layer.

Application Layer

The application layer (layer 7) is the layer closest to the user. Because it is the highest layer in the OSI model, it does not provide services to other layers, but it does communicate with user applications and selects the appropriate network applications for those user applications. In addition, layer 7 identifies and establishes the availability of application resources in order to synchronize applications, to negotiate error recovery, and to provide data integrity.

Table 2.2 lists common user and network applications.

Any of the user applications can require services from one or more of the network applications. For example, a database application on one server may require

Table 2.2 Common user and network applications.	
User Application	**Network Application**
Word Processing	Email
Spreadsheet	File Transfer-FTP
Presentation Graphics	Client/Server Process
Database	Remote Access
Computer-Aided Design	Telnet/rlogin

remote access to a database on another server and also the ability to transfer database information between the two.

On the other hand, some user applications can include network application functions. For example, a word processor application that includes the network components necessary to email files (a network application) would be considered an application at layer 7 of the OSI model.

Presentation Layer

The presentation layer (layer 6) ensures that information it receives from the application layer is readable by the application layer of the destination peer. Simply put, the presentation layer concerns itself primarily with how the data is represented to the application. The presentation layer accomplishes this task by performing several functions:

➤ It performs code formatting and conversion to ensure that applications have readable information.

➤ It negotiates data transfer syntax between applications that use different data formats.

➤ It performs data encryption and decryption to ensure that the data cannot be viewed or altered by unauthorized parties.

➤ It performs data compression to make optimal use of its *channel* (a single communication path on a system).

 The primary services provided by the presentation layer are data representation, data encryption, and data compression.

The presentation layer must support a wide variety of data types. Table 2.3 lists some of the common data types and standards supported in layer 6 of the OSI model.

Table 2.3 Presentation layer data types and standards.	
Data Type	**Standards**
Text and Data	ASCII, EBCDIC, Encrypted
Sound and Video	MIDI, MPEG, QuickTime
Graphics and Images	PICT, TIFF, GIF, JPEG

It is important to know the different standards at the presentation layer.

Session Layer

The session layer (layer 5) establishes, manages, and terminates sessions between applications. A *session* consists of a dialogue between presentation layers on two or more different systems. The session layer also synchronizes and coordinates service requests and responses between the systems. Common layer 5 protocols include:

➤ **Network file system (NFS)** Developed by Sun Microsystems, NFS provides transparent remote access to network resources via TCP/IP on Unix workstations.

➤ **Structured query language (SQL)** Developed by IBM, SQL provides a simple method of accessing information on local or remote systems.

➤ **Remote procedure call (RPC)** RPCs are procedures that are built on a client and executed on a local or remote server.

Note: The application, presentation, and session layers provide standardization so that applications can share data and communicate with one another more easily. Layers 7, 6, and 5 do not concern themselves with how the data will arrive at its destination.

Transport Layer

The transport layer (layer 4) sits between the upper layers and the lower layers. Layer 4 is not concerned with applications, data presentation, or session management. As its name implies, the transport layer provides end-to-end data transport services to the upper layers. To further clarify, layer 4 provides the following service to the upper layers:

➤ It segments upper-layer applications.

➤ It establishes an end-to-end connection.

➤ It sends segments from one end host to another.

➤ It ensures reliable data transport.

Segment Upper-Layer Applications

One service provided by the transport layer is the capability to segment upper-layer applications. Layer 4 accomplishes this task by transporting the data segment by segment. Each segment created is autonomous. Different applications send successive segments on a first-come, first-served basis to the transport layer. The applications can destine the segments for a single system or several different systems. To illustrate, a file transfer can occur between two different systems. Conversely, a single email message may be sent to one or more recipients. The transport layer tracks and manages the various segments sent to and from both applications using port numbers. These port numbers are standard for each application and must be set by the application before the transport layer receives the segment. Because the source and destination applications use a predefined port number, the transport layers at the source and destination systems can easily pass the segments to and from the appropriate upper-layer applications.

Establish End-To-End Connections

The second service the transport layer provides is to establish an end-to-end connection between the source and destination systems. Layer 4 establishes this connection through a series of *handshakes*, which involve one system making a request to another system prior to a connection being established. Handshakes occur during the establishment of a connection between two systems and address matters such as synchronization and connection parameters.

Send Segments From One Host To Another

Another service that is provided by the transport layer occurs after the connection has been established and data transfer between the two systems has begun. It is the transport layer that is responsible for sending the segments from one system to another and checking that all of the segments arrive at the destination. As data is transferred between the two systems, data can be discarded for many reasons, but the most common reason is *congestion*. This may occur during data transfer if one computer generates traffic faster than the network can transfer it. Also, if several computers simultaneously send traffic to a single destination or through a single gateway, that destination or gateway may not be able to process the data fast enough. The transport layer handles congestion by *flow control*, a mechanism to ensure that a sending system does not overwhelm the receiving system with data.

 As the transport layer sends segments from one system to another, it can use any of the three methods of flow control:

➤ Buffering

➤ Multiplexing

➤ Parallelization

Buffering

The first method of flow control involves *buffering*. Each system has a certain amount of memory available for buffering information. The transport layer of the receiving system ensures that sufficient buffers are available and that data is not transmitted at a rate that exceeds the rate at which the receiving system can process it. When the buffers on the receiving system are full, a "not ready" message is sent to the sending system to suspend the data transmission until the data in the buffers has been processed. A "ready" message is sent from the receiving system to the sending system once the data in the buffers has been processed.

Multiplexing

The second method of flow control involves *multiplexing*. Occasionally, the upper layers require slower service than a channel can provide. As a result, the channel's bandwidth goes under-utilized. In this case, the transport layer multiplexes conversations; it does this by interweaving packets from different segments and transmitting them. The transport layer at the receiving end sorts the packets (using the header information that was encapsulated) and recreates the original segments.

Parallelization

The third method of flow control involves *parallelization*. If the upper layers require faster service than a channel can provide, the transport layer may be able to combine multiple channels (paralleling the flow of the data) and to increase the effective bandwidth for the upper layers.

Note: *Operating systems such as Unix and MVS support parallelization, whereas some PC operating systems do not.*

Ensure Reliable Data Transport

The final service that is provided by the transport layer involves the reliable transport of the segments. Reliable transport depends upon a connection-oriented relationship between the sending and receiving systems to ensure the following tasks are completed successfully:

➤ Send an acknowledgment to the sending system for each segment that was successfully received.

➤ Retransmit any segments that were not acknowledged by the receiving system.

➤ Discard any duplicate segments.

➤ Put segments back into their original sequence at the receiving system.

➤ Provide congestion avoidance and control.

Thus, reliable transport ensures that segments are not lost, damaged, duplicated, or received out of sequence. Upon successful receipt of segments, the receiving system sends acknowledgments back to the sending system.

Practice Questions

Question 1

What is the correct order for the OSI model?

- ○ a. Application, session, presentation, transport, network, physical, data link
- ○ b. Application, network, presentation, transport, session, physical, data link
- ○ c. Application, presentation, session, transport, network, data link, physical
- ○ d. Application, network, transport, presentation, session, physical, data link

Answer c is the correct order. Answers a, b, and d are incorrect because they are out of order.

Question 2

Which of the following tasks is an example of encapsulation?

- ○ a. Putting the header and/or trailer on an incoming frame.
- ○ b. Putting a header and/or a trailer on an incoming segment.
- ○ c. Putting a header and/or a trailer on an outgoing frame.
- ○ d. Stripping a header and/or trailers from an incoming frame.

Answer c is correct. Encapsulation involves *placing* control information on an *outgoing* PDU. The PDU can be either a frame, segment, packet, or segment. Answers a and b are incorrect because they involve an incoming PDU. Answer d is incorrect because it involves stripping control information from a PDU.

Question 3

> Which of the following layers is most concerned with selecting the appropri-
> ate network applications for user applications?
>
> O a. Application
>
> O b. Presentation
>
> O c. Session
>
> O d. Transport

Answer a is correct. The application layer provides services for user applications. The presentation layer's chief concern is data representation. The session
layer mainly performs session management. The transport layer primarily focuses on aspects of data transport. Therefore, answers b, c, and d are incorrect.

Question 4

> Which of the following tasks is an example of de-encapsulation?
>
> O a. Stripping the header and trailer from an incoming frame.
>
> O b. Putting a header and a trailer on an incoming segment.
>
> O c. Stripping a header and a trailer from an outgoing frame.
>
> O d. Putting a header and trailers on an outgoing frame.

Answer a is correct. De-encapsulation involves *removing* control information
from *incoming* PDUs. Answers b and d are incorrect because they involve putting control information on the PDU. Answer c is incorrect because it involves
an outgoing PDU.

Question 5

> A data, segment, packet, frame, and bits conversion process includes which
> layers (in order)?
>
> O a. Presentation, session, transport, network, physical
>
> O b. Session, transport, network, data link, physical
>
> O c. Presentation, session, transport, network, data link
>
> O d. Session, network, transport, data link, physical

Answer b is correct. The session layer sends data to the transport layer. The transport layer converts the data to segments. The network layer converts segments into packets. The data link layer converts packets into frames. The physical layer converts frames into bits. Therefore, answers a, c, and are incorrect.

Question 6

Which of the following layers is most concerned with getting an entire segment through a network from source to the final destination?

O a. Application

O b. Presentation

O c. Session

O d. Transport

Answer d is correct. The transport layer handles different aspects of data transport, including end-to-end communication, sending segments from one host to another, and reliable transport. The application layer provides services for user applications. Therefore, answer a is incorrect. The presentation layer's chief concern is data representation. Therefore, answer b is incorrect. The session layer mainly performs session management. Therefore, answer c is incorrect.

Question 7

Which of the following is NOT a service provided by the session layer?

O a. Establishing a session

O b. Ensuring that the segment sent is error free

O c. Ending a session

O d. Keeping the sending and receiving station from sending segments at the same time

Answer b is correct. The session layer provides services to establish sessions, to end sessions, and to manage the dialogue between the sending and receiving stations. Ensuring that the segment sent is error free and is handled within the transport layer. Therefore, answers a, c, and d are incorrect.

Question 8

> Which of the following is not a service provided by the presentation layer? [Choose the two best answers]
>
> ❏ a. Data representation
>
> ❏ b. Data compression
>
> ❏ c. Dialog management
>
> ❏ d. Data transmission
>
> ❏ e. Data encryption

Answers c and d are correct. The session layer handles dialog management. Therefore, answer c is correct. The transport layer handles data transmission. Therefore, answer d is correct. The Presentation layer concerns itself with data representation, data compression, and data encryption. Therefore, answers a, b, and e are incorrect.

Question 9

> The transport layer of the OSI model is concerned with? [Choose the two best answers]
>
> ❏ a. Ensuring data reliability
>
> ❏ b. Compressing data
>
> ❏ c. Establishing an end-to-end connection
>
> ❏ d. Segmenting upper-layer applications
>
> ❏ e. Synchronizing service requests

Answers a, c, and d are correct. The transport layer ensures data reliability, establishes end-to-end connectivity, and segments upper-layer applications. The presentation layer performs data compression. Therefore, answer b is incorrect. The session layer synchronizes service requests. Therefore, answer e is incorrect.

Question 10

> Peer-to-peer communication involves?
>
> ○ a. Each layer communicating with its adjacent layers in a single system.
>
> ○ b. Each layer communicating with its corresponding layer a single system.
>
> ○ c. Each layer communicating with its adjacent layers in another system.
>
> ○ d. Each layer communicating with its corresponding layer in another system.

Answer d is correct. Peer-to-peer communication occurs when a layer in one system communicates with the same layer in another system. In other words, the network layer in system A communicates with the network layer (its peer layer) in system B. Answers a and b are incorrect because peer-to-peer communication cannot occur with a single system. Answer c is incorrect because peer-to-peer communication does not occur between adjacent layers.

Question 11

> Reasons why the industry uses a layered model include? [Choose all answers that apply]
>
> ❏ a. Enhancements for one layer can be isolated from the other layers.
>
> ❏ b. Designs and development efforts can be made in a modular fashion.
>
> ❏ c. Network operations and troubleshooting can be simplified.
>
> ❏ d. Standard interfaces can be defined for vendor compatibility.

Answers a, b, c, and d are correct.

Need To Know More?

 Stallings, William: *Handbook of Computer Communications Standards: The Open Systems Interconnection (OSI Model and OSI-Related Standards) Vol. 1*. Prentice-Hall, 1990. ISBN 0-02415-521-7.

 The official Cisco Documentation Web site provides more information regarding the OSI model. See the first chapter of the "Networking Fundamentals" Web page at **www.cisco.com/public/documentation.html**.

 Review the Web pages on the OSI model at **http://whatis.com/osi.htm**. These Web pages offer additional information and illustrations on the OSI model.

The OSI Model: Physical, Data Link, And Network Layers

3

Terms you'll need to understand:

√ Logical link sub-layer (LLC)

√ Media access control sub-layer (MAC)

√ Service access point (SAP)

√ Frame relay

√ Integrated services digital network (ISDN)

√ Point-to-point protocol (PPP)

√ Connection-oriented network services

√ Connectionless network services

√ Synchronous data link control (SDLC)

√ High-level data link control (HDLC)

√ RS-232

√ V.35

√ High speed serial interface (HSSI)

√ Public switched telephone network (PSTN)

Techniques you'll need to master:

√ Differentiating between connection-oriented and connectionless network services

√ Describing the differences between data link layer addresses and network layer addresses

√ Identifying the functions of a network layer address

√ Identifying the functions of a data link layer address

√ Identifying the key inter-networking functions of the OSI network layer

√ Describing how the OSI network layer performs its functions in a router

√ Describing the difference between a routing and a routed protocol

This chapter describes the functions of the physical, data link, and network layers of the OSI model. The information in this chapter focuses on providing the right details to help you study and pass the CCNA exam. In many cases, the information presented will not provide a comprehensive explanation of specific technologies and concepts. However, you'll find a reference to other sources of information on each topic at the end of the chapter.

Network Layer

The primary purpose of the network layer is to determine the best path from one network to another and to route messages in that direction; therefore, the network layer is considered the domain of routing. The process of routing includes path determination and packet switching. Path determination requires the use of routing protocols to optimize the routing process. In addition, the network layer employs routed protocols that provide a logical two-part addressing scheme to identify paths and assign costs to different destinations. The steps in path determination and packet switching are discussed in the next sections; however, remember that the primary purposes of the network layer are:

➤ Packet switching

➤ Path determination

Path Determination

The network layer performs path determination via routers, routing protocols, and routed protocols. A router utilizes a routing protocol to determine the best path to take to get from itself to a destination. Typically, routing protocols utilize layer 3 or logical addressing—an inherent part of most routed protocols—to identify and differentiate between two destinations. Before we continue to discuss the process of path determination, let's look at the difference between a routed and a routing protocol.

Routing Protocols Vs. Routed Protocols

Routing protocols apply a set of rules to a network topology to determine the best path to a destination from a given reference point. In addition, they communicate topology information to other routers in their networks. Routing protocols utilize all the topology information that they receive to produce *routing tables*; these contain information describing a variety of paths and their costs for reaching a specific address. The number of paths to a given address is dependent on the routing protocol being implemented, and the cost of a path is specific to each routing protocol. It is not unlikely that two routing protocols used in the same internetwork might derive different paths and costs to the same destination. The value of the costs is based on the metrics used in their calculation. The most common metrics include hop count, bandwidth, delay, reliability, and mean time between failures (MTBF). Some examples of routing protocols include Routing Information Protocol (RIP), open shortest path first (OSPF), and enhanced interior gateway routing protocol (EIGRP).

A *routed protocol* provides the information required for the routing protocol to determine the topology of the internetwork and the best path to a destination. The routed protocol provides this information in the form of a logical address and other fields within a packet. The information contained in the packet allows the router to direct user traffic. The most common routed protocols include Internet Protocol and Internet Packet Exchange.

Logical Addressing

Network layer addressing is most commonly referred to as *logical addressing* (versus the physical addressing of the data link layer). Whereas the physical address of a device cannot be changed without removing or changing the hardware, a logical address can be reconfigured as required. A logical address consists of two parts: the network and the node. Routers use the network part of the logical address to determine the best path to the network of a remote device. Some routing protocols count the number of networks that must be crossed to reach a destination and make that value the cost of the path. For example, Figure 3.1 shows three routers labeled A through C supporting four networks. Each connection between a router is labeled with a network number starting at 1 and ending with 4. Table 3.1 shows the routing table of router A.

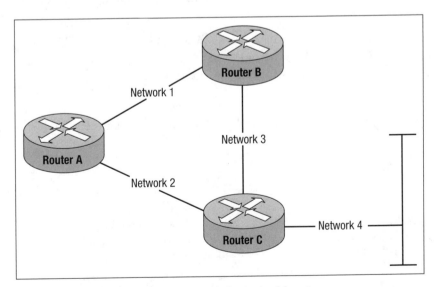

Figure 3.1   Path determination with logical addressing.

Table 3.1	Router A's routing table.	
Destination	**Next Hop**	**Number Of Hops**
Network 1	None	Directly connected
Network 2	None	Directly connected
Network 3	Router B	1
Network 3	Router C	1
Network 4	Router C	2
Network 4	Router B	3

In this scenario, router A is trying to determine the best path to send a packet to network 4. The routing protocol uses the path with the fewest number of hops (networks) between itself and the destination as the metric for determining the optimal route. The routing table provided in Table 3.1 indicates the cost of reaching network 4, which is 3 hops, by sending the packet to router B, whereas the cost of sending it through router C is only 2 hops. Because the path with the lowest number of hops is most desirable for this routing protocol, the packet is forwarded to router C.

The node part of the logical address is used to identify a specific device on a network. To continue the previous example, once router C has received the message destined for network 4, it must determine how to differentiate between all the nodes on network 4. The router uses the node part of the logical address to determine the physical address of the destination node and sends the message directly to that node.

The utilization of this type of 2-part network layer addressing scheme has allowed networks to scale to enormous sizes. Table 3.2 highlights the difference in addressing between IP and IPX logical addressing.

It is very important to be able to distinguish between the network portion and the node portion of IP and IPX addresses.

Novell IPX addresses do not necessarily have to have 8 decimal characters. Often Novell IPX address will use less than 8 characters to represent the network address.

Table 3.2	IP versus IPX logical addressing.		
Protocol	**Network**	**Interface/Node**	**Example**
TCP/IP	Uses up to 30-bits to indicate the Network Number.	The number of bits used for the node is dependent on the number of bits used for the network.	172.29.15.4. 172.29 = Network 15.4 = Node
Novell IPX	Uses up to 32-bits to indicate the network address. Can be up to 8 hex characters.	Uses the 48-bit hexadecimal MAC address.	8BCDF45E.0011.0434.44FF 8BCDF45E = Network 0011.0434.44FF = Interface

Note: Each address is broken into a network and a node portion. IP uses a 32-bit classfull-addressing scheme; IPX uses up to a 70-bit classless addressing scheme. The details of IPX and IP are presented in Chapters 7, 8, and 9. However, note that IP uses a dotted decimal notation to represent the network and node values, whereas IPX uses a hexadecimal notation. The node portion of the IPX address is the MAC address of the destination node.

Routing Protocol Algorithms And Metrics

Routing protocols use algorithms to generate a list of paths to a particular destination and the cost associated with that path. The cost of a path is determined by the values of the metrics used as input to the algorithm. The metrics used differs, depending on the routing protocol implemented. However, some of the most common metrics include hop count, link speed, reliability, and mean time between failures (MTBF). Metrics are either dynamically or administratively set. The reliability of a circuit is an example of an administratively set metric, because a system administrator is required to set the metric. Hop count is an example of a dynamically set metric, because the routing protocol determines this value by communicating with other routers. When the number of hops changes, this metric will be updated. Metrics and logical addresses are the inputs to routing algorithms and a routing table that displays destination network addresses, and the best path to take to reach that destination is produced. An illustration of this process is shown in Figure 3.2.

Packet Switching

The final purpose of the network layer is to perform *packet switching* from one network to another. The process of packet switching refers to a router receiving a packet on one network interface and switching it to another interface in

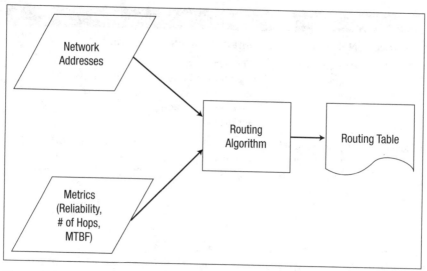

Figure 3.2 Routing algorithm process.

route to its destination. This process relies on the determination of an optimal path by the routing protocol so that the best interface can be identified for reaching the packet's destination. Once the best path has been identified, the router takes the packet from one interface and forwards it out the interface on the most optimal path to the packet's destination.

Data Link Layer

The data link layer is responsible for the transport of data across a physical media. The data link layer packages data in the format of frames. This layer is divided into two sub-layers: the logical link control (LLC) sub-layer and the media access control (MAC) sub-layer. The LLC and MAC sub-layers work together to perform all the functions required of the data link layer. The data link layer performs these functions:

➤ Allows the upper layers of the OSI model to work independently of the type of media used at the physical layer.

➤ Provides optional flow control and frame sequencing.

➤ Provides error notification.

➤ Performs physical hardware addressing to ensure that all devices in an internetwork have a unique identification.

Different wide area network (WAN) and local area network (LAN) protocols have been developed for the data link layer. Figure 3.3 displays the topologies of a number of different LAN protocols. The difference between a WAN and

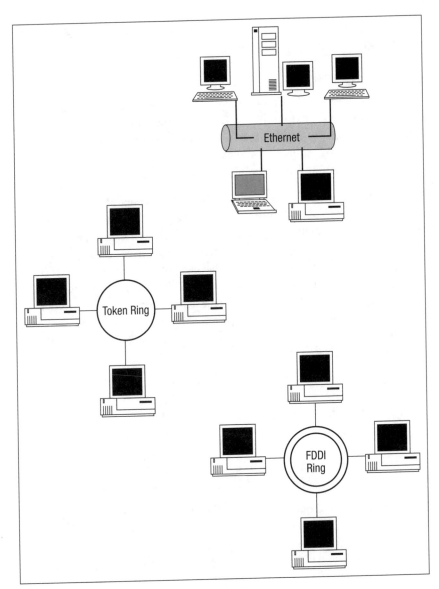

Figure 3.3   Local area network topologies.

LAN protocol is the purpose of the link. *LAN protocols* are designed to provide efficient media access for a number of workstations, printers, and servers. *WAN protocols* are designed to provide data transport over some geographic distance. WAN links are typically slower than LAN protocols because of the physical distance of their connections. This chapter does not describe any of the LAN or WAN protocols in detail. It is not necessary to have a detailed knowledge of each of the LAN topologies and functions that each performs for the exam.

However, these are foundation skills that should be mastered before attempting to conquer some of the more difficult technologies.

LAN Protocols

The three most popular LAN protocols used today are Ethernet, token ring, and fiber distributed data interface (FDDI). However, in the last few years Ethernet has begun to dominate. LAN protocols operate at the data link layer and utilize the MAC address to allow computers and other devices to communicate among one another. A summary of these protocols follows:

➤ **Ethernet bus** A LAN protocol that allows a number of devices to communicate with each other by competing for the use of a shared media. Ethernet uses the concept of *carrier sense multi access/collision detection* (*CSMA/CD*) to govern when a device can send data. Basically, when a computer wants to send a message, it must listen to media (most often the media is Category Five Cable); if it does not hear that another computer is sending a message, it will send its message. The computer continues to listen to the media to ensure that its message did not collide with another computer's message. Ethernet typically runs at 10Mb, 100Mb, or 1,000Mb data rates.

➤ **Token Ring** IBM created the Token Ring protocol in 1970 to support its mainframe environments. Token Ring is a LAN protocol that allows a number of devices to communicate by circulating a token around a ring and only allowing a computer to send a message if it has the token. After a computer has sent a message, it must release the token and wait for it to circulate the ring before sending another message. Token Ring typically runs at 4MB and 16MB data rates.

➤ **Fiber distributed data interface (FDDI)** A FDDI topology is very similar to token ring except that it uses two rings that operate in a counter rotating direction. The opposing direction of each ring creates a "self-healing" LAN media. It is self-healing, because under normal operation conditions only one ring is used to pass the token and user traffic. However, if part of the primary ring is broken traffic is transferred to the opposing ring and the direction of traffic is reversed. In addition, FDDI utilizes fiber optic cables to give it 100Mb capacity.

WAN Protocols

WAN protocols primarily function at the data link and physical layers. Chapters 11 and 12 are devoted to describing the more common WAN protocols (frame relay, ISDN, and PPP) in detail. However, the following is a brief synopsis of the main WAN protocols:

➤ **Synchronous data link control (SDLC)** SDLC is primarily used for terminal to mainframe communication. SDLC requires that one device be labeled as the primary station and all other devices be labeled as secondary stations. Communication can only occur between the primary and secondary stations.

➤ **High-level data link control (HDLC)** HDLC provides for networks that require communication to occur between many different devices, versus the central facility approach of SDLC. HDLC provides for multipoint communication as well as point-to-point communication between two devices.

➤ **Integrated services digital network (ISDN)** ISDN was developed to maximize the utilization of the current public switched telephone network (PSTN). ISDN calls for the use of digital facilities across the current copper wiring used by current voice analog services.

➤ **Frame relay** Frame relay provides digital communication for packet switched networks. Frame relay does not require a high level of error checking because of the use of digital facilities. In addition, it allows for the connection of multiple WAN sites via a single connection; this aggregation drastically reduces hardware and circuit costs.

➤ **Point-to-Point** Point-to-Point provides communication between two networks or nodes or any combination of the two. It allows for encryption, multiple protocol support, and error control, and is commonly used for WAN connections using leased lines.

Logical Link Control Sub-Layer

The LLC sub-layer performs more of the software functions of the data link layer. Its primary function is to allow the upper-layers to communicate with other devices in connectionless or connection-oriented environments. Because confusion often occurs regarding the difference between connection-oriented and connectionless communication, an explanation of the difference between the two follows.

Connection-Oriented Vs. Connectionless Communication

Connection-oriented communication occurs when two devices create a virtual connection between themselves. What is the difference between a virtual and a physical connection? In a *physical connection*, two devices are physically connected via some type of media such as a copper wire. A *virtual connection* occurs when two devices are not directly physically linked, but perform setup and maintenance procedures during the communication process to ensure the other device is still communicating or receiving messages. *Connectionless communication* occurs when two devices that are not physically or virtually connected communicate with each other in a best effort manner.

The difference between connection-oriented and connectionless communication can be illustrated by observing two people communicating via smoke signals.

With connectionless communication, person A sends a smoke signal any time he or she desires and assumes that person B received the message. With connection-oriented communication, person A first must request a conversation with person B by sending a smoke signal. Person A will respond with a smoke signal if he or she is willing to communicate. In addition, any time that person A or B sends a message the other must respond to the message indicating that it was received.

Functions Of The Logical Link Layer

The logical link layer:

➤ **Allows upper layers to perform independently of the LAN/WAN protocol or physical media** The LLC sub-layer allows upper-layer protocols like IP and IPX to act independently of the LAN topology or protocol. This is a major benefit because you can change the LAN protocols or media without affecting the upper-layers. This autonomy is available because the LLC is not tied to a specific MAC protocol.

➤ **Provides service access points (SAPs) for the lower MAC sub-layer to communicate with the upper-layer functions** The LLC provides a common set of service access points so that the MAC sub-layer can send information to the upper-layer services. The SAPs help the LLC determine where to send the data received from the MAC sub-layer.

➤ **Performs flow control for upper-layer protocols** The data link layer is capable of using ready/not ready codes to indicate when either it or its upper-layers are capable of receiving more information. This allows communicating devices to throttle back on the communication data rate and minimize the amount of data that has to be sent twice due to dropped packets.

➤ **Performs sequencing of frames** The data link layer is capable of re-sequencing any frames that are received in the wrong order.

Media Access Control Sub-Layer

The MAC sub-layer interfaces with the physical layer and media. In comparison to the LLC sub-layer, the MAC sub-layer is responsible for performing more of the hardware functions of the data link layer. It functions as follows.

The MAC sub-layer maintains the physical address of a device. The physical address is also referred to as the *MAC address*. The MAC address is a 48-bit address expressed as 12 hexadecimal digits: The first six digits contain the unique identification of the manufacturer and the last six digits are the serial number assigned by the manufacturer. Typically, a workstation has a piece of hardware called a *network interface card (NIC)* that has a MAC address burned into the read only memory (ROM). The MAC address uniquely identifies this interface from any other interface in the world. The Institute of Electrical and Electronic Engineers (IEEE) developed a set of unique identification codes and distributes them to manufacturers. Each manufacturer vendor is assigned a different identification code. An example of a MAC address is shown in Table 3.3.

The first column shows the entire physical address; it is typically shown in this format. The second column displays the first six digits; these identify the IEEE assigned manufacturer code. And finally, the last column displays the last six digits that are assigned by the manufacturer as a product serial number.

Framing

The MAC sub-layer is also responsible for framing data as it is received or transmitted onto the physical media. All WAN/LAN protocols implement specific frame formats; however, they all perform a subset of the following functions:

➤ Add a header and or trailer to the transmitted packet, indicating the protocol, frame length, and error checking mechanism.

➤ Perform error checking on received frames.

➤ Strip the header off the received frame and pass the data to the LLC.

➤ Determine if any frames on the physical layer are destined for this device.

Table 3.3   MAC address example.

MAC Address	Manufacturer Code	Serial Number
FF34.2345.12AB	FF34.23	45.12AB
45AB.2348.ABDD	45AB.23	48.ABDD

Physical Layer

The physical layer performs the mechanical and electrical engineering functions of the OSI model. Because physical layer specifies the conversion of 1s and 0s into an electrical current or pulse of light, it must communicate with its peer layers regarding the signals for activating, maintaining, and deactivating a physical circuit. Numerous standards are specified for the physical layer. The following is a list of three of the more common standards:

➤ **RS-232** Used for serial data transmission for speeds of 19.2Kbps or less. RS-232 connects two devices communicating over a serial link with either a 25-pin (DB-25) or 9-pin (DB-9) serial interface.

➤ **V.35** Used for serial data transmission for speeds up to 4Mbps. The V.35 standard was created by the International Telecommunication Union-Telecommunication Standardization Sector (ITU-T).

➤ **HSSI** The high speed serial interface (HSSI) standard is designed for serial connections that require high data transmission rates. This standard allows for high-speed communication and runs at speeds up to 52Mbps.

Practice Questions

Question 1

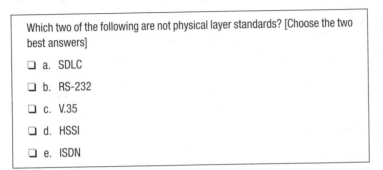

Which two of the following are not physical layer standards? [Choose the two best answers]

❑ a. SDLC

❑ b. RS-232

❑ c. V.35

❑ d. HSSI

❑ e. ISDN

Answers a and e are correct. SDLC and ISDN are not physical layer standards; in fact, they are WAN protocols that function at the data link layer. RS-232 is a physical layer standard for data transmission speeds of 19.2Kbps or less. Therefore, answer b is incorrect. V.35 is a physical layer standard for data transmission speeds up to 4Mbps. Therefore, answer c is incorrect. Finally, HSSI is a physical layer standard desired for serial connections at very high data rates. Therefore, answer d is incorrect.

Question 2

Which two answers are functions of the OSI model's network layer? [Choose the two best answers]

❑ a. Sequencing of frames

❑ b. Path determination

❑ c. Packet switching

❑ d. The electrical and mechanical functions required to send data

Answers b and c are correct. The network layer of the OSI model performs both path determination and packet switching. Path determination is the process of identifying the best path to a destination across an internetwork. Packet switching is the process of moving a packet from one network interface to another. Sequencing of frames is a function of the data link layer. Therefore, answer a is incorrect. Typically, if the word frame is used in an OSI model question, the answer is going to have something to do with the data link layer. Finally, the electrical and mechanical functions required to send data refers to the functions performed by the physical layer of the OSI model. Therefore, answer d is incorrect.

Question 3

> Which is an example of a physical (MAC) address?
>
> ○ a. AL45.5555.2334
>
> ○ b. 23CD4.23AB.F1
>
> ○ c. 00.FB12.0023.4512
>
> ○ d. A1B5.5AA4.FF21
>
> ○ e. 172.29.12.14

Answer d is correct. The physical (MAC) address is a 48-bit address represented as 12 hexadecimal digits. AL45.5555.2334 has 12 digits; however, L is not a hexadecimal character. Therefore, answer a is incorrect. 23CD4.23AB.F1 only has 11 characters and is in the wrong format. Therefore, answer b is incorrect. 00.FB12.0023.4512 has too many digits to represent a 48-bit address. Therefore, answer c is incorrect. Finally, 172.29.12.14 is an IP address and not a MAC address. Therefore, answer e is incorrect.

Question 4

> Which answer is not a characteristic of the data link layer?
>
> ○ a. Transports data across a physical link.
>
> ○ b. Performs physical addressing.
>
> ○ c. Determines the network topology.
>
> ○ d. Performs flow control.
>
> ○ e. Establishes, manages, and terminates sessions between end hosts.

Answer e is correct. The session layer of the OSI model is responsible for establishing, managing, and terminating sessions between end hosts. The data link layer is responsible for the transport of data across a physical link. Therefore, answer a is incorrect. The data link layer does perform physical addressing in the form of a MAC address. Therefore, answer b is incorrect. The data link layer does determine the network topology with such protocols as Ethernet and token ring. Therefore, answer c is incorrect. The data link layer does perform flow control with ready/ready not codes. Therefore, answer d is incorrect.

Question 5

Which three protocols are examples of data link layer protocols? [Choose the three best answers]

❏ a. HDLC

❏ b. FTP

❏ c. SQL

❏ d. Token ring

❏ e. ISDN

Answers a, d, and e are correct. HDLC (high-level data link control) is a WAN protocol used in communication between stations. Therefore, answer a is correct. Token ring is a LAN protocol/topology controlled by the data link layer. Therefore, answer d is correct. ISDN (integrated services digital network) is a layer 2 protocol that utilizes the existing copper wire of the PSTN to provide digital data services. Therefore, answer e is correct. FTP (file transfer protocol) is an application protocol that performs file transfers between an FTP server and a FTP host. FTP is not a data link layer protocol. Therefore, answer b is incorrect. SQL (structured query language) is a session layer protocol that is used to make database calls. Therefore, answer c is incorrect. This is a very typical question of the CCNA exam. It is necessary to know the protocols that exist at each layer of the OSI model.

Question 6

Given the following physical address, what is the vendor code of this address?

BBD1.4822.53AA

○ a. BBD148

○ b. 2253AA

○ c. BBD1

○ d. 53AA

○ e. 4822

Answer a is correct. The first six digits of the physical address represent the vendor code. The last six numbers of the physical address represent the serial number, not the vendor code. Therefore, answer b is incorrect. Answers c, d, and e have no meaning on their own and are therefore, incorrect.

Question 7

Which two answers are characteristics of connection-oriented communication? [Choose the two best answers]

❑ a. Setup and maintenance procedures are performed to ensure delivery of messages.

❑ b. A physical circuit exists between the two communicating devices.

❑ c. It is a best effort type of communication.

❑ d. A virtual connection exists between the two devices.

Answers a and d are correct. Both a virtual connection and setup and maintenance functions are performed during connection-oriented communication. A physical circuit is not necessary for connection-oriented communication. Therefore, answer b is incorrect Answer c is a characteristic of connectionless communication, not of connection-oriented communication, and therefore is incorrect.

Question 8

Which of the following are examples of layer 3 addressing? [Choose the two best answers]

❑ a. 172.29.5.12

❑ b. BB455467.0000.B333.A232

❑ c. 0000.B333.A232

❑ d. S0:

Answers a and b are correct. 172.29.5.12 is an example of an IP logical address or a network layer address. BB455467.0000.B333.A232 is an example of an IPX logical address or a network layer address. 0000.B333.A232 is an example of a physical or layer 2 address, not a network or layer 3 address. Therefore, answer c is incorrect. S0: has no meaning. Therefore, answer d is incorrect.

Question 9

Which of the following are considered routing protocols? [Choose the two best answers]

❏ a. OSPF

❏ b. IPX

❏ c. IP

❏ d. EIGRP

❏ e. Token Ring

Answers a and d are correct. Both open shortest path first (OSPF) and enhanced interior gateway routing protocol (EIGRP) are routing protocols. IPX and IP designate routed protocols. Therefore, answers b and c are incorrect. Token Ring is a layer 2 topology/protocol. Therefore, answer e is incorrect.

Question 10

Which of the following are not examples of a WAN protocol? [Choose the two best answers]

❏ a. Frame relay

❏ b. ATM

❏ c. Ethernet

❏ d. FDDI

❏ e. ISDN

Answers c and d are correct. Both Ethernet and FDDI are examples of LAN protocols, not WAN protocols. While FDDI and Ethernet are layer two protocols, they are used for local area networks versus wide area networks. Frame Relay, Asynchronous Transfer Mode (ATM), and ISDN are WAN protocols. Therefore, answers a, b, and e are incorrect.

Need To Know More?

Chappell, Laura. *Introduction to Cisco Router Configuration*. Cisco Systems Inc., Macmillan Publishing Company, 1998. ISBN 0-7645-3186-7. The first three chapters cover some great OSI material

Comer, Douglas E.: *Internetworking with TCP/IP: Principles, Protocols, and Architectures Vol 1*. Prentice Hall, 1995. ISBN 0-1321-6987-8.

Lammle, Todd, Donald Porter, and James Chellis. *CCNA Cisco Certified Network Associate*. Sybex Network Press, Alameda, CA, 1999. ISBN 0-7821-2381-3. This book is full of helpful information.

Syngress Media, with Richard D. Hornbaker, CCIE: *Cisco Certified Network Associate Study Guide*. Osborne/McGraw-Hill, Berkeley, CA, 1998. ISBN 0-07-882487-7. This book is a great study tool.

The first chapter of the Cisco "Networking Fundamentals" Web page provides more information regarding the OSI model.

The official Cisco documentation Web site, **www.cisco.com/public/documentation.htm**, provides valuable information on the following pages:

www.cisco.com/univercd/cc/td/doc/cisintwk/ito_doc/55016.htm

www.cisco.com/univercd/cc/td/doc/cisintwk/ito_doc/55771.htm

www.cisco.com/univercd/cc/td/doc/cisintwk/ito_doc/55031.htm

www.cisco.com/univercd/cc/td/doc/cisintwk/ito_doc/55773.htm

www.cisco.com/univercd/cc/td/doc/cisintwk/ito_doc/55150.htm

www.cisco.com/univercd/cc/td/doc/cisintwk/ito_doc/55780.htm

www.cisco.com/univercd/cc/td/doc/cisintwk/ito_doc/55172.htm

Router Basics

Terms you'll need to understand:

- √ EXEC
- √ Router modes
- √ Console
- √ Random access memory (RAM)
- √ Non-Volatile Random Access Memory (NVRAM)
- √ Flash
- √ Read only memory (ROM)
- √ Interfaces
- √ Cisco Discovery Protocol (CDP)
- √ Telnet
- √ Ping
- √ Traceroute

Techniques you'll need to master:

- √ Logging into a router in both user and privileged modes
- √ Logging out of a router
- √ Understanding the help facility
- √ Utilizing the context-sensitive help facility
- √ Using the command history and editing features
- √ Explaining the command modes available on a router
- √ Understanding the components and functions of a router
- √ Examining router elements (RAM, ROM, CDP, show, and more)
- √ Understanding the Cisco Discovery Protocol
- √ Accessing a router remotely
- √ Testing the network connectivity of a router

This chapter introduces basic router components and functions. The topics covered include logging into a router, using the help facility, accessing the command history, and using editing features. It also presents the basic components and functions of a router and discusses how to examine those components. In addition, this chapter introduces discovering, accessing, and testing routers in a network.

User Interface

This section provides background on the user interface of a router. In addition, it describes the capabilities of the help facility, command history manipulation, and enhanced command line editing features.

The Cisco Internetwork Operating System (IOS) provides a robust user interface—called *EXEC*—for its routers; this interface interprets the commands that are entered and performs the corresponding tasks. For security reasons, EXEC supports two types of access to router commands: user mode and privileged mode.

User Mode

Upon logging in to a router, you are automatically placed into *user mode*. EXEC commands in user mode allow information to be displayed, but router configuration settings cannot be changed. User mode commands are a subset of the privileged mode commands. Table 4.1 contains a listing of available commands while in user EXEC mode. The actual number and type of commands

Table 4.1   User EXEC mode commands.

User Command	Function
access-enable	Create a temporary Access-List entry.
clear	Reset functions.
connect	Open a terminal connection.
disable	Turn off privileged commands.
disconnect	Disconnect an existing network connection.
enable	Turn on privileged commands.
exit	Exit from the EXEC.
help	View description of the interactive help system.
lat	Open a lat connection.
lock	Lock the terminal.

(continued)

Table 4.1   User EXEC mode commands (continued).

User Command	Function
login	Log in as a particular user.
logout	Exit from the EXEC.
mrinfo	Request neighbor and version information from a multicast router.
mstat	Show statistics after multiple multicast traceroutes.
mtrace	Trace reverse multicast path from destination to source.
name-connection	Name an existing network connection.
pad	Open a X.29 PAD connection.
ping	Send echo messages.
ppp	Start IETF point-to-point protocol (PPP).
resume	Resume an active network connection.
rlogin	Open a rlogin connection.
show	Show running system information.
slip	Start serial-line IP (SLIP).
systat	Display information about terminal lines.
telnet	Open a Telnet connection.
terminal	Set terminal line parameters.
tn3270	Open a tn3270 connection.
traceroute	Trace route to destination.
tunnel	Open a tunnel connection.
where	List active connections.
x3	Set X.3 parameters on PAD.
xremote	Enter XRemote mode.

displayed varies based upon the router configuration and Cisco IOS level. In addition, generating a list may require multiple screens of output. When that occurs, a "—More—" prompt is displayed as the last line of the screen to indicate that additional information is waiting to be displayed. To display the next line of information, press the Return or Enter key. To display the next screen of information, press the spacebar. Pressing any other key stops the listing (a few exceptions exist, such as the Shift key).

A greater-than symbol ">" indicates that the router is in user mode. For example, if the hostname of the router is RouterA, the user mode prompt is RouterA>.

Use the **exit** or **logout** command to log out of the router.

Privileged Mode

Typically, you must enter a password before you can place the router in privileged EXEC mode. *Privileged mode* allows execution of all of the user mode commands, as well as setting configuration parameters, performing extensive testing, and accessing the other router modes.

Table 4.2 contains a listing of available commands while in privileged EXEC mode. The actual number and type of commands displayed varies based upon the router configuration and Cisco IOS level.

Table 4.2 Privileged EXEC mode commands.	
EXEC Command	**Function**
access-enable	Create a temporary Access-List entry.
access-template	Create a temporary Access-List entry.
bfe	For manual emergency modes setting.
clear	Reset functions.
clock	Manage the system clock.
configure	Enter configuration mode.
connect	Open a terminal connection.
copy	Copy configuration or image data.
debug	Access debugging functions (see also **undebug**).
disable	Turn off privileged commands.
disconnect	Disconnect an existing network connection.
enable	Turn on privileged commands.
erase	Erase flash or configuration memory.
exit	Exit from the EXEC.
help	View description of the interactive help system.
lat	Open a lat connection.
lock	Lock the terminal.
login	Log in as a particular user.

(continued)

Table 4.2   Privileged EXEC mode commands (continued).

EXEC Command	Function
logout	Exit from the EXEC.
mrinfo	Request neighbor and version information from a multicast router.
mstat	Show statistics after multiple multicast traceroutes.
mtrace	Trace reverse multicast path from destination to source.
name-connection	Name an existing network connection.
ncia	Start/Stop NCIA server.
no	Disable debugging functions.
pad	Open a X.29 PAD connection.
ping	Halt and perform a cold restart.
resume	Resume an active network connection.
rlogin	Open a rlogin connection.
rsh	Execute a remote command.
sdlc	Send SDLC test frames.
send	Send a message to other TTY lines.
setup	Run the SETUP command facility.
show	Show running system information.
slip	Start serial-line IP (SLIP).
start-chat	Start a chat-script on a line.
systat	Display information about terminal lines.
tarp	Access TARP (Target ID Resolution Protocol) commands.
telnet	Open a Telnet connection.
terminal	Set terminal line parameters.
test	Test subsystems, memory, and interfaces.
tn3270	Open a tn3270 connection.
traceroute	Trace route to destination.
tunnel	Open a tunnel connection.
undebug	Disable debugging functions (see also **debug**).
verify	Verify checksum of a Flash file.
where	List active connections.
which-route	Do OSI route table lookup and display results.

(continued)

Table 4.2 Privileged EXEC mode commands (continued).	
EXEC Command	**Function**
write	Write running configuration to memory, network, or terminal.
x3	Set X.3 parameters on PAD.
xremote	Enter XRemote mode.

A pound sign "#" indicates that the router is in privileged mode. For example, if the hostname of the router is RouterA, the privileged mode prompt is RouterA#.

Use the **enable** command to enter privileged mode and the **disable** command to return to user mode.

Context-Sensitive Help

The previous tables illustrate one of the help features available within Cisco IOS. Entering a question mark, "?", at the command prompt generates a list of available commands for that EXEC mode. Context-sensitive help provides assistance while entering commands. Syntax checking, command prompting, and keyword completion are some of the context-sensitive help that is available within Cisco IOS. Table 4.3 highlights several types of context-sensitive help.

Table 4.3 Context-sensitive help.	
Command	**Function**
?	Display a list of all commands available within a command mode.
help	Display a brief description of the help system for any command mode.
<abbreviated command> ?	Display a list of commands that begin with a specific character string.
<abbreviated command> <Tab>	Complete a partial command name.
<command> ?	Display a list of the command's possible keywords.
<command> <keyword> ?	Display a list of the keyword's possible arguments.

The following information highlights the different types of context-sensitive help available to someone who would like to set the system clock on a router.

```
r2#c
% Ambiguous command:   "c"
```

This command abbreviation is not specific enough to be interpreted. Because several commands begin with the letter "c", the command interpreter does not know which command to execute.

```
r2#clok
Translating "clok"
% Unknown command or computer name, or unable to find computer
   address
```

EXEC does not recognize the way this command is typed. Or, EXEC interprets the entry as a computer name and attempts to open a Telnet session, but is unable to resolve the name to an address.

```
r2#c?
clear   clock   configure   connect   copy
```

The abbreviated command followed by a question mark "?" lists all commands in this router mode that begin with "c".

```
r2#clock ?
   set  Set the time and date
```

The command followed by a space then a question mark "?" lists all possible keywords for that command.

```
r2#clock set
% Incomplete command.
```

This command and keyword combination requires at least one argument to complete the command string.

```
r2#clock set ?
   hh:mm:ss  Current Time
```

The command and keyword followed by a space and a question mark "?" list the next possible arguments for the keyword.

```
r2#clock set 23:45:00
% Incomplete command.
```

Another incomplete command message is returned because another argument is required for this command and keyword combination.

```
r2#clock set 23:45:00 ?
  <1-31>  Day of the month
  MONTH   Month of the year
```

A space and a question mark "?" at the end of the incomplete command string reveal additional arguments that are required for this command and keyword combination.

```
r2#clock set 23:45:00 31 12
                         ^
% Invalid input detected at '^' marker.
```

The caret "^" beneath a character indicates a syntax error. EXEC expected the word "December" to be entered instead of the number "12".

```
r2#clock set 23:45:00 31 December
% Incomplete command.
```

Another incomplete command message is returned because another argument is required for this command and keyword combination.

```
r2#clock set 23:45:00 31 december ?
  <1993-2035>  Year
```

A space and a question mark "?" at the end of the incomplete command string reveal additional arguments that are required for this command and keyword combination.

```
r2#clock set 23:45:00 31 december 1999 ?
<cr>
```

Entering a space and a question mark "?" after the command, keyword, and arguments returned a carriage return symbol. This indicates that the command line is syntactically correct, no additional values must be entered for this command, and that pressing Return or Enter executes the command string.

```
r2# clock set 23:45:00 31 december 1999
```

In the previous example, the command syntax is checked each time that a command is entered.

Command History

EXEC also provides a record of recent commands that have been executed. The command history feature is available in many of the router modes. The commands are stored in a buffer as a list; the most recent commands are inserted at the bottom of the list and older commands appear toward the top of the list. Table 4.4 lists the tasks that can be performed with this feature.

For example, pressing the up arrow retrieves the most recent command executed. Repeatedly pressing the up arrow scrolls through the command history from the most recent command to the oldest command. Pressing the down arrow then scrolls through command history from the oldest to the most recent.

Note: *Command history is enabled by default. The default history size is 10 commands.*

Editing Commands

EXEC includes an enhanced editing mode that supports several editing key functions. Used along with the command history, the editing commands prove quite handy. You can recall commands from the command history, edit them, then re-execute them without re-entering the entire command line. Table 4.5 describes the editing commands.

Table 4.4   Command history.

Keystroke	Task
Ctrl+P or up arrow	Recall the last or previous command.
Ctrl+N or down arrow	Recall a more recent command.
show history command	Display the command history buffer.
terminal history size <number of lines>	Set the command history buffer size.

Table 4.5   Editing commands.

Keystroke	Task
Ctrl+A	Move to the beginning of the command line.
Ctrl+E	Move to the end of the command line.
Esc+F	Move forward one word.
Esc+B	Move backward one word.
Ctrl+F	Move forward one character.
Ctrl+B	Move backward one character.

In addition, the enhanced editing command feature includes horizontal scrolling for long command lines. Should the cursor reach the right margin while you enter a command, the command line shifts 10 characters to the left. A dollar sign "$" at the beginning of the command line indicates that the line has been shifted. Each time the cursor reaches the right margin, the command line will be shifted. You can then use the keystrokes listed in Table 4.5 to edit the line.

Enhanced editing is enabled by default. You can disable it with the **terminal no editing** command and reenable it with the **terminal editing** command.

Most laptop computers support functionality that can copy a previous command string and paste it on the command line so it can be re-executed or edited.

Router Elements

This section describes the various interface modes that you may work in on a router. It also provides an overview of the different components within a router and explains how to examine the status of each of those components.

Router Modes

Regardless of how you access a router (through the console port, a modem connection, or through a router interface), you can place it on one of several modes. Other router modes exist beyond the user and privileged modes discussed earlier. Each router mode enables specific functions to be performed. The different types of router modes include user, privileged, setup, RXBOOT, global configuration, and other configuration modes, as shown in Table 4.6.

User Mode

As stated earlier, *user mode* provides a display-only environment. You can view limited information about the router, but cannot change the configuration.

Privileged Mode

Privileged mode enables you to perform an extensive review of the router. This mode supports testing commands, debugging commands, and commands to manage the router configuration files.

Table 4.6	Router modes.		
Mode	**Function**	**How Accessed**	**Prompt**
User	Limited display	Log in to the router	Router>
Privileged	Display, testing, debugging, configuration file manipulation	From user mode, enter the **enable** command	Router#
Setup	Create initial router configuration	During router startup if the configuration file is missing from NVRAM (console access only)	Interactive dialog prompts
RXBOOT	Perform router recovery	Press Break key during router startup (console access only)	>
Global	Perform simple configuration	From privileged EXEC mode, enter the **configure** command	Router (config)#
Others	Perform complex and multiline configuration	From within global configuration mode, the command entered varies	Router (config-<mode>)#

Setup Mode

Setup mode is triggered on router startup when no configuration file resides in Non-Volatile Random Access Memory (NVRAM). This mode executes an interactive prompted dialog to assist in creating an initial router configuration.

RXBOOT Mode

A router's maintenance mode is called *RXBOOT mode* or *ROM monitor mode*. This mode facilitates recovery functions when the router password is lost or the IOS file stored in Flash has been erased or is corrupt. Pressing the Break key (from a console terminal directly connected to the router) within the first 60 seconds of startup also allows you to place the router in this mode.

Global Configuration Mode

You perform simple configuration tasks in *global configuration mode*. For example, router names, router passwords, and router banners are configured in this mode.

Other Configuration Modes

You perform complex router configuration tasks in several other configuration modes. You enter interface, sub-interface, controller, and routing protocol configurations from within these other modes.

Router Components

Every router contains several components that comprise its configuration. These components are: RAM, NVRAM, Flash, ROM, and interfaces.

RAM

Random access memory (RAM) serves as a working storage area for the router. RAM contains data such as routing tables, various types of cache and buffers, as well as input and output queues. RAM also provides storage for temporary memory for the router's active IOS and configuration file (the *running config*). However, the entire content of RAM is lost if the router is powered down or restarts.

NVRAM

Conversely, *non-volatile RAM (NVRAM)* retains its content when the router is powered down or restarts. NVRAM stores permanent information, such as the router's backup configuration file. The startup config is retrieved from NVRAM during startup and loaded into RAM.

Flash

Flash stores the Cisco IOS image and associated microcode. Flash is erasable, reprogrammable *read only memory (ROM)* that retains its content when the router is powered down or restarts. Several copies or versions of an IOS image can be contained in Flash memory. It is Flash that allows software to be upgraded without adding, removing, or replacing chips on the processor.

ROM

Like Flash, ROM contains a version of IOS—usually an older version with minimal functionality. It also stores the bootstrap program and power-on diagnostic programs. However, software upgrades can only be performed by replacing chips on the CPU.

Interfaces

Interfaces provide the network connections where packets move in and out of the router. Depending on the model of router, interfaces exist either on the motherboard or on separate, modular interface cards. Figure 4.1 shows the various router components and the router elements they contain.

Router Status

Routine administration of a router involves examining the status of the router. The **show** command enables you to view the status of the router's components.

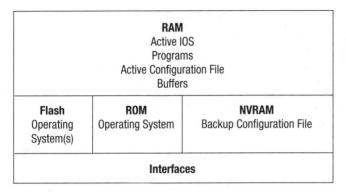

Figure 4.1 The Router components.

You can execute **show** from either user or privileged mode. However, the keywords used with the **show** command are different in user and privileged mode. Figure 4.2 illustrates some of the more common **show** command keywords and the router components they are associated with.

The **show version** command displays the hardware configuration, software version, boot images, and names and sources of configuration files, as shown in Listing 4.1.

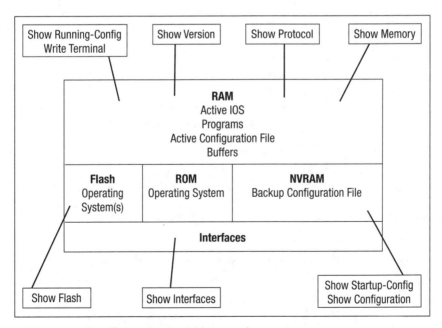

Figure 4.2 The **show** command keywords.

Listing 4.1   The **show version** command.

```
r2#show version
Cisco Internetwork Operating System Software
IOS (tm) 2500 Software (C2500-IS-L), Version 11.3(7)T,
RELEASE SOFTWARE (fc1)
Copyright (c) 1986-1998 by cisco Systems, Inc.
Compiled Tue 01-Dec-98 12:21 by ccai
Image text-base: 0x0303A9D8, data-base: 0x00001000

ROM: System Bootstrap, Version 11.0(10c)XB1, PLATFORM SPECIFIC
RELEASE SOFTWARE
(fc1)
BOOTFLASH: 3000 Bootstrap Software (IGS-BOOT-R),
Version 11.0(10c)XB1, PLATFORM
SPECIFIC RELEASE SOFTWARE (fc1)

r2 uptime is 2 days, 7 hours, 17 minutes
System restarted by reload
System image file is "flash:c2500-is-l_113-7_T",
booted via flash

cisco 2500 (68030) processor (revision M) with
6144K/2048K bytes of memory.
Processor board ID 06972781, with hardware revision 00000000
Bridging software.
X.25 software, Version 3.0.0.
1 Ethernet/IEEE 802.3 interface(s)
1 Token Ring/IEEE 802.5 interface(s)
2 Serial network interface(s)
32K bytes of non-volatile configuration memory.
8192K bytes of processor board System flash (Read ONLY)

Configuration register is 0x2102

r2#
```

The **show memory** command displays statistics about the router's memory, as shown in Listing 4.2.

Listing 4.2   The **show memory** command.

```
r2#show memory
              Head   Total(b)   Used(b)    Free(b)  Lowest(b)  Largest(b)
Processor    87510   5733104    809476    4923628   4872780   4890708
       I/O  600000   2097152    488444    1608708   1476032   1532904
```

Processor memory

Address	Bytes	Prev.	Next	Ref	PrevF	NextF	Alloc PC	What
87510	1068	0	87968	1			31A0B86	List Elements
87968	2868	87510	884C8	1			31A0B86	List Headers
884C8	3884	87968	89420	1			314B0E0	TTY data
89420	2000	884C8	89C1C	1			314D52E	TTY Input Buf
89C1C	512	89420	89E48	1			314D55E	TTY Output Buf
89E48	3000	89C1C	8AA2C	1			31B31BA	Interrupt Stack
8AA2C	44	89E48	8AA84	1			36C16D8	*Init*
8AA84	1068	8AA2C	8AEDC	1			31A0B86	messages
8AEDC	88	8AA84	8AF60	1			31AFBAC	Watched Boolean
8AF60	88	8AEDC	8AFE4	1			31AFBAC	Watched Boolean
8AFE4	88	8AF60	8B068	1			31AFBAC	Watched Boolean
8B068	88	8AFE4	8B0EC	1			31AFBAC	Watched Boolean
8B0EC	1032	8B068	8B520	1			31B796A	Process Array
8B520	1000	8B0EC	8B934	1			31B7D1C	Process Stack
8B934	480	8B520	8BB40	1			31B7D2E	Process
8BB40	128	8B934	8BBEC	1			31AFDBC	Process Events
8BBEC	44	8BB40	8BC44	1			36C16D8	*Init*
8BC44	1068	8BBEC	8C09C	1			31A0B86	List Elements

--More--

The **show protocols** command displays the network layer protocols and addresses that are configured on the router, as shown in Listing 4.3.

Listing 4.3   The **show protocols** command.

```
r2#show protocols
Global values:
  Internet Protocol routing is enabled
Ethernet0 is up, line protocol is up
  Internet address is 172.16.57.1/24
Serial0 is administratively down, line protocol is down
Serial1 is administratively down, line protocol is down
TokenRing0 is administratively down, line protocol is down
r2#
```

The **show running-config** command displays the active configuration file. Use **write terminal** if the router's IOS version is 10.3 or earlier. The **write terminal** command is also supported in later versions of IOS, as shown in Listing 4.4.

Listing 4.4   The **show running-config** command.

```
r2#show running-config
Building configuration...
Current configuration:
!
```

```
version 11.3
service timestamps debug uptime
service timestamps log uptime
no service password-encryption
!
hostname r2
!
interface Ethernet0
 description Engineering LAN Segment
 ip address 172.16.57.1 255.255.255.0
!
interface Serial0
 no ip address
 no ip mroute-cache
 shutdown
 no fair-queue
!
interface Serial1
 no ip address
 shutdown
!
interface TokenRing0
 no ip address
 shutdown
!
ip classless
!
!
line con 0
line aux 0
line vty 0 4
 login
!
end

r2#
```

The **show startup-config** command displays the backup configuration file. Use **show configuration** command if the router's IOS version is 10.3 or earlier. The **show configuration** command is also supported in later versions of IOS, as shown in Listing 4.5.

Listing 4.5   The **show startup-config** command.

```
r2#show startup-config
Using 424 out of 32762 bytes
!
version 11.3
```

```
service timestamps debug uptime
service timestamps log uptime
no service password-encryption
!
hostname r2
!
interface Ethernet0
 description Engineering LAN Segment
 ip address 172.16.57.1 255.255.255.0
!
interface Serial0
 no ip address
 no ip mroute-cache
 shutdown
 no fair-queue
!
interface Serial1
 no ip address
 shutdown
!
interface TokenRing0
 no ip address
 shutdown
!
ip classless
!
!
line con 0
line aux 0
line vty 0 4
 login
!
end

r2#
```

The **show interfaces** command displays statistics for all of the interfaces on the router or a specific interface, as shown in Listing 4.6.

Listing 4.6   The **show interfaces** command.

```
r2#show interface ethernet 0
Ethernet0 is up, line protocol is up
  Hardware is Lance, address is 00e0.1e60.9d9f (bia 00e0.1e60.9d9f)
  Description: Engineering LAN Segment
  Internet address is 172.16.57.1/24
  MTU 1500 bytes, BW 10000 Kbit, DLY 1000 usec,
     reliability 255/255, txload 1/255, rxload 1/255
```

```
Encapsulation ARPA, loopback not set, keepalive set (10 sec)
ARP type: ARPA, ARP Timeout 04:00:00
Last input 00:00:01, output 00:00:03, output hang never
Last clearing of "show interface" counters never
Queueing strategy: fifo
Output queue 0/40, 0 drops; input queue 0/75, 0 drops
5 minute input rate 0 bits/sec, 0 packets/sec
5 minute output rate 0 bits/sec, 0 packets/sec
    42 packets input, 9697 bytes, 0 no buffer
    Received 42 broadcasts, 0 runts, 0 giants, 0 throttles
    0 input errors, 0 CRC, 0 frame, 0 overrun, 0 ignored, 0 abort
    0 input packets with dribble condition detected
    80 packets output, 16167 bytes, 0 underruns
    0 output errors, 0 collisions, 2 interface resets
    0 babbles, 0 late collision, 0 deferred
    0 lost carrier, 0 no carrier
    0 output buffer failures, 0 output buffers swapped out
r2#
```

The **show flash** command displays information about the Flash memory device, as shown in Listing 4.7.

Listing 4.7   The show flash command.

```
r2#show flash

System flash directory:
File  Length    Name/status
  1   7181580   c2500-is-l_113-7_T
[7181644 bytes used, 1206964 available, 8388608 total]
8192K bytes of processor board System flash (Read ONLY)

r2#
```

Cisco Discovery Protocol

The *Cisco Discovery Protocol (CDP)* is a proprietary protocol that enables network administrators to view a summary protocol and to address information about other directly connected Cisco routers (and some Cisco switches). CDP operates at the data link layer and connects physical media and network layer protocols. Any physical media supporting the Subnetwork Access Protocol (SNAP) can be used to connect CDP devices. Because CDP resides at the data link layer, it enables two or more devices; that support different network layer protocols to still learn about each other.

Figure 4.3 provides a further illustration of CDP. Router A discovers router B via network 1 and router C via network 2 if CDP is enabled on all those three

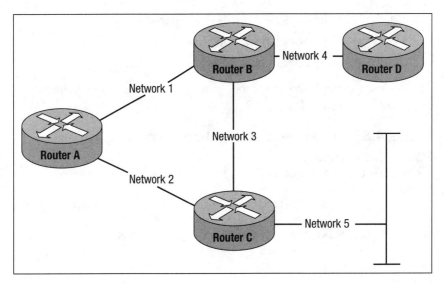

Figure 4.3   A CDP.

routers. However, router A will not discover router D, because routers A and D are not directly connected.

CDP Configuration

By default, CDP communication begins automatically on startup. However, you can still enable or disable CDP on a router's interface. The commands **cdp enable** and **no cdp enable** respectively enable and disable CDP on an interface. If CDP is enabled on an interface, that interface will advertise and discover its directly connected neighbors. This process involves exchanging frames at the data link layer, and the information discovered is stored in a router's cache memory. The **show cdp interface** command displays CDP configuration and status information.

CDP Information

Because the router stores the CDP information discovered in its cache memory, you can retrieve the information with a **show** command. Two common commands exist for displaying CDP information: **show cdp neighbors** and **show cdp entry**. The **show cdp neighbors** command provides a summary of all the CDP information from a router's directly connected neighbors.

The CDP neighbor information includes:

➤ Neighbor's device ID

➤ Local port type and number

➤ Holdtime value (in seconds)

> ➤ Neighbor's network device capability
> ➤ Neighbor's hardware platform
> ➤ Neighbor's remote port type and number

The following example lists the output generated from the **show cdp neighbors** command, as shown in Listing 4.8.

Listing 4.8 The **show cdp neighbors** command.

```
r2#show cdp neighbors
Capability Codes:R - Router, T - Trans Bridge, B - Source Route
Bridge
                S - Switch, H - Host, I - IGMP, r - Repeater

Device ID Local Intrfce  Holdtme  Capability  Platform  Port ID
r2             Eth 1       155         R         2500      Eth 0
r4             Eth 1       125         R         2500      Eth 0
r2#
```

The **show cdp entry** command provides additional detail about one device. As a result, the device ID (that is currently defined as a CDP neighbor) must be included as an argument in the **show cdp entry** command. The following example lists the output generated from the **show cdp entry <device id>** command:

```
r2#show cdp entry r4
-------------------------
Device ID: r4
Entry address(es):
  IP address: 172.16.41.4
Platform: cisco 2500,  Capabilities: Router
Interface: Ethernet1,  Port ID (outgoing port): Ethernet0
Holdtime : 173 sec

Version :
Cisco Internetwork Operating System Software
IOS (tm) 2500 Software (C2500-JS-L), Version 11.2(15),
RELEASE SOFTWARE (fc1)
Copyright (c) 1986-1998 by cisco Systems, Inc.
Compiled Tue 07-Jul-98 22:22 by tmullins

r2#
```

The **show cdp entry** command output includes all the layer 3 addresses configured on the neighboring router's directly connected interface.

Note: The holdtime value indicates the age of the CDP information.

Testing Other Routers

Several methods exist in accessing and testing connectivity to other routers. The approach to testing and troubleshooting should follow the principles of the OSI model. As discussed in Chapters 2 and 3, each layer depends on its lower layers for successful communication with its peer layers at the remote host. In other words, if layer 3 on one system can communicate with layer 3 on another system, then layers 1 and 2 of both systems are operating properly.

Several useful tools are available on the router to assist in testing and troubleshooting problems, including: **telnet, ping, traceroute,** and the **show interfaces** commands.

Telnet

Telnet operates at the application layer and is an application that provides a virtual terminal. You can connect to a remote router that supports TCP/IP. Telnet helps answer the question, "Can I access the router remotely across the internetwork?" If a Telnet session can be established, all the lower layers are operating properly. If not, one of the lower layers on the local or remote router is experiencing problems. The following example depicts the **telnet** command:

```
r2#telnet 172.16.41.4
Trying 172.16.41.4... Open
User Access Verification

Password:
r4>
```

Ping

Ping operates at the network layer. It is a basic echo protocol that determines whether IP packets are being received by the remote hosts and the response time across the internetwork. Simply put, ping checks end-to-end connectivity. Ping sends a specific number echo request and waits a specified time for an equal number of echo replies. Ping helps answer the question, "Are my packets being routed successfully?" If 100 percent of the echo replies are received, all of the lower layers are operating properly. If not all of the replies are received, an internetwork routing problem or a problem with the lower layers may exist. The following figure lists an example of a basic **ping** command output:

```
r2#ping 172.16.41.4

Type escape sequence to abort.
Sending 5, 100-byte ICMP Echos to 172.16.41.4, timeout is 2 seconds:
```

```
!!!!!
Success rate is 100 percent (5/5), round-trip min/avg/max = 4/4/4 ms
r2#
```

In this previous example, the exclamation points indicate that a successful echo reply was received. A period indicates a time-out condition and that the echo reply was not received.

Traceroute

When you need to know where data is traveling in a network, **traceroute** is the perfect command. Like the **ping** command, traceroute sends packets to the remote destination host and awaits replies. However, traceroute tests each step along the network path. It sets the Time To Live (TTL) value (which is a hop count value) to one of the three packets it sends to the first hop. When an intermediate router receives these packets, it decrements each packet's TTL value by one. The packets now have a TTL value of zero which generates an error message. The intermediate router sends an error message back to the source device for each packet it received. The source device then increments the TTL value to two and sends three more packets out again.

The first intermediate router receives the packets, decrements the TTL value by one, and forwards the packets. This process continues—with each router that receives traceroute packets sending error messages back to the source router as the TTL value reaches zero. Traceroute can then determine not only response times from the error messages it receives, but it can also identify the last router along the network path that was reached successfully. Traceroute helps answer the question, "What route are my packets taking?" Like the **ping** command, if all the error messages are received (including from the remote destination host), then the network layer and all lower layers are working well. If some of the error messages time out, you will be able to quickly identify where the problem is occurring. The following example lists output from the **traceroute** command:

> *Note: The "msec" indicates a successful traceroute reply received. An asterisk "*" indicates a timeout condition.*

```
r2#traceroute 172.16.50.4

Type escape sequence to abort.
Tracing the route to 172.16.50.4

  1 172.16.41.4    4 msec   4 msec   4 msec
  2 172.16.50.4    4 msec   5 msec   4 msec
r2#
```

Show Interfaces

As discussed earlier in this chapter, the **show interfaces** command displays statistics for all of the interfaces on the router. This command helps to answer the question, "Is my network link operating properly?" However, two aspects exist for each interface: a physical aspect and a logical aspect. The physical aspect includes the interface hardware and operates at the physical layer. The logical aspect includes the interface software and operates at the data link layer. The hardware makes the actual network connection between devices, whereas the software transmits frames between devices. Therefore, two items must be verified when testing at the physical and data link layers: carrier detect signal and keepalive frames, respectively. *Carrier detect signal* triggers a line status that you can verify using the **show interfaces** command. The transmission of *keepalive frames* triggers the line protocol and can also be verified using the **show interfaces** command. The following lists an example of the **show interfaces** command output:

```
r2#show interface ethernet 0
Ethernet0 is up, line protocol is up
  Hardware is Lance, address is 00e0.1e68.4011 (bia 00e0.1e68.4011)
--More--
r2#
```

In the previous example, line status is "up" (the interface hardware is currently active) and line protocol is "up" (the software processes that handle the line protocol believe the interface is usable). In other words, interface Ethernet0 is up/up and the carrier detect signal and keepalive frames are being communicated. However, this status only verifies that layers 1 and 2 are working properly; it does not indicate that any layers above them are working properly. Table 4.7 lists the different line status/line protocol combinations you may encounter.

Table 4.7 Line status and protocol combinations.	
Line Status/Line Protocol Combination	**Description**
Ethernet0 is up, line protocol is up	Interface is operational.
Ethernet0 is up, line protocol is down	Network connection problem exists.
Ethernet0 is down, line protocol is down	Physical interface problem exists.
Ethernet0 is administratively down, line protocol is down	Interface has been disabled or shut down.

Practice Questions

Question 1

> Which of the following commands will allow you to review the contents of NVRAM? [Choose the two best answers]
>
> ❑ a. **show configuration**
>
> ❑ b. **show protocols**
>
> ❑ c. **show version**
>
> ❑ d. **show running-config**
>
> ❑ e. **show startup-config**

Answers a and e are correct. The **show configuration** and **show startup-config** commands display the router's backup configuration file from NVRAM. The **show protocols, show version,** and **show running-config** commands will allow you to review the contents of RAM not NVRAM. Therefore, answers b, c, and d are incorrect.

Question 2

> Which of the following router components contains the router's operating system image?
>
> ○ a. Flash
>
> ○ b. NVRAM
>
> ○ c. RAM
>
> ○ d. Interfaces

Answer a is correct. Flash contains the operating system images used by the router. If no image resides in Flash, the image in ROM will be used. Interfaces provide the network connections for the router. Therefore, answer d is incorrect. NVRAM and RAM contain the backup configuration and active configuration files respectively. Therefore, answers b and c are incorrect.

Question 3

Which of the following prompts indicates that the router is in privileged mode?

○ a. Router>

○ b. Router#

○ c. Router(config)#

○ d. Router:

Answer b is correct. Router# is correct because a pound sign (#) immediately following the router's hostname (in this case "Router") indicates that the router is in privilege mode. A greater than sign (>) after the hostname indicates the router is in user mode. Therefore, answer a is incorrect. The text "(config)#" after the hostname indicates that the router is in global configuration mode. Therefore, answer c is incorrect. A colon (:) after the hostname is not a valid router mode indicator. Therefore, answer d is incorrect.

Question 4

The command **show cdp neighbors** does not display which of the following?

○ a. Neighbor's device ID

○ b. Neighbor's hardware platform

○ c. Neighbor's IOS version

○ d. Neighbor's port type and number

○ e. Local port type and number

Answer c is correct. The neighbor's IOS version is displayed by the **show cdp entry** command. Answers a, b, d, and e are displayed by the **show cdp neighbors** command and are therefore incorrect responses to the question.

Question 5

> Which of the following router commands displays the keyword needed for the command **"clock"**?
>
> ○ a. **"cl?"**
>
> ○ b. **"cl ?"**
>
> ○ c. **"clock?"**
>
> ○ d. **"clock ?"**

Answer d is correct. **"clock ?"** will display the keyword needed to complete the command. The **"cl?"** and **"clock?"** keystrokes will display the commands beginning with the text "cl" and "clock" respectively. Therefore, answers a and c are incorrect. The **"cl ?"** keystroke is an ambiguous command and returns an error. Therefore, answer b is incorrect.

Question 6

> CDP operates at which layer?
>
> ○ a. Transport
>
> ○ b. Network
>
> ○ c. Data link
>
> ○ d. Physical

Answer c is correct. CDP operates at the data link layer. Although CDP can communicate over a variety of physical media, CDP does not operate at the physical layer. Therefore, answer d is incorrect. CDP allows a network device to exchange frames with other directly connected network devices. It enables those network devices (which may support different network layer protocols) to discover each other's protocol and address information and capabilities. But CDP does not operate at the network layer. Therefore, answer b is incorrect. Answer a is incorrect because CDP does not operate at the transport layer and is not concerned with end-to-end connectivity like other transport layer protocols.

Question 7

Which command, when executed successfully, does not verify that two routers are routing packets between them successfully?

○ a. **ping**

○ b. **show interface**

○ c. **trace**

○ d. **telnet**

Answer b is correct. Although the **show interface** command displays the status of the interfaces on a router, it does not indicate whether packets are reaching their destination. The **ping** and **trace** commands verify routing by sending and receiving packets across the network. Therefore, answer a is incorrect. In order for the **telnet** command to be successful, packets must be sent and received properly, so it also verifies routing. Therefore, answer d is incorrect.

Question 8

In order to display the list of possible commands in privileged mode, which of the following sequence of keystrokes must be typed at the prompt?

○ a. "help"

○ b. "h"

○ c. "CTRL+H"

○ d. "?"

Answer d is correct. The question mark "?" will display the list of possible commands when it is typed at the prompt, regardless of the router's current mode. The "help" and "h" commands display a brief description of the help system for any command mode. Therefore, answers a and b are incorrect. The "CTRL+H" keystroke displays nothing. Therefore, answer c is incorrect.

Question 9

Which of the following router components contain versions of the router's configuration file? [Choose the two best answers]

❑ a. Flash

❑ b. NVRAM

❑ c. RAM

❑ d. ROM

Answers b and c are correct. NVRAM contains the backup configuration file for the router, while RAM contains the router's active configuration file. FLASH and ROM do not contain a configuration file. They contain the router's operating system image files. Therefore, answers a and d are incorrect.

Question 10

Which of the following commands will allow you to review the contents of RAM? [Choose the three best answers]

❑ a. **show configuration**

❑ b. **show protocols**

❑ c. **show version**

❑ d. **show running-config**

❑ e. **show startup-config**

Answers b, c, and d are correct. The **show protocols, show version,** and **show running-config** commands allow you to review the contents of RAM. The **show configuration** and **show startup-config** commands allow you to review the router's backup configuration file from NVRAM not RAM. Therefore, answers a and e are incorrect.

Need To Know More?

 Router Products Configuration Guide. Cisco Internetwork Operating System, Release 11.0. Customer order number: DOC-RPCG 11.0. Text Part Number: 78-2032-01. Chapters 2 and 3 provide additional detail on the Cisco IOS user interface commands.

 Syngress Media, with Richard D. Hornbaker, CCIE. *Cisco Certified Network Associate Study Guide.* Osborne/McGraw-Hill, Berkeley, CA, 1998. ISBN 0-07-882487-7.

 The official Cisco Documentation Web site hosted by Cisco, **www.cisco.com**, contains helpful information. From the home page, search for "user exec mode" or "privileged exec mode" and you'll be presented with a choice of several pages of detailed information.

 With the Cisco's documentation CD-ROM, you can immediately access Cisco's entire library of end user documentation, selected product news, bug databases, and related information. The documentation CD-ROM is produced monthly.

Router Configuration And Software Management

5

Terms you'll need to understand:

√ Running configuration file

√ Startup configuration file

√ Trivial File Transfer Protocol (TFTP)

√ **Enable secret** password

√ **Service password-encryption**

√ Boot field

√ Configuration register

√ ROM monitor

Techniques you'll need to master:

√ Managing configuration files from the privileged exec mode

√ Copying and moving configuration files

√ Setting up the router passwords, identification, and banner

√ Identifying the main Cisco IOS commands for router startup

√ Performing the initial configuration using the setup command

√ Loading software from various sources on Cisco routers

√ Backing up and upgrading software on Cisco routers

√ Configuring a router via the initial setup sequence

This chapter focuses on a number of very important and often applied skills in networking. The ability to manage configuration files, to load and copy Cisco Software, and to understand the impact of these types of commands is vital for success. More important, you need to master these crucial skills to avoid causing a disaster in your company's network. Understanding the many password types and security levels used on Cisco routers is important. Finally, this chapter describes and illustrates the steps required to set up a router via the initial setup sequence.

Managing Configuration Files

The process of managing configuration files is somewhat straightforward; however, it has been made difficult by the many different versions of Cisco Software and the wide variety of architectures used in Cisco hardware. This section will bring light to these subjects and present an overview of the different types of configuration files, the commands used to move, display, and copy these files, and highlight some of the areas that can cause confusion when managing configuration files.

The material presented in this chapter assumes the implementation of Cisco IOS release 11.0 or later. Don't worry, the CCNA exam uses this assumption as well.

Types Of Configuration Files

Cisco IOS Software uses and requires a configuration file to determine how a router is to function. Typically, a network administrator enters the commands necessary for his or her environment into a router configuration file. Only two types of configuration files exist for the context of the CCNA exam:

➤ The running configuration file exists in random access memory (RAM) and contains the commands that Cisco IOS uses to drive the actions of the router. See Chapter 4 for a description of the different parts of a Cisco router.

Note: RAM is erased during power cycles or software reloads. Therefore, the running configuration file is erased as well.

➤ The startup configuration file exists in non-volatile random access memory (NVRAM) and is the backup for the running configuration file.

Configuration files reside in NVRAM and that running configuration files exist in RAM.

The router will always use the running configuration file to execute. However, any time a router is restarted (cycling power or reloading the software), the running configuration file is erased and the startup configuration file is the only remaining configuration file. Therefore, during the boot sequence of a router, the router copies the startup configuration file to the running configuration file (NVRAM to RAM). Thus, it is paramount that any time a change is made to a running configuration that it is copied to the startup configuration. Many ways of preventing this from happening exist; these are discussed in this chapter.

Displaying The Running And Startup Configuration

The purpose of displaying a running or startup configuration is to determine the configuration commands being executed on a router. Use the **show running-config** or **show startup-config** command to show the running configuration and startup configuration files respectively. Displaying the running configuration shows the commands being executed at the time the show command is executed, as shown in Listing 5.1.

Listing 5.1   An example of displaying the running configuration.

```
Router#show running-config
Building configuration...
Current configuration:
Last configuration change at 03:25:38 UTC Sat Jan 1 2000
version 11.2
no service password-encryption
no service udp-small-servers
no service tcp-small-servers
hostname Router
enable secret 5 $1$2uUP$2I.LOxxD3wnX.7WDMHzb60
enable password cisco
no ip domain-lookup

interface Serial0
 ip address 138.144.2.2 255.255.255.0
 encapsulation frame-relay
```

```
 bandwidth 2000
 frame-relay lmi-type cisco

interface Serial1
 no ip address
 shutdown
!
interface TokenRing0
 ip address 138.144.3.1 255.255.255.0
 ring-speed 16
!
interface TokenRing1
 ip address 138.144.4.1 255.255.255.0
 ring-speed 16
!
router igrp 1
 network 138.144.0.0
!
no ip classless
!
snmp-server community public RO
!
line con 0
line aux 0
line vty 0 4
password  cisco
login
!
end
```

*Note: The 'Router#' prompt indicates that the command is initiated
from the privilege exec (enable) command line. It is important to know
what mode a command should be executed from.*

Configuring The Running And Startup Configuration Files

The running configuration file often requires changes while the router is
functioning. Cisco IOS is designed to accept changes to a running or startup
configuration without restarting (reloading) or cycling the power of the router.
The following commands are used to manipulate the configuration files:

➤ **Router# configure terminal** Allows a user to add, change, or delete
commands in the running configuration while the router is executing.

➤ **Router# configure memory** Allows a user to add, change, or delete
commands in the startup configuration.

Making changes to the running configuration file will immediately affect the behavior of a router.

Backing Up And Restoring Configuration Files

Configuration files are copied and moved constantly in most networks. One common method of copying files is with the use of a *Trivial File Transfer Protocol* (*TFTP*) server. Cisco routers use a TFTP server to load IOS and to copy software and configuration files. To copy a file using TFTP, one device needs to be executing TFTP server software and the other device the client software. Cisco routers are equipped with both functions. Network administrators often need to back up a running or a startup configuration file on a central server. The following command sequence accomplishes this goal:

```
Router# copy running-config TFTP
Remote host []? 172.15.12.2 (IP Address of TFTP Server)
Name of configuration file to write [router-confg]? <Return>
Write file Router-confg on host 172.15.12.2? [confirm] <Return>
Building configuration…
Writing Router-confg !!!!!!!!!!!!!!!!!![OK]
```

> *Note:* Pay attention to the order and syntax of commands during the test. The function of a command can completely change, depending on the syntax.

The reverse process occurs when a configuration file is copied from a central server to an executing router. This process is most often used when a router has gone dead or someone has accidentally deleted the configuration file on the router. If the running configuration was backed up on a TFTP server, it is really simple to restore the configuration file. The first step for restoring the configuration on a router is to determine IP connectivity from the central server to the router. This might require the use of a ping test and/or the configuration of an IP address on the router. The following command sequence is used for restoring a running configuration file:

```
Router# copy TFTP running-config
Host or network configuration file [host]? <Return>
Address of remote host [255.255.255.255]? 172.15.12.2 (TFTP Server)
Name of configuration file [Router-confg]?Router-confg (File name)
Configure using Router-confg from 172.15.12.2? [confirm] <Return>
Loading Router-confg from 172.15.12.2 (via serial 1): !!!!!
[OK - 875/32723]
Router#
```

Exercise caution when performing configuration file changes across networks, especially to remote sites. Visit Cisco's Web site and utilize the search engine to identify anything that you might need to be aware of while performing configuration backups or restores in your network. Always be sure to find hardware-specific features before changing configuration files or Cisco IOS software.

Another method of backing up a running configuration is to save it to NVRAM. You should complete this process after every change to the running configuration, unless a good reason exists to keep the startup configuration different. By copying the running configuration to NVRAM, you are ensuring that if the router is reloaded or the power is cycled, it will boot with the same configuration that you are currently executing. The following command sequence is required for this process:

```
Router#copy running-config startup-config
Building configuration...
[OK]
Router#copy running-config startup-config
```

The startup configuration file can also be copied into RAM, thereby overwriting the running configuration file by performing the following command:

```
Router# Copy startup-config running-config
```

> *Note:* *It is necessary to know all of the backup and restore commands for the CCNA exam. Be sure to pay special attention to the syntax of these commands. It is easy to forget the sequence of words for the different commands.*

Finally, the startup configuration file can be completely erased. When this occurs, the router boots into setup mode the next time it is reloaded:

```
Router#erase startup-config
```

Router Passwords

The router passwords on the Cisco router provide security against snooping users; Cisco IOS passwords were never intended to resist a determined, intelligent attack. Many programs exist (Cisco is aware of these programs) that can crack the MD5 encryption algorithm Cisco IOS employs. Cisco always recommends that some type of user authentication protocol be used to enhance the security of Cisco routers. RADIUS and TACACS are two of the more popular authentication methods that major corporations use today. Cisco Routers utilize five different password types to provide security.

Enable And Enable Secret Passwords

The **enable password** and **enable secret** password commands are designed to provide an additional layer of security for passwords. Both commands allow you to establish an encrypted password that requires users to enter to access enable mode. The enable secret mode was developed because it uses an improved encryption algorithm. The **enable secret** password overrides the **enable password** when it is present. An **enable secret** password can be entered by performing the following command.

```
Router(config)#enable secret phoenix
Router#
```

The **enable password** and **enable secret** commands also provide for security levels. These options are not part of the objectives set by the CCNA exam, and therefore, will not be presented in this book.

Console And Auxiliary Passwords

The **console** and **auxiliary** passwords restrict user mode access via the console or auxiliary ports on the router:

```
Router(config)#line aux 0
Router(config-line)#login
Router(config-line)#password phoenix
```

The login command designates that you want a user to have to enter a password every time he or she connects to the router via the auxiliary port. The login command can be added to the console port to require a password login as well. The console password is set with the same command format as the "AUX" password, except the keyword "AUX" is changed to "CON."

Virtual Terminal Password

The **virtual terminal** or **vty** password restricts user mode access via a Telnet session. The **virtual terminal** password must be set, or a user will not be able to log into the router with a Telnet session. Multiple virtual terminal sessions can be engaged at one time. A separate password can be additionally specified for each virtual terminal session:

```
Router(config-line)#line vty 0 4
Router(config-line)#login
Router(config-line)#password phoenix
```

This command sequence designates five virtual terminals that all use the password **phoenix**.

Of the five different types of passwords, only the **enable secret** password is encrypted by default. For the remaining passwords, you must use the **service password-encryption** command. This command encrypts the enable, console, auxiliary, and virtual terminal passwords:

```
Router(config)#service password-encryption
```

Passwords that have already been set in the configuration file will not become encrypted; only passwords that are entered after the **service password-encryption** command has been entered will be encrypted. The **service password-encryption** command does not provide a high level of network security, but helps keep unauthorized individuals from viewing a password in a configuration file.

Router Identification And Banner

A router's name is referred to as the *host name*. The default host name for all Cisco routers is "Router." You can change the host name of a router in global configuration mode by entering the **hostname** command. The **hostname** is changed with the following commands.

```
Router(config)#hostname Phoenix
Phoenix(config)#
```

Notice that the host name changed from "Router" to "Phoenix" immediately after executing the command.

The **banner motd** command allows you to display a message-of-the-day (motd) every time you log into the router. Even though the banner message was designed to convey day-to-day messages, it is typically used for displaying security messages for legal reasons:

```
Phoenix(config)#banner motd * Authorized Access Only,
 All Violations Will Be Prosecuted *
Phoenix(config)#
```

> *Note:* The "*c*" before the word "authorized" and after the word "Only" represents the start and finish of the text to be displayed as the banner.

In this scenario, the next time you Telnet into the router, the message of the day banner will display the following message:

```
Authorized Access Only, All Violations Will Be Prosecuted.
User Access Verification
Password:
```

A description can be added to every interface using the **description** command. Typically, an interface description, which is limited to 80 characters, is used to describe the function of the interface:

```
Phoenix(config)#interface s0
Phoenix(config-line)#description 56K between Phoenix and San Diego
Phoenix(config-line)#
```

The next time someone views the running configuration file, they will see the description:

```
interface Serial0
description 56K connection between Phoenix and San Diego
ip address 138.144.2.2 255.255.255.0
encapsulation frame-relay
bandwidth 2000
frame-relay lmi-type cisco
```

Cisco IOS Commands For Router Startup

The first time a Cisco router is powered on the startup configuration file is blank, so it will boot into the initial configuration dialog. This dialog is designed to walk a novice through the basic steps and requirements of configuring a Cisco router. However, before the initial configuration dialog is started, the router performs the boot sequence.

Router Boot Sequence

The router boot sequence is as follows:

1. The router checks the system hardware for proper functioning, including the CPU, interfaces, NVRAM, RAM, and other hardware circuitry:

```
%SYS-5-RELOAD: Reload requested
System Bootstrap, Version 11.0(10c)XB1, PLATFORM SPECIFIC
RELEASE SOFTWARE (fc1)
Copyright (c) 1986-1997 by Cisco Systems
2500 processor with 2048 Kbytes of main memory
```

2. The bootstrap program is a small application that resides in read only memory (ROM); its purpose is to find Cisco IOS. In the preceding message, the software version of the bootstrap application and the amount of main memory available are displayed:

```
ROM: System Bootstrap, Version 11.0(10c)XB1, PLATFORM
SPECIFIC RELEASE SOFTWARE (fc1)
BOOTFLASH: 3000 Bootstrap Software (IGS-BOOT-R), Version
11.0(10c)XB1,
PLATFORM SPECIFIC RELEASE SOFTWARE (fc1)
```

3. After the Bootstrap application has found an IOS (where the bootstrap searches for the IOS is dependent on the configuration register settings and possibly the Boot System commands that are covered later in this chapter), it loads the IOS from NVRAM to RAM. The router displays the software version, copyright, compilation date, and hardware features:

```
Router uptime is 3 days, 14 hours, 49 minutes
System restarted by reload
System image file is "flash:11-2-13.img", booted via flash
Host configuration file is "example-config", booted via TFTP
from 172.16.24.134

cisco 2500 (68030) processor (revision L) with 2048K/2048K
bytes of memory.
Processor board ID 07112268, with hardware revision 00000000
Bridging software.
SuperLAT software copyright 1990 by Meridian Technology Corp.
X.25 software, Version 2.0, NET2, BFE and GOSIP compliant.
TN3270 Emulation software.
2 Ethernet/IEEE 802.3 interface(s)
2 Serial network interface(s)
32K bytes of non-volatile configuration memory.
16384K bytes of processor board System flash (Read ONLY)
Configuration register is 0x2102
```

4. The IOS determines what types of hardware interfaces exist and are supported on the router and displays it on the console terminal.

Note: If you have a hardware interface that the router does not recognize, you probably need to upgrade the software version or replace the hardware.

5. After the hardware has been inventoried, the router loads the configuration that resides in NVRAM. The commands in the configuration
file are executed one line at a time. The router displays an error message
for any command that is not supported by this version of software. If a
configuration file does not exist in NVRAM and the router has not been
set up to copy a configuration from a TFTP server, it is designed to
enter the initial configuration dialog.

Initial Configuration Dialog

The *initial configuration dialog* is a menu driven command and response query
designed to configure a router with a bare bones configuration. The dialog will
start anytime a configuration file is not found in NVRAM during the boot
sequence as described previously. The two instances when a configuration file
will not exist in NVRAM are the first time the router is powered on, or if the
router was reloaded subsequent to erasing the startup configuration file.

```
Would you like to enter the initial configuration
dialog? [yes] <Return>
First, would you like to see the current interface
summary? [yes] <Return>
Any interface listed with OK? Value "NO" does not have a
valid configuration
Interface    IP-Address    OK?    Method    Status    Protocol
Serial 0     unassigned    NO     not set   up        down
Serial 1     unassigned    NO     not set   up        down
Ethernet 1   unassigned    NO     not set   up        down
Ethernet 2   unassigned    NO     not set   up        down
Configuring global parameters:
```

The above interface summary indicates that the router has two serial and two
Ethernet interfaces. In this example, we will configure both serial interfaces
and neither of the Ethernet interfaces. None of the four interfaces has been
assigned IP addresses, which is indicated by the "unassigned" listed under the
IP Address column. The status of the interface is set to "up" because this is the
default value. We must manually shut down the interface to turn it off. However,
the protocol is listed as "down" because no active connections are on the interface.
After the interface summary is displayed, the next step in the initial configuration
dialog is to configure the host name, passwords, routing protocols, and IP
addressing, as shown in Listing 5.2.

Listing 5.2   Configuring hostname, passwords, routing
protocols, and IP addresses.

```
Enter host name [Router]" Phoenix
The enable secret is a one-way cryptographic secret used instead
```

```
of the enable password when it exists.
Enter enable secret: Phoenix
The enable password is used when no enable secret exists and when
Using older software and some boot images.
Enter enable password: Cisco
Enter the virtual terminal  password: Telnet
Configure SNMP Network Management? [yes]: no
Configure IP? [yes]<Return>
        Configure IGRP Routing? [yes]: no
        Configure RIP Routing? [yes]: no
Configure Interface ters:
        Configuring interface Ethernet 0:
        Is this interface in use? [yes] no
        Configuring interface Ethernet 1:
        Is this interface in use? [yes] no
        Configuring interface Serial 0:
        Is this interface in use? [yes] <Return>
        Configure IP on this interface? [yes] <Return>
        Configure IP unnumbered on this interface? [no] : <Return>
        IP Address for this interface: 172.29.3.4
        Number of bits in subnet field [8]: <Return>
        Class B network is 172.29.0.0, 8 subnet bits; mask is
          255.255.255.0
        Configuring interface Serial 1:
        Is this interface in use? [yes] <Return>
        Configure IP on this interface? [yes] <Return>
        Configure IP unnumbered on interface? [no] : <Return>
        IP Address for this interface: 172.29.4.3
        Number of bits in subnet field [8]: <Return>
        Class B network is 172.29.0.0, 8 subnet bits; mask is
          255.255.255.0
```

Now we have configured the two serial interfaces, set up our passwords, and chosen any routing protocols that we wanted to utilize. However, in this example we did not turn on either Routing Information Protocol (RIP) or Interior Gateway Routing Protocol (IGRP) for simplicity. The router will then show us the configuration that we created:

```
The following configuration command script was created:
Hostname Phoenix
Enable secret 5 09371034073401823
Enable password Cisco
Line vty 0 4
Password Telnet
No snmp-server
!
ip routing
```

```
!
interface Ethernet 0
Shutdown
No ip address
Interface Ethernet 1
Shutdown
No ip address
Interface Serial 0
Ip address 172.29.3.4 255.255.255.0
Interface Serial 1
Ip address 172.29.4.3 255.255.255.0
!
end
Use this configuration? [yes/no]: yes
```

We have now completed the initial configuration dialog and successfully configured the Phoenix router with IP addressing.

Loading Cisco IOS Software

The sequence in which a router searches for a software image is dependent on the value of the *configuration register*; this is a 16-bit software configuration register that can be changed to set system parameters. The values in it are stored in NVRAM and are not erased during a reload or a power cycle. Some of the parameters that can be changed by modifying the configuration register are:

➤ Enable or disable the break function

➤ Control broadcast addresses

➤ Enable booting from a TFTP server

➤ Set the console terminal baud rate

➤ Recover a lost password

➤ Manipulate the boot commands

The last four bits of the configuration register are referred to as the *boot field*. The configuration register is typically shown in hexadecimal value, so only the last digit represents the 4 bits of the boot field. The value of the boot field determines the order in which the router looks for software. The default value for the boot field, as well as two other popular configuration register values and their functions are listed in Table 5.1.

When the boot field value is set to 0 (hexadecimal), the router will not boot. The user must execute the **boot** command from the ROM Monitor prompt. Typically, this configuration register setting is used for programming.

Table 5.1		Configuration register boot values and functions.
Configuration Register	Boot Field	Description
0x2100	0	The router will not boot unless you enter the **boot** command to the system bootstrap or ROM monitor program.
0x2101	1	The router will boot from ROM. The software version in ROM is usually a subset image (with the exception of the 7000) of IOS.
0x2102 – 0x210F	2 thru F	The router will look at the startup configuration file for **boot** command instructions.

When the boot field value is set to 1 (hexadecimal), the router will boot from the IOS image maintained in ROM. This image is usually a subset image of the full IOS stored in flash. However, this image usually contains the required functionality for loading new software into NVRAM.

When the boot field value is set to any value between 2 and F (hexadecimal), the router will boot based on the **boot** commands in the startup configuration file.

The configuration register can be viewed from exec mode and changed from configuration mode. The **show version** command displays this value highlighted on the last line of its output as shown in Listing 5.3.

Listing 5.3   The configuration register.

```
Phoenix#show version
%SYS-5-CONFIG_I: Configured from console by console
Cisco Internetwork Operating System Software
IOS (tm) 2500 Software (C2500-J-L), Version 11.2(13), RELEASE
SOFTWARE (fc1)
Copyright (c) 1986-1998 by cisco Systems, Inc.
Compiled Tue 31-Mar-98 12:27 by tlane
Image text-base: 0x0303F1E4, data-base: 0x00001000

ROM: System Bootstrap, Version 11.0(10c)XB1,
PLATFORM SPECIFIC RELEASE SOFTWARE (fc1)
BOOTFLASH: 3000 Bootstrap Software (IGS-BOOT-R), Version 11.0(10c)XB1,
 PLATFORM SPECIFIC RELEASE SOFTWARE (fc1)

Phoenix uptime is 8 minutes
System restarted by reload
System image file is "flash:11-2-13.img", booted via flash
```

```
cisco 2500 (68030) processor (revision L) with 2048K/2048K bytes
of memory.
Processor board ID 07112268, with hardware revision 00000000
Bridging software.
SuperLAT software copyright 1990 by Meridian Technology Corp.
X.25 software, Version 2.0, NET2, BFE and GOSIP compliant.
TN3270 Emulation software.
2 Ethernet/IEEE 802.3 interface(s)
2 Serial network interface(s)
32K bytes of non-volatile configuration memory.
16384K bytes of processor board System flash (Read ONLY)
Configuration register is 0x2101
```

Entering configuration mode and executing the **config-register** command will change the value of the configuration register:

```
Phoenix#conf t
Enter configuration commands, one per line. End with CNTL/Z.
Phoenix(config)
Phoenix(config)#config-register 0x2102
```

After the configuration register has been changed, you can check its value at the next reload by executing the **show version** command again, as shown in Listing 5.4.

Listing 5.4   The configuration register's value.

```
Phoenix#show version
%SYS-5-CONFIG_I: Configured from console by console
Cisco Internetwork Operating System Software
IOS (tm) 2500 Software (C2500-J-L), Version 11.2(13),
RELEASE SOFTWARE (fc1)
Copyright (c) 1986-1998 by cisco Systems, Inc.
Compiled Tue 31-Mar-98 12:27 by tlane
Image text-base: 0x0303F1E4, data-base: 0x00001000

ROM: System Bootstrap, Version 11.0(10c)XB1,
PLATFORM SPECIFIC RELEASE SOFTWARE (fc1)
BOOTFLASH: 3000 Bootstrap Software (IGS-BOOT-R), Version 11.0(10c)XB1,
 PLATFORM SPECIFIC RELEASE SOFTWARE (fc1)

Phoenix uptime is 8 minutes
System restarted by reload
System image file is "flash:11-2-13.img", booted via flash

cisco 2500 (68030) processor (revision L)
with 2048K/2048K bytes of memory.
```

```
Processor board ID 07112268, with hardware revision 00000000
Bridging software.
SuperLAT software copyright 1990 by Meridian Technology Corp.
X.25 software, Version 2.0, NET2, BFE and GOSIP compliant.
TN3270 Emulation software.
2 Ethernet/IEEE 802.3 interface(s)
2 Serial network interface(s)
32K bytes of non-volatile configuration memory.
16384K bytes of processor board System flash (Read ONLY)
Configuration register is 0x2101 (will be 0x2102 at next reload)
```

Boot System Commands

Typically, a router boots from the commands in the startup configuration. A few different variations of **boot** commands are based on the hardware platform. However, the overall command types remain primarily the same. You can tell your bootstrap program to search for Cisco IOS in three places: flash (NVRAM), network (TFTP Server), or ROM. Cisco has created a different startup configuration command for each of these scenarios. These commands are listed in Table 5.2.

The **boot system ROM** command forces the router to boot the system from the IOS maintained in ROM.

The **boot system flash** command forces the router to boot the system from the IOS image specified or the first image in flash if no image is specified. Listing its file name after the **boot system flash** command specifies an image.

The **boot system** command followed by a file name and an IP address boots the router by loading IOS from a remote TFTP server. By adding this command, you can often prevent a major outage if your current IOS becomes corrupt. All you need to do is to recycle the power, and the new image will be found. This scenario will not work if a network outage has occurred between this router and the TFTP server.

Table 5.2 Boot system commands and examples.		
Boot System Commands	**Location**	**Example**
boot system ROM	ROM	Phoenix(config)#boot system ROM
boot system flash {file name}	Flash	Phoenix(config)#boot system flash version11-3
boot system {file name} {IP Address}	TFTP Server	Phoenix(config)#boot system IOS11.3 172.29.3.4

The router executes each boot system command in the order in which they were entered. Therefore, as soon as the first command locates a valid and non-corrupt IOS image, no other boot system commands will be executed.

Upgrading Cisco IOS Software

Cisco IOS is constantly being revised to add new features or to fix bugs in previous versions. The process of upgrading software on a Cisco router can be broken down into three main steps:

1. Back up current Cisco IOS.

2. Copy new Cisco IOS to router.

3. Reload Cisco router and verify new IOS.

Back Up Current IOS

The first part of backing up the current IOS involves determining what version of IOS is running on the router and the file name of the software image. It is also necessary to note the size available in flash memory. The new version of IOS must not be larger than the total flash memory on the router. The **show version** command displays this information, as shown in Listing 5.5.

Listing 5.5   Backing up the current IOS.

```
Phoenix#sh vers
Cisco Internetwork Operating System Software
IOS (tm) 2500 Software (C2500-J-L), Version 11.2(13),
RELEASE SOFTWARE (fc1)
Copyright (c) 1986-1998 by cisco Systems, Inc.
Compiled Tue 31-Mar-98 12:27 by tlane
Image text-base: 0x0303F1E4, data-base: 0x00001000
ROM: System Bootstrap, Version 11.0(10c)XB1,
PLATFORM SPECIFIC RELEASE SOFTWARE (fc1)
BOOTFLASH: 3000 Bootstrap Software (IGS-BOOT-R), Version 11.0(10c)XB1,
PLATFORM SPECIFIC RELEASE SOFTWARE (fc1)

Phoenix uptime is 7 minutes
System restarted by reload
System image file is "flash:11-2-13.img", booted via flash

cisco 2500 (68030) processor (revision L)
with 2048K/2048K bytes of memory.
Processor board ID 07112268, with hardware revision 00000000
Bridging software.
SuperLAT software copyright 1990 by Meridian Technology Corp.
```

```
X.25 software, Version 2.0, NET2, BFE and GOSIP compliant.
TN3270 Emulation software.
2 Ethernet/IEEE 802.3 interface(s)
2 Serial network interface(s)
32K bytes of non-volatile configuration memory.
16384K bytes of processor board System flash (Read ONLY)
Configuration register is 0x2102
```

From the above command listing, we can determine that we have 16,384K bytes of flash memory available. Therefore, we can copy any software image less or equal to 16,384K bytes to this device. The name of the file name is provided above as "11-12-13.img." After the memory requirements and the file name have been determined, copy the old image to a TFTP server. This step gives you a fallback procedure in case the new software image is corrupt:

```
Phoenix#copy flash TFTP
System flash directory:
File  Length    Name/status
  1   7969232   11-2-13.img
[7969296 bytes used, 8807920 available, 16777216 total]
Address or name of remote host [255.255.255.255]? 172.16.24.134
Source file name? 11-2-13.img
Destination file name [11-2-13.img]? <Return>
Verifying checksum for '11-2-13.img' (file # 1)... OK
Copy '11-2-13.img' from Flash to server
  as '11-2-13.img'? [yes/no]y
!!!!!!!!!!!!!!!!!!!!!!!!!!!!!!!!!!!!!!!!!!!!!!!!!!!!!!!!!!!!!!!!!!!!!!!!!!
!!!!!!!!!!!!!!!!!!!!!!!!!!!!!!!!!!!!!!!!!!!!!!!!!!!!!!!!!!!!!!!!!!!!!!!!!!
!!!!!!!!!!!!!!!!!!!!!!!!!!!!!!!!!!!!!!!!!!!!!!!!!!!!!!!!!!!!!!!!!!!!!!!!!!
!!!!!!!!!!!!!!!!!!!!!!!!!!!!!!!!!!!!!!!!!!!!!!!!!!!!!!!!!!!!!!!!!!!!!!!!!!
!!!!!!!!!!!!!!!!!!!!!!!!!!!!!!!!!!!!!!!!!!!!!!!!!!!!!!!!!!!!!!!!!!!!!!!!!!
!!!!!!!!!!!!!!!!!!!!!!!!!!!!!!!!!!!!!!!!!!!!!!!!!!!!!!!!!!!!!!!!!!!!!!!!!!
!!!!!!!!!!!!!!!!!!!!!!!!!!!!!!!!!!!!!!!!!!!!!!!!!!!!!!!!!!!!!!!!!!!!!!!!!!
!!!!!!!!!!!!!!!!!!!!!!!!!!!!!!!!!!!!!!!!!!!!!!!!!!!!!!!!!!!!!!!!!!!!!!!!!!
!!!!!!!!!!!!!!!!!!!!!!!!!!!!!!!!!!!!!!!!!!!!!!!!!!!!!!!!!!!!!!!!!!!!!!!!!!
!!!!!!!!!!!!..!!!!!!!!!!!!!!!!!!!!!!!!!!!!!!!!!!!!!!!!!!!!!!!!!!!!!!!!!!!!
!!!!!!!!!!!!!!!!!!!!!!!!!!!!!!!!!!!!!!!!!!!!!!!!!!!!!!!!!!!!!!!!!!!!!!!!!!
!!!!!!!!!!!!!!!!!!!!!!!!!!!!!!!!
Upload to server done
Flash copy took 00:04:36 [hh:mm:ss]
```

Upgrade IOS

After the current IOS has been backed up to a TFTP server and the available memory checked on the router, you can proceed with the upgrade of the IOS. The new IOS must reside on the TFTP server, as shown in Listing 5.6.

Listing 5.6   Upgrading the IOS.

```
Phoenix#copy TFTP flash
Proceed? [confirm]<Return>

System flash directory:
File  Length   Name/status
  1   7969232  11-2-14.img
[7969296 bytes used, 8807920 available, 16777216 total]
Address or name of remote host [172.16.24.134]?<RETURN>
Source file name? 11-2-14.img
Destination file name [11-2-14.img]?
Accessing file '11-2-14.img' on 172.16.24.134...
Loading 11-2-14.img from 172.16.24.134 (via Ethernet1): ! [OK]

Erase flash device before writing? [confirm]
Flash contains files. Are you sure you want to erase? [confirm]

System configuration has been modified. Save? [yes/no]:
% Please answer 'yes' or 'no'.

System configuration has been modified. Save? [yes/no]: y
Building configuration...
[OK]

Copy '11-2-14.img' from server
  as '11-2-14.img' into Flash WITH erase? [yes/no]y

%SYS-5-RELOAD: Reload requested
%SYS-4-CONFIG_NEWER: Configurations from version 11.2 may not be
correctly understood.
%FLH: 11-2-14.img from 172.16.24.134 to flash ...

System flash directory:
File  Length   Name/status
  1   7969232  11-2-14.img
[7969296 bytes used, 8807920 available, 16777216 total]
Accessing file '11-2-14.img' on 172.16.24.134...
Loading 11-2-14.img from 172.16.24.134 (via Ethernet1): ! [OK]
Erasing device... eeeeeeeeeeeeeeeeeeeeeeeeeeeeeeeeeeeeeeeeeeeeeeeeeeeeee
ee ...erased
Loading 11-2-14.img from 172.16.24.134 (via Ethernet1): !!!!!!!!!!!!
!!!!!!!!!!!!!!!!!!!!!!!!!!!!!!!!!!!!!!!!!!!!!!!!!!!!!!!!!!!!!!!!!!!!!!!!!
!!!!!!!!!!!!!!!!!!!!!!!!!!!!!!!!!!!!!!!!!!!!!!!!!!!!!!!!!!!!!!!!!!!!!!!!!
!!!!!!!!!!!!!!!!!!!!!!!!!!!!!!!!!!!!!!!!!!!!!!!!!!!!!!!!!!!!!!!!!!!!!!!!!
!!!!!!!!!!!!!!!!!!!!!!!!!!!!!!!!!!!!!!!!!!!!!!!!!!!!!!!!!!!!!!!!!!!!!!!!!
!!!!!!!!!!!!!!!!!!!!!!!!!!!!!!!!!!!!!!!!!!!!!!!!!?!<!!!!!!!!!!!!!!!!!!!!!
```

```
!!!!!!!!!!!!!!!!!!!!!!!!!!!!!!!!!!!!!!!!!!!!!!!!!!!!!!!!!!!!!!!!!!!!!!!!!!!
!!!!!!!!!!!!!!!!!!!!!!!!!!!!!!!!!!!!!!!!!!!!!!!!!!!!!!!!!!!!!!!!!!!!!!!!!!!
[OK - 7969232/16777216 bytes]
Verifying checksum... OK (0xF865)
Flash copy took 0:07:00 [hh:mm:ss]
```

Reloading The Router

Depending on what type of router mode you have, when you copy a new version of software to the router, the router will either reload itself or return with the Router# prompt. If the router returns with a prompt, use the **Router# reload** command to restart the router and load the new software. The router reload command is as follows:

```
Router# reload
```

Practice Questions

Question 1

> Which command would allow you to add, modify, or delete the commands in the startup configuration file?
>
> ○ a. **show startup-config**
>
> ○ b. **show running-config**
>
> ○ c. **configure terminal**
>
> ○ d. **configure memory**

Answer d is correct. The **configure memory** command allows you to enter commands into the startup configuration file stored in NVRAM. Answers a and b are incorrect because they only allow you to view the startup and running configuration files, respectively. Answer c is incorrect because it allows you to add, modify, or delete the commands in the running configuration file, but not in the startup configuration file.

Question 2

> Which command would be used to restore a configuration file to RAM on a Cisco router?
>
> ○ a. **router#copy TFTP running-config**
>
> ○ b. **router>copy TFTP running-config**
>
> ○ c. **router#copy TFTP startup-config**
>
> ○ d. **router>copy TFTP running-config**

Answer a is correct. To restore a configuration file, the file must be copied from a TFTP server to the Cisco router. This is a trick question, because you must be in privileged exec mode to perform this function. Answers b and d are incorrect because the answer implies that the command is initiated from exec mode; you can determine this by the ">" symbol (versus the "#" symbol) at the end of the word "router" in answers a and d.

Question 3

Which of the following commands will display the running configuration file to a console terminal?

- ○ a. **router>show running-config**
- ○ b. **router#show startup-config**
- ○ c. **router#show flash**
- ○ d. **router>show version**
- ○ e. None of the above

Answer e is correct. The command to display a running configuration file to a console terminal is **show running-config**. Answer a is incorrect because this command is being executed from the exec mode. The **show running-config** command can only be executed from the privileged exec mode. Answer b displays the startup configuration file to the console monitor, and therefore, is incorrect. Answer c is incorrect because it displays any IOS images or configuration files stored in flash. Answer d displays software version and hardware on this router and therefore is incorrect.

Question 4

If you need to copy the currently executing configuration file into NVRAM, which command would accomplish this goal?

- ○ a. **router#copy startup-config running-config**
- ○ b. **router#copy startup-config TFTP**
- ○ c. **router#copy running-config startup-config**
- ○ d. **router>copy startup-config running-config**

Answer c is correct. The startup configuration file exists in NVRAM. So, to copy a configuration file to NVRAM, the current startup configuration file must be overwritten. Answer a is incorrect because the **startup-config** is not the currently executing image and this command is attempting to right the configuration file to RAM. Answer b is incorrect because the **startup-config** is not the currently executing configuration file and TFTP does not exist in NVRAM. Answer d is incorrect for the same reason as answer a, and because the command is being executed from exec mode.

Question 5

Which of the following commands would not set a password on a Cisco router?

○ a. **router(config)#enable secret**

○ b. **router(config-line)#password phoenix**

○ c. **router(config)#service encryption password**

○ d. **router(config)#enable password**

Answer c is correct. The **service encryption password** command is used to encrypt passwords in configuration files. Answer a is incorrect because it is used to set the **enable secret password**. Answer d is incorrect because it is used to set the **enable password**. Finally, answer b is incorrect because this command is used to set either the **telnet, auxiliary,** or **console** passwords, dependent on which line configuration mode the router is in when the command is executed.

Question 6

In which of the following scenarios would a router boot into the initial configuration dialog after its power has been cycled? [Choose the two best answers]

❏ a. Someone had copied the startup configuration file to a TFTP server.

❏ b. The running configuration file was copied to the startup configuration file.

❏ c. It is the first time this router has ever been powered on.

❏ d. The **write erase** command was executed immediately before powering down the router.

Answers c and d are correct. The initial configuration dialog starts anytime a configuration file cannot be found in NVRAM. This occurs when a write erase has been performed on the startup configuration file or when it is the first time the router is being powered on. Copying the running configuration to the startup configuration will not cause the router to boot into initial configuration dialog, and therefore, answer b is incorrect. Answer a is incorrect because copying a startup configuration file to a TFTP server will not cause a router to boot into the initial configuration dialog.

Question 7

Which of the following configuration register values would force a router to boot from ROM?

○ a. 0x2103

○ b. 0x210F

○ c. 0x2101

○ d. 0x2104

Answer c is correct. A configuration register with the value of 0x2101 forces a router to boot from ROM. Only when the boot field has a value of 1 or 0 will the router boot from ROM. Answers b, c, and d are incorrect because all these values would cause the router to look at the boot commands in the configuration file to determine what IOS to load.

Question 8

Where does the running configuration file exist in a Cisco route?

○ a. NVRAM

○ b. ROM

○ c. RAM

○ d. Flash memory

Answer c is correct. The running configuration file exists in RAM. This file is erased if a router is reloaded or its power is cycled. Answer b cannot be correct because ROM is a read only device and configuration files are constantly being updated. Answer a is incorrect because NVRAM is used to maintain the startup configuration file, not the running configuration file. Finally, answer d is incorrect because flash memory stores a copy of the IOS software, not running configurations.

Question 9

Which is the correct command to back up Cisco IOS software?

- ○ a. **router#copy running-config startup-config**
- ○ b. **router(config)#copy TFTP flash**
- ○ c. **router#copy flash TFTP**
- ○ d. **router#copy flash NVRAM**

Answer c is correct. To back up Cisco IOS, you must copy it to either a TFTP server or another storage device. Answer a is incorrect because it deals with configuration files, not Cisco IOS software. Answer b is incorrect because this command would be used to restore Cisco IOS to a router. Answer d is incorrect because **copy flash NVRAM** is not a command.

Question 10

Which of the following is not a valid Cisco command?

- ○ a. **router>show version**
- ○ b. **router#show running-config**
- ○ c. **router#show startup-config**
- ○ d. **router#show RAM**

Answer d is correct. **show RAM** is not a Cisco IOS command. Answers a, b, and c are incorrect because they are Cisco commands.

Need To Know More?

 Chappell, Laura: *Introduction to Cisco Router Configuration*. Cisco Systems Inc., Macmillan Publishing Company, 1998. ISBN 0-7645-3186-7. A great introduction to Cisco Router configuration.

 Lammle, Todd, Donald Porter, and James Chellis. *CCNA Cisco Certified Network Associate*. Sybex Network Press, Alameda, CA, 1999. ISBN 0-7821-2381-3. This book is full of helpful information.

 Syngress Media, with Richard D. Hornbaker, CCIE. *Cisco Certified Network Associate Study Guide*. Osborne/McGraw-Hill, Berkeley, CA, 1998. ISBN 0-07-882487-7. This book is a great study tool.

 The Cisco Web page, **www.cisco.com**, also provides some helpful information. Use the search engine to search for the following topics: password configuration, 2500 software upgrade, and managing configuration files.

Routing
Protocols

Terms you'll need to understand:

√ Route table

√ Metric

√ Routing protocol

√ Convergence

√ Routing loop

√ Distance vector

√ Link state

√ Hop count

√ Counting to infinity

√ Split horizon

√ Hold-down timers

√ Route poisoning

Techniques you'll need to master:

√ Understanding the path determination function of a router

√ Understanding the switching function of a router

√ Explaining the goals of routing protocols

√ Listing the types of routing protocols

√ Understanding the problems distance vector and link state routing protocols encounter when dealing with network topology changes

√ Describing techniques to increase the stability of distance vector and link state routing protocols

√ Configuring a router with the RIP routing protocol

√ Configuring a router with the IGRP routing protocol

√ Explaining the services of separate and integrated multiprotocol routing

This chapter presents information on routing protocols. Because the path determination and switching functions of a router rely upon routing protocols, we'll discuss the goals and types of routing algorithms and protocols. We review strengths and weaknesses of two popular routing algorithms and highlight techniques to mitigate those weaknesses. In addition, we'll list router configuration commands to enable routing protocols.

Routing Activities

As we have already discussed, routing occurs within the network layer (layer 3) of the OSI model. By sending packets from source network to destination network, the network layer gives its best effort in the delivery of end-to-end services. Getting packets to their next hop requires a router to perform two basic activities: path determination and packet switching.

Path determination involves reviewing all available paths to a destination network and choosing the optimal route on which to send a packet. Network topology information used to determine optimal routes is collected and stored in *route tables*, which contain information such as destination network, next hop, and an associated *metric* (or the cost of sending packets to that next hop).

Packet switching involves changing a packet's physical destination address to that of the next hop; however, the packet's destination logical address remains constant during the packet switching process. Review Chapter 3 for more specific examples of path determination and packet switching.

Routing Algorithms And Protocols

Routers choose the optimal or best route based on the available route information. A *routing algorithm* aids in the collection of route information and determination of the best path. These algorithms may vary in several aspects. They may differ based upon the goals they were designed to achieve with an internetwork. In addition, several types of routing algorithms exist to suit specific internetwork requirements. Finally, the metrics used by different routing algorithms also vary.

A *routing protocol* is a standard method of implementing a particular routing algorithm. For purposes of our discussions, routing protocols mean the routing algorithm or the protocol that implements it.

Goals Of Routing Protocols

As the needs of internetworks changed, new routing protocols were created to meet those needs and goals. For example, a routing protocol that functioned well in a small internetwork five years ago may experience problems in the large internetworks in use today.

 Routing protocols have been designed to meet one or more of the following design goals:

➤ Flexibility

➤ Optimality

➤ Rapid convergence

➤ Robustness

➤ Simplicity

Flexibility

A routing protocol should be flexible. It should be able to quickly adapt to its ever-changing network environment. Should a network segment go down, a flexible routing protocol would detect that event and determine the next best path to use while the segment is down. When the network segment becomes available, the routing protocol should update its route table to reflect that event also. Flexible routing protocols can also adapt to changes in network variables, such as network bandwidth and delay.

Optimality

The optimality of a routing protocol gauges its ability to correctly choose the best route. The metrics used by the protocol impact its optimality. For example, one protocol may heavily weight number of hops as its metric, whereas another may use a combination of number of hops and network delay.

Rapid Convergence

Convergence occurs once all routers within an internetwork agree on the optimal routes through the internetwork. Network events like routes going down or becoming available cause routers to recalculate optimal paths and distribute update messages about network routes. These messages permeate the entire network until all routes converge and agree on optimal routes. Slow convergence of the routing protocol can cause problems such as a routing loop.

A *routing loop* occurs when two or more routers have not yet converged and are broadcasting their inaccurate route tables. In addition, they most likely are still switching packets based on their inaccurate route tables. Figure 6.1 illustrates this case. An event has just occurred within the network—router A lost its path to network 5. While router A is updating its route table, it receives an update from router B that says network 5 is one hop away.

Router A increments the counter by one and adds this new information to its route tables. In turn, router A broadcasts its updated route table to router C, which updates its table and broadcasts the erroneous information to router D. Router D updates its table and propagates the misinformation to router B. Figure 6.2 illustrates this situation.

This cycle will continue ad infinitum. If any packets traversing the network are destined for network 5, it will loop between router A and router B until the packet becomes too old and is discarded.

Robustness

Robust and stable routing protocols perform correctly during unusual and un-predictable network events. High utilization, hardware failures, or incorrect configurations can create significant problems within a network. A robust routing protocol will be stable during a variety of network situations.

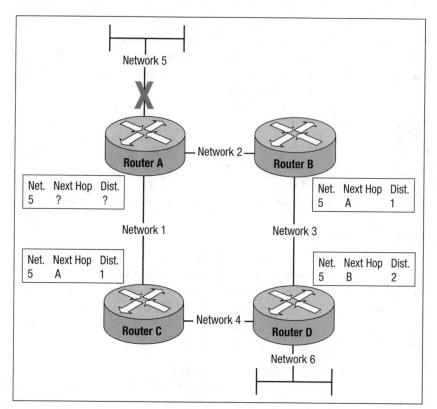

Figure 6.1 The routing loop.

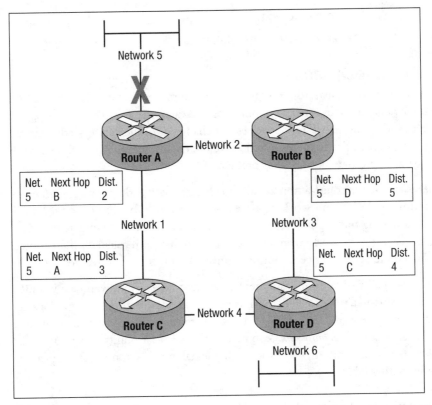

Figure 6.2 The routing loop update.

Simplicity

Simplicity of a routing protocol refers to its ability to operate efficiently. Because routing protocols collect and store route information, the protocol is competing for the router's limited physical resources. A routing protocol must perform its functions with minimal administrative overhead.

Types Of Routing Protocols

Routing protocols can also be categorized by type. The type of routing protocol deployed within an internetwork should be based on the organizational requirements.

Type of routing protocols include:

➤ Static or dynamic

➤ Single-path or multipath

➤ Flat or hierarchical

➤ Interior or exterior

➤ Distance vector or link state

Static Or Dynamic

A network administrator configures static routes manually. When defining a *static route*, the administrator configures destination network, next hop, and appropriate metrics. The route does not change until the network administrator changes it. Static routes function well in environments where the network is simple and network traffic is predictable.

Dynamic routes adjust automatically to changes within the internetwork environment. When network changes occur, routers begin to converge by recalculating routes and distributing route updates. The route update messages permeate the network, which causes more routers to recalculate their routes. This route update process continues until all routers have converged.

Occasionally, static routes augment dynamic routes. In a dynamically routed environment, a router will discard a packet if the destination network does not appear in the route table. However, a static route can be configured to handle this situation. A *default route* can be established (that points to a router) that will receive and attempt to process all packets for which no route appears in the routing table.

Single-Path Or Multipath

When calculating the optimal path for a particular network, some routing protocols will simply choose the best *single-path* to a destination network. Others will allow more than one optimal path if the paths have equal metric values. A *multipath protocol* enables traffic multiplexing using the multiple paths and offers additional advantages over single-path protocols, such as reliability.

Flat Or Hierarchical

A routing environment is considered *flat* if all routers are peers to each other. Routers using a flat routing protocol may communicate with any other router in the network as directly as possible. Like static routing, a flat routing protocol functions well in simple and predictable network environments.

On the other hand, a *hierarchical* routing environment contains several routers that comprise a backbone. Most traffic from non-backbone routers usually traverses the backbone routers (or at least travels to the backbone) in order to reach another non-backbone router. Within a hierarchical routing environment, autonomous systems (sometimes referred to as *domains* or *areas*) can be established. Being part of the same autonomous system enables a group of routers to share network topology information with each other, but that same information is not shared outside the group. Although several layers or tiers may exist within the hierarchy, the routers at the highest level comprise the backbone. Typically the network backbone comprises its own autonomous system or domain.

Interior Or Exterior

An *interior routing* protocol operates within a single autonomous system or domain. These protocols are typically implemented within an organization's private network. Routers that are running interior routing protocols are considered *intradomain routers*; they only need to know about other routers within their domain. Conversely, an *exterior routing* protocol conveys routing information between domains; exterior routing protocols are in use within the Internet. *Interdomain routers* need to know how to route traffic between autonomous systems and can protect errors or problems with one domain from impacting another.

Distance Vector Or Link State

Distance vector protocols require each router to send all or a large part of its route table to its neighboring routers. *Link state* protocols require that each router send the state of its own interfaces to every router in the internetwork. Distance vector protocols are simple and straightforward, but they converge slowly, which can cause routing loops. Link state protocols converge quickly, but they require more of the router's CPU and memory resources. Distance vector and link state routing protocols are widely used. They will be explored further later in the chapter.

Each routed protocol can be implemented in one or more routing protocols. It is actually the routing protocols (or standard set of rules) that enable the router to determine the best path. Common routing protocols include:

➤ Routing Information Protocol (RIP)

➤ Interior Gateway Routing Protocol (IGRP)

➤ Open Shortest Path First (OSPF)

➤ Enhanced Interior Gateway Routing Protocol (EIGRP)

➤ Border Gateway Protocol (BGP)

➤ Exterior Gateway Protocol (EGP)

BGP and EGP are both exterior routing protocols and differ significantly from their interior counterparts. Table 6.1 lists the common interior routing protocols and their characteristics.

Table 6.1 Interior routing protocols.					
Routing Protocol	Static Or Dynamic	Single-Path Or Multipath	Flat Or Hierarchical	Interior Or Exterior	Distance Vector Or Link State
RIP	Dynamic	Single-path	Flat	Interior	Distance vector
IGRP	Dynamic	Multipath	Flat	Interior	Distance vector
OSPF	Dynamic	Multipath	Hierarchical	Interior	Link state
EIGRP	Dynamic	Multipath	Flat	Interior	Advanced distance vector

Note: *IGRP and EIGRP are Cisco proprietary routing protocols. They are only supported on Cisco routers.*

Routing Metrics

Routing protocols use many different metrics to determine the optimal route. These variables can be used individually or in combination with one another to create the metric defined within a given routing protocol.

Metrics used in routing protocols include:

➤ Bandwidth

➤ Delay

➤ Load

➤ Path length

➤ Reliability

Bandwidth

The available capacity of a network link is known as its *bandwidth.* Typically, a 10Mbps Ethernet link is preferable to a 56Kb Frame Relay link. However, if other metrics such as delay are considered, the Ethernet link may not be the optimal path.

Delay

Network delay refers to the amount of time necessary to move a packet through the internetwork from source to destination. Delay is a conglomeration of several other variables, including physical distance between source and destination, bandwidth and congestion of intermediate links, and port queues of intermediate routers.

Load

Load is an indication of how busy a network resource is. CPU utilization and packets processed per second are two valuable factors when calculating the load.

Path Length

In some routing protocols, *path length* refers to the sum of the costs of each link traversed up to the destination network. Other routing protocols refer to path length as the *hop count*, which is the number of passes through a router that a packet makes on its way to the destination network.

Reliability

This metric allows the network administrator to arbitrarily assign a numeric value to indicate a reliability factor for the link. Some network links go down more than others; some are easily repaired and become available relatively quickly. The reliability metric is simply a method to capture an administrator's experience with a given network link.

 A routed protocol such as IP or IPX is concerned with the movement of user traffic. A routing protocol such as RIP or OSPF is concerned with maintaining route tables.

Distance Vector Vs. Link State

This section highlights the similarities and differences between two types of widely used routing protocols: distance vector and link state.

Distance Vector Overview

As discussed previously, a distance vector routing protocol sends all or part of its route table across the network, but only to its neighbors. The route table contains the distance and direction to any network within its domain. Figure 6.3 provides an overview of the distance vector process.

Periodically, router A broadcasts its entire route table to its neighbors, router B and router C. Router B will update the route information it received by incrementing the metric value, which is usually the hop count, by one. Router B then compares the route information it just received and updated with the

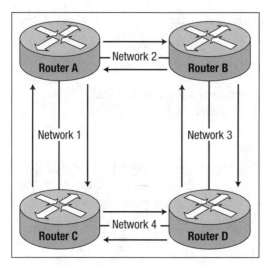

Figure 6.3 The distance vector process overview.

existing route information from its route table. Router B replaces existing route information with an updated entry only if the updated route information has a lower calculated metric. Router B then broadcasts its route table to its direct neighbors—router D and router A. This process occurs regularly and in all directions for all directly connected neighbors. Although this process enables routers to accumulate network distance information, the routers do not know the network's exact topology.

Note: The default value for RIP updates to occur is every 30 seconds.

Link State Overview

A *link state* routing protocol (sometimes referred to as *shortest path first*) sends only the state of its own network links across the network, but it sends this information to every router within its domain. This process enables routers to learn and maintain full knowledge of the network's exact topology and how it is interconnected. Figure 6.4 provides an overview of the link state process.

Link state routing protocols rely upon several components to acquire and maintain knowledge of the network:

➤ Router C broadcasts and receives *link state packets* to and from other routers via the network. Link state packets contain the status of a router's links or network interfaces.

➤ Router C builds a topology database of the network.

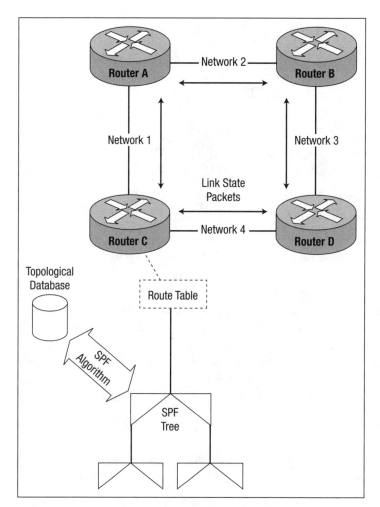

Figure 6.4   The Link state process overview.

➤ Router C runs a SPF algorithm against the database and generates a SPF tree of the network with router C as the root of the tree.

➤ Router C populates its route table with optimal paths and ports to transmit data through to reach each network.

Network Discovery

When a router starts up, it must undergo a *network discovery* process. This process enables the router to begin communicating with other routers on the network.

Figure 6.5 illustrates the network discovery process for distance vector protocols. Router A has just started up and is configured to run a distance vector.

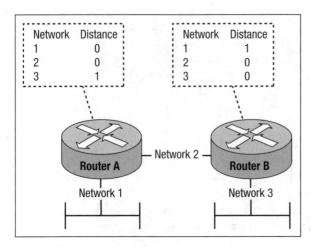

Network	Distance
1	0
2	0
3	1

Network	Distance
1	1
2	0
3	0

Router A — Network 2 — Router B

Network 1   Network 3

Figure 6.5   The distance vector network discovery.

It begins the discovery process by identifying its neighbor—router B. Router A begins populating its route table with its directly connected networks—networks 1 and 2, which receive a metric of 0. It passes its route table to router B and receives router B's entire route table. Router A will increment the distances of each entry by one hop. After the distances have been updated, router A will already have better routes to networks 1 and 2, but not network 3. Router A will increment the distance to network 3 by a one hop and store it in its route table.

The network discovery process for link state protocols is similar to that of distance vector protocols. Instead of route tables, routers exchange link state packets and use that information to build their topology databases, SPF trees, and route tables. Refer to Figure 6.4 for an example of the link state discovery process.

Regardless of whether a router uses a distance vector or link state routing protocol, the router will dynamically discover its network environment. It can then use its route table to perform the packet switching function.

Topology Changes

After the router has discovered the network, it must also keep up with network topology changes. Depending on the protocol used, a router transmits route information periodically or when a network event occurs. Routers detect changes in the network topology via these updates.

Most distance vector protocols handle topology changes through regularly scheduled updates. After a specified interval, a router broadcasts its route table to its neighbor. Route recalculation occurs if necessary and updates in the network topology are broadcast. The route distribution timers are not synchronized across routers.

Link state protocols rely upon network events to address topology changes. If a router detects a network event (such as one of its neighbors being no longer reachable or it becomes aware of a new neighbor), it triggers an update. The router broadcasts the state of its links to all other routers within the domain. Upon receiving the update, other routers will update their topology database and broadcast the state of their links also. Once all updates have been received, each router updates its SPF tree and route tables accordingly. It is at this point that the network has converged. Event-triggered updates have a ripple effect within a network.

Distance Vector Problems

The fact that route updates with a distance vector protocol occur after a specified interval can become problematic. With RIP, route updates are broadcast every 30 seconds by default. As a result, distance vector protocols converge slowly. Previously in this chapter, routing loops and the problems they create were discussed. Routing loops create a condition know as *counting to infinity*, where the distance metric is continually incremented because the network has not fully converged. Refer to Figures 6.1 and 6.2 for examples of a routing loop and counting to infinity.

Distance Vector Remedies

One technique to remedy a count to infinity situation involves a maximum hop count. Although this count will not prevent a routing loop, it does reduce the time that the routing loop exists. A maximum hop count, when reached, forces a router to mark a network unreachable, rather than incrementing the distance metric as represented in Figure 6.6.

Routing loops also occur when information is broadcast back to a router that contradicts information that the router previously sent. Refer to Figure 6.7 as an example. Router A sends information about network 5 to router B. *Split horizon* prevents a router from sending information it received about a network back to its neighbor that originally sent the information. For example, split horizon prohibits router B and router C from sending any information about network 5 back to router A.

Route poisoning occurs when a router detects that a network is down and immediately marks it as unreachable. This route update is broadcast throughout the network. While the other routers slowly converge, the router maintains this poisoned route in its route table and ignores updates from other routers about better routes to the network. The poisoned route is removed after several update cycles. Route poisoning works well with another technique called *holddown timers*.

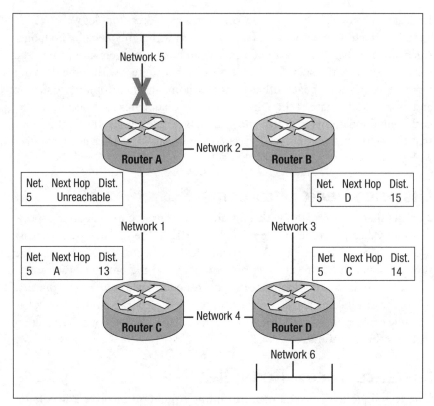

Figure 6.6 The maximum hop count.

A *hold-down timer* indicates that no updates to a particular route should be accepted until the timer expires. A hold-down condition is triggered when a router receives an update from its neighbor indicating that a reachable network has just gone down. The router marks the network as unreachable and starts its hold-down timer. While the timer is active, updates from any other router are ignored. Only updates from the neighboring router (that initially indicated the network unreachable) about the unreachable network are accepted while the timer is active. If the neighboring router indicates the network is reachable again, the router stops the hold-down timer and updates its route table. Once the hold-down timer expires, the router marks the network reachable and receives updates from any router.

The following techniques help stabilize distance vector protocols:

➤ Maximum hop count

➤ Split horizon

➤ Route poisoning

➤ Hold-down timers

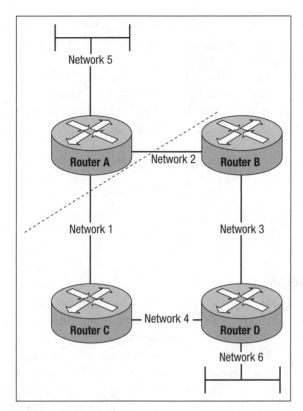

Figure 6.7 Split horizon.

Link State Problems

Because link state routing protocols have knowledge of the entire network and converge quickly, they do not suffer from the same problems as distance vector protocols. One problem that impacts link state protocols is the significant memory and processor resources required from the router itself when acquiring and maintaining full knowledge of large networks. As updates move through the network, each router must receive the update, recalculate its information, and send its own link information. Of course this type of overhead impacts the ability of the router to move user data packets through the network.

A second shortcoming of link state protocols is the amount of network bandwidth that can be consumed while the network converges. Routers flood updates about the state of their links to every other router in the network, so the amount of bandwidth consumed is significant. As routers collect link information from each other, the amount of bandwidth available for end user communications is reduced. This high level of bandwidth utilization typically occurs on initialization of the network or when several routers start up simultaneously.

Additional problems can occur during the link state update process itself. It is imperative that each router receives all of the packets in a timely manner and that the updates are synchronized. For example, if one part of the network receives route information before another part, convergence may take longer or SPF trees and route tables may store inaccurate information. Additionally, as routers attempt to move link state packets through the network, they may be doing so without fully constructed SPF trees or route tables.

The following problems may occur within networks using link state protocols:

➤ Router resource usage

➤ Network bandwidth consumption

➤ Update synchronization

Link State Remedies

One remedy for link state problems involves minimizing the resources required to build and maintain route tables. The time between periodic updates can be lengthened to reduce the processing resources required. Also, routers can be identified to serve as border routers. The border routers can then exchange route summaries with other border routers and each core router to reduce the bandwidth consumed during the update process and to isolate update processes to hierarchical areas. The border router then passes updates to the routers within its area. Another technique involves coordinating link state updates. Time stamps and a sequence number can be attached to the link state packet. Routers then realize when they receive inaccurate or old link state packets.

The following techniques help stabilize link state protocols:

➤ Minimize router resource usage by lengthening update frequency or exchanging route summaries.

➤ Coordinate updates with time stamps or sequence numbers.

Both distance vector and link state routing protocols have demonstrated their worth over time. Each has advantages that may suit a particular network design perfectly. Several factors must be considered when choosing a routing protocol, including business policies and operational issues. Table 6.2 provides a quick comparison of distance vector and link state routing protocols.

Table 6.2 Distance vector versus link state routing protocols.	
Distance Vector	**Link State**
Sees the network from its neighbor's perspective.	Sees the entire network from its own perspective.
Distance metrics accumulate from router to router.	Calculates shortest path to other routers.
Route updates occur periodically.	Route updates are event-triggered.
Convergence is slow.	Convergence is fast.
Broadcasts entire route table to neighbors.	Broadcasts link status information to all other routers.

Routing Protocol Configuration And Review

This section highlights the basic router commands necessary to add the RIP and IGRP routing protocols to a router configuration.

RIP

Table 6.3 lists the router configuration commands necessary to enable RIP on a router.

The **show IP protocol** command displays detailed information about each IP routing protocol that has been configured on the router.

Table 6.3 RIP configuration commands.		
Task	**Router Prompt**	**Command**
Enter global configuration mode	RouterA#	**configure terminal**
Enter RIP routing protocol configuration mode	RouterA (config)#	**router rip**
Configure network 172.16.0.0 to be advertised	RouterA (config-router)#	**network 172.16.0.0**
Exit configuration mode	RouterA (config-router)#	**<CTRL>Z**

Listing 6.1 displays the results of the **show IP protocol** command after RIP has been configured.

Listing 6.1   RIP configuration display.

```
RouterA#
RouterA#show ip protocol <Return>
Routing Protocol is "rip"
  Sending updates every 30 seconds, next due in 2 seconds
  Invalid after 180 seconds, hold down 180, flushed after 240
  Outgoing update filter list for all interfaces is not set
  Incoming update filter list for all interfaces is not set
  Redistributing: rip
  Default version control: send version 1, receive any version
    Interface       Send  Recv   Key-chain
    Ethernet0        1     1 2
    Loopback0        1     1 2
    Serial0          1     1 2
  Routing for Networks:
    172.16.0.0
  Routing Information Sources:
    Gateway          Distance      Last Update
    172.16.24.252       120        00:00:12
  Distance: (default is 120)

RouterA#
```

> *Note:*   *Notice that by default, RIP sends updates every 30 seconds. Also, the RIP hold-down timer is set to 180 seconds and a neighbor router has an IP address of 172.16.24.252.*

IGRP

Table 6.4 lists the router configuration commands necessary to enable IGRP on a router.

Table 6.4   IGRP configuration commands.

Task	Router Prompt	Command Syntax
Enter global configuration mode	RouterA #	**configure terminal**
Enter IGRP routing protocol configuration mode for autonomous system 1	RouterA (config)#	**router igrp 1**
Configure network 172.16.0.0 to be advertised	RouterA (config-router)#	**network 172.16.0.0**
Exit configuration mode	RouterA (config-router)#	**<CTRL>Z**

Listing 6.2 displays the results of the **show IP protocol** command after IGRP has been configured.

Listing 6.2   IGRP configuration display.

```
RouterA#
RouterA#show ip protocol <Return>
Routing Protocol is "igrp 1"
  Sending updates every 90 seconds, next due in 7 seconds
  Invalid after 270 seconds, hold down 280, flushed after 630
  Outgoing update filter list for all interfaces is not set
  Incoming update filter list for all interfaces is not set
  Default networks flagged in outgoing updates
  Default networks accepted from incoming updates
  IGRP metric weight K1=1, K2=0, K3=1, K4=0, K5=0
  IGRP maximum hopcount 100
  IGRP maximum metric variance 1
  Redistributing: igrp 1
  Routing for Networks:
    172.16.0.0
  Routing Information Sources:
    Gateway          Distance       Last Update
    172.16.24.252       100         00:00:15
  Distance: (default is 100)
RouterA#
```

Note: Notice that by default, IGRP sends updates every 90 seconds. Also, the IGRP maximum hop count is set to 100 and a neighbor router has an IP address of 172.16.24.252.

Advanced Distance Vector Protocol

Both distance vector and link state routing protocols have performed well under a variety of network conditions. Based on the specific needs of an organization, one may be more preferable than the other. However, as discussed earlier, each type has shortcomings. An *advanced distance vector protocol* combines the strengths of distance vector and link state protocols. Enhanced Interior Gateway Routing Protocol (EIGRP) is Cisco's proprietary advanced distance vector protocol.

Like distance vector protocols, advanced distance vector protocol uses distance metrics, but the metrics are more accurate than simple hop counts for determining the best path. In the event that distance metrics are equal for multiple best paths, routers supporting advanced distance vector protocol will add both or all routes to its route table and load balance traffic across those routes. But unlike distance vector protocols, an advanced distance vector protocol does not periodically send route updates across the network. It relies upon topology changes to trigger when route updates are to be sent.

Like link state protocols, an advanced distance vector protocol converges quickly. However, it is much more efficient in its use of a router's resources and its use of network bandwidth when sending route updates.

In addition to resolving some of the shortcomings of distance vector and link state protocols, advanced distance vector protocols support integrated routing.

Integrated Routing

Although a router can support multiple routing and routed protocols, it keeps those protocols isolated. The protocols have no knowledge or impact upon each other. This concept is referred to as "ships-in-the-night routing." *Integrated routing* permits these different protocols to have knowledge of each other. It also allows different protocols to share resources. Rather than using several routing protocols to support multiple routed protocols, integrated routing enables a network administrator to use a single routing protocol to support multiple routed protocols.

Benefits of integrated routing include:

➤ Carrying route updates that can be used by multiple routing protocols.

➤ Minimizing the use of network and router resources.

➤ Maintaining separate route tables for each routing protocol.

➤ Simplifying network administration.

➤ Supporting path selection and packet switching for multiple routed protocols.

EIGRP also supports integrated routing, and supports IP, Novell IPX, and AppleTalk protocols. Table 6.5 lists the router configuration commands necessary to enable EIGRP on a router.

Listing 6.3 displays the results of the **show IP protocol** command after EIGRP has been configured.

Listing 6.3   EIGRP configuration display.

```
RouterA#
RouterA#show ip protocol <Return>
Routing Protocol is "eigrp 1"
```

```
Outgoing update filter list for all interfaces is not set
Incoming update filter list for all interfaces is not set
Default networks flagged in outgoing updates
Default networks accepted from incoming updates
EIGRP metric weight K1=1, K2=0, K3=1, K4=0, K5=0
EIGRP maximum hopcount 100
EIGRP maximum metric variance 1
Redistributing: igrp 1, eigrp 1
Automatic network summarization is in effect
Routing for Networks:
  172.16.0.0
Routing Information Sources:
  Gateway          Distance      Last Update
  172.16.24.252          90      0:00:06
Distance: internal 90 external 170
RouterA#
```

Note: *Notice that EIGRP does not periodically send updates. Also, the EIGRP maximum hop count is set to 100 by default and a neighbor router has an IP address of 172.16.24.252.*

Table 6.5 EIGRP configuration commands.

Task	Router Prompt	Command
Enter global configuration mode	RouterA#	**configure terminal**
Enter EIGRP routing protocol configuration mode for autonomous system 1	RouterA (config)#	**router eigrp 1**
Configure network 172.16.0.0 to be advertised	RouterA (config-router)#	**172.16.0.0**
Exit configuration mode	RouterA (config-router)#	**<CTRL>Z**

Practice Questions

Question 1

> Which of the following are basic functions of a router? [Choose the two best answers]
>
> ❑ a. Packet switching
>
> ❑ b. Packet filtering
>
> ❑ c. Path determination
>
> ❑ d. Rapid convergence

Answers a and c are correct. Routers packet switch once they have determined the best path. Path determination is the process of choosing the best network path among all available network paths. Packet filtering is a technique for controlling inbound and/or outbound packets to or from a router. Therefore, answer b is incorrect. Rapid convergence is a design goal of some routing protocols. Therefore, answer d is incorrect.

Question 2

> Network routing information distributed among routers is stored in which of the following?
>
> ○ a. Flash
>
> ○ b. Route table
>
> ○ c. Metric table
>
> ○ d. NVRAM

Answer b is correct. Route tables contain information about destination networks and the next hop along the optimal path to get there. Flash contains the operating system images used by the router. Therefore, answer a is incorrect. Metric information is contained within a router's route table. Therefore, answer c is incorrect. NVRAM contains the router's active configuration files. Therefore, answer d is incorrect.

Question 3

Which of the following is not an interior routing protocol?

○ a. RIP

○ b. IGRP

○ c. OSPF

○ d. BGP

Answer d is correct. BGP is designed to communicate route information between autonomous systems; therefore, it is an exterior routing protocol. RIP, IGRP, and OSPF are routing protocols used to communicate route information within an autonomous system. Therefore, answers a, b, and c are incorrect.

Question 4

Which of the following routing protocols communicates route information by sending the state of its links to all routers in its domain?

○ a. BGP

○ b. RIP

○ c. IGRP

○ d. OSPF

Answer d is correct. OSPF is a link state routing protocol that passes the state of its links to all routers within its domain. BGP is an exterior routing protocol that communicates reachability information between domains. Therefore, answer a is incorrect. RIP and IGRP are distance vector protocols that send all or part of their route tables to their neighbors. Therefore, answers b and c are incorrect.

Question 5

> Which of the following conditions is a problem experienced by distance vec-
> tor routing protocols?
>
> ○ a. Split horizon
>
> ○ b. Route poison
>
> ○ c. Counting to infinity
>
> ○ d. Maximum hop count
>
> ○ e. Hold-down timers

Answer c is correct. Counting to infinity can result from the slow convergence
inherent with distance vector protocols. Split horizon, route poison, maximum
hop count, and hold-down timers are techniques to reduce the occurrence and
impact of the counting to infinity situation. Therefore, answers a, b, d, and e
are incorrect.

Question 6

> What router command will display the routing protocol settings (such as tim-
> ers and neighbors) configured on a router?
>
> ○ a. **show protocol**
>
> ○ b. **show routing protocol**
>
> ○ c. **show ip protocol**
>
> ○ d. **show running-config**

Answer c is correct. The **show ip protocol** command displays all routing protocols active on the router. In addition, it displays other values such as timers,
neighbors, and when the next update will be sent. The **show protocol** command displays the information about routed protocols such as IP and IPX.
Therefore, answer a is incorrect. The **show running-config** command displays
some routing protocol information, such as the networks that are being advertised to other routers. Therefore, answer d is incorrect. The **show routing-config**
command is invalid. Therefore, answer b is incorrect.

Question 7

Which techniques will help mitigate the shortcoming of link state protocols? [Choose the two best answers]

❑ a. Maximum hop count

❑ b. Minimize router resource usage

❑ c. Coordinate updates

❑ d. Route poisoning

Answers b and c are correct. Lengthening the update frequency or exchanging router summaries at specific border routers helps minimize router resource usage. Therefore, answer b is correct. Also, attaching time stamps or sequence numbers on link state packets helps coordinate update information between routers. Therefore, answer c is correct. A maximum hop count and route poisoning address problems with distance vector protocols. Therefore, answers a and d are incorrect.

Question 8

Which router commands, if executed from the global configuration prompt, will enable RIP routing for network 172.16.0.0?

○ a. **router rip 1** and **network 172.16.0.0**

○ b. **router rip all**

○ c. **router rip** and **network 172.16.0.0**

○ d. **network 172.16.0.0**

Answer c is correct. The **router rip** command enables RIP routing and the **network 172.16.0.0** command enables the router to advertise that network to other routers. Answers a and b are incorrect because the **router rip** command requires no additional parameters. Answer d is incorrect because you must first enter routing protocol configuration mode before configuring a network to be advertised.

Question 9

> Which router commands, if executed from the global configuration prompt, will enable IGRP routing for autonomous system 1 and network 172.16.0.0?
>
> ○ a. **router igrp 1** and **network 172.16.0.0**
>
> ○ b. **router igrp 172.16.0.0**
>
> ○ c. **router igrp** and **network 172.16.0.0**
>
> ○ d. **network 172.16.0.0**

Answer a is correct. The **router igrp 1** command enables IGRP routing for autonomous system 1 and the **network 172.16.0.0** command enables the router to advertise that network to other routers. The **router igrp** command requires an autonomous system to be specified, so answers b and c are incorrect. Answer d is incorrect because you must first enter routing protocol configuration mode before configuring a network to be advertised.

Question 10

> Which of the following statements is a benefit of integrated routing?
>
> ○ a. Supporting path selection and packet switching for multiple routed protocols.
>
> ○ b. Carrying route updates that can be used by multiple routing protocols.
>
> ○ c. Minimizing the use of network and router resources.
>
> ○ d. Maintaining separate route tables for each routing protocol.
>
> ○ e. All of the above

Answer e is correct. All of the answers are benefits of integrated routing. Simplifying network administration and replacing the native routing algorithm are also benefits of integrated routing.

Question 11

> Which of the following conditions are problems experienced by link state routing protocols? [Choose the three best answers]
>
> ❑ a. Split horizon
>
> ❑ b. High router resource usage
>
> ❑ c. High network bandwidth consumption
>
> ❑ d. Unsynchronized updates
>
> ❑ e. Hold-down timers

Answers b, c, and d are correct. Problems with high router resource usage and high network bandwidth can occur during convergence as link state packets flood the network. If link state packet updates are not synchronized, inaccurate SPF trees and route tables may result and/or convergence may take longer. Split horizon and hold-down timers are techniques for reducing problems in distance vector routing protocols. Therefore, answers a and e are incorrect.

Need To Know More?

 Moy, John T. *OSPF: Anatomy of an Internet Routing Protocol.* Addison-Wesley Publishing Co., 1998. ISBN 0-20163-472-4. This book gives detailed information on various Internet routing protocols, then focuses specifically on OSPF.

 Parkhurst, William R. *Cisco Router OSPF: Design and Implementation Guide.* McGraw Hill, 1998. ISBN 0-07048-626-3. This book reviews routing protocol configuration commands and also discusses advanced topics, such as route redistribution between routing protocols.

 The Computer and Information Science Web site at Ohio State University, **www.cis.ohio-state.edu/hypertext/information/ rfc.html,** provides information on Internet Request for Comments (RFC) documents. For detailed information on a distance vector routing protocol, look up RFC 1058, which describes RIP. RFCs 1388 and 1723 provide updated information on RIP. For detailed information on a link state routing protocol, review RFC 1131, which lists the OSPF specification. RFC 1247 provides updated information on OSPF.

 The official Cisco Documentation Web site, **www.cisco.com/ public.technotes/tech_protocol.shtml,** discusses the routing protocol Web pages for IGRP/EIGRP and OSPF. You can also review more information on exterior routing protocols such as BGP and EGP.

TCP/IP

Terms you'll need to understand:

✓ Transfer Control Protocol (TCP)

✓ Internet Protocol (IP)

✓ Defense Advanced Research Projects Agency (DARPA)

✓ Advanced Research Project Agency network (ARPAnet)

✓ File Transfer Protocol (FTP)

✓ Simple Mail Transfer Protocol (SMTP)

✓ Telnet

✓ Domain Name System (DNS)

✓ TCP three-way handshake

✓ TCP windowing

✓ User Datagram Protocol (UDP)

✓ Address Resolution Protocol (ARP)

✓ Reverse Address Resolution Protocol (RARP)

✓ Internet Control Message Protocol (ICMP)

Techniques you'll need to master:

✓ Identifying the functions of the TCP/IP transport-layer protocols

✓ Identifying the functions of the TCP/IP network-layer protocols

✓ Describing the TCP/IP stack

✓ Explaining the function of the TCP/IP protocols ARP, RARP, and ICMP

This chapter and Chapter 8 discuss the *Transmission Control Protocol/Internet Protocol (TCP/IP)* suite of protocols. The birth and evolution of the Internet was made possible by the creation of the TCP/IP protocol suite. This chapter begins by providing a brief background of TCP/IP; understanding its humble beginnings allows you to truly appreciate the enormity of its use in our world today.

To continue to build upon the foundation of internetworking, the TCP/IP protocol suite is mapped to the OSI model. Each of the TCP/IP protocols maps roughly to one of the seven layers of the OSI model. Each of the TCP/IP layers is discussed and broken down to a level of detail to prepare for the CCNA exam. The purpose and function of many of the TCP/IP protocols are discussed in this chapter. IP addressing is covered in detail in Chapter 8.

Background And History Of TCP/IP

The importance of TCP/IP in today's society was not expected during its early development. In the early 1970s, Stanford University received funding from the Defense Advanced Research Project Agency (DARPA) to create a protocol that could exploit the advantages of a packet-switched network and allow communications between dissimilar networks.

DARPA wanted a protocol that could connect different networks while having the robustness to choose among multiple paths to a final destination. DARPA believed that the flexibility inherent to a packet-switched network might be the solution. Stanford University consequently produced the Internet Protocol suite to fulfill these wishes. Meanwhile, DARPA built a hardware infrastructure designed to use the Internet Protocol as the software and called it *ARPAnet*, which later evolved into the Internet. The Internet Protocol suite is commonly referred to as TCP/IP in reference to the two best known protocols.

The Internet Protocol suite was developed to operate across the networks of a wide variety of institutions. The Internet Protocol suite allowed networks with different information formats, data rates, error characteristics, and data unit sizes to share a common suite of protocols. It is the adaptability of the Internet Protocol suite that has made it the most widely used protocol today. Nearly every computer vendor supports at least part of this suite. The TCP/IP suite of protocols has literally evolved from a government funded research program into packet-switched networks into a ubiquitous media.

TCP/IP Stack And The OSI Model

TCP/IP is based on a nonproprietary model and allows all vendors to develop applications that are based on the model. The TCP/IP protocol suite has four layers that roughly map to the seven layers of the OSI model; however, it performs all the functions of the OSI model. The mapping of the TCP/IP suite of protocols to the OSI model is shown in Figure 7.1.

Note that the application layer of the TCP/IP protocol suite maps to the application, presentation, and session layers of the OSI model. The TCP/IP application layer performs the functions described by the OSI model for all three layers. The transmission and network layers of the TCP/IP protocol suite perform the functions described by the OSI model for the transmission and network layers. Finally, the network interface of the TCP/IP protocol performs the same functions as the data link and physical layers of the OSI model.

Application Layer

The application layer consists of a set of services that provides ubiquitous access to all types of networks. Applications utilize the services to communicate with other devices and remote applications. A large number of TCP/IP services is provided at the application layer. However, Table 7.1 lists the most important protocols when studying for the CCNA exam.

 Memorize the port numbers for these protocols. You will find knowing these protocols by name and number will save you a lot of time for the CCNA test as well as in your career.

OSI 7 Layer Model	TCP/IP 4 Layer Model	Services/ Protocols	
Application		Telnet	FTP
Presentation	Application	TFTP	NFS
		SMTP	DNS
Session			
Transport	Transport	TCP	UDP
Network	Network	IP	ICMP
Data Link	Network Interface	ARP	RARP
Physical			

Figure 7.1 TCP/IP mapping to the OSI model.

Table 7.1 TCP/IP application layer services.		
Service	**Function**	**Port Number**
FTP	File transfer	21
TFTP	File transfer	69
Telnet	Terminal emulation	23
SMTP	Simple Mail Transfer Protocol	25
SNMP	Simple Network Management Protocol	162
DNS	Domain Name System	53

File Transfer Protocol

File Transfer Protocol (*FTP*) is used to copy a file from one host to another host regardless of the physical hardware or operating system of each device. FTP identifies a client and server during the file transfer process. In addition, it provides a guaranteed transfer by using the services of TCP. The services that TCP provides are explained in more detail in the next section of this chapter.

Trivial File Transfer Protocol

Trivial File Transfer Protocol (*TFTP*) was designed to be a lean FTP service. The goal was to develop a protocol that could fit into the limited ROM space of diskless machines. TFTP is a connectionless protocol that uses the services of the *User Datagram Protocol* (*UDP*) for transport. TFTP is used to copy files from one host (server) to another host (client). In many cases, TFTP is used to copy software to a device as it boots up. The function of the TFTP services for Cisco routers is illustrated in Chapter 5. A list of some of the commands that use TFTP is as follows:

➤ **copy tftp startup-config**

➤ **copy tftp running-config**

➤ **copy tftp flash**

➤ **copy startup-config tftp**

➤ **copy running-config tftp**

➤ **copy flash tftp**

The steps for performing these commands was shown in Chapter 5. It is important to completely understand the proper situation in which to use each of these commands. For example, one must know that copying a file to the startup-config will write the file to the flash memory and copying a file to the running-config will write the file to the random access memory (RAM).

Telnet

The Telnet service allows a user to act as though he or she has a terminal attached to another device. This process is referred to as *terminal emulation*. Telnet is a very useful protocol in internetworking, because it allows network administrators to view and configure remote devices in the network from one location. Telnet uses the services of TCP to provide a connection-oriented session. An example of using the Telnet service between two devices follows:

```
Router#telnet 204.99.4.36
Trying 204.99.4.36 ... Open
Phoenix>
```

Simple Mail Transfer Protocol

Simple Mail Transfer Protocol (SMTP) is used to pass mail messages between devices. It uses TCP connections to pass the email we've all grown to love between two mail hosts.

Simple Network Management Protocol

Simple Network Management Protocol (SNMP) is used to obtain data on remote devices. Typically, a network management station uses SNMP to poll the devices in a network and to retrieve data regarding the devices' current and past conditions. SNMP uses five different types of messages to monitor the condition of devices. With SNMP, the network management machine is referred to as the *manager* and all the remote devices are considered *agents* of the manager. Each of the agents maintains a *Management Information Database (MIB)* locally that constantly stores information about that device. The manager systematically polls each of its agents, requesting information from their databases; it then manipulates and organizes the data into a useful format for reporting or display on the network management monitor.

Domain Name System

Domain Name System (DNS) is used to translate host names or computer names into IP addresses such as **www.coriolis.com** or vice versa. DNS is a hierarchical database of names and their associated IP addresses. DNS is what allows people to enter a word-based address for any device on the Internet. When this occurs, that person's device requests a DNS lookup from a DNS server. The DNS server replies with the IP address associated with that word-based address.

Transport Layer

The *transport layer* provides an end-to-end connection between two devices during communication by performing sequencing, acknowledgments, checksums, and flow control. The transport layer allows the application layer to ignore the complexities of the network and focus on its primary job. This layer also is responsible for sending data that it receives from the network layer to the appropriate application. An application using the services of the transport layer can use two different protocols: User Datagram Protocol (UDP) and Transfer Control Protocol (TCP). Both of these fulfill the transport layer responsibilities, however, they provide two very different levels of service.

Transfer Control Protocol

TCP provides a connection-oriented and reliable service to the applications that use its services. TCP was designed to add some reliability into the world of IP networking. A description of the main functions of TCP follows:

➤ **Segments application layer data stream** TCP accepts data from applications and segments it into a desirable size for transmission between itself and the remote device. The segment size is determined while TCP is negotiating the connection between the two devices. Either device can dictate the segment size.

➤ **Provides acknowledgment timers** TCP maintains timers to identify when packets have taken too long to get to their destination. When an acknowledgment is not received for an IP packet before the expiration of the timer, TCP resends the packet to the destination. Therefore, if a packet gets lost in a network, TCP resends it until the remote device sends an acknowledgment of the packet's receipt or a defined limit of acknowledgments is reached.

➤ **Enables sequence number checking** TCP/IP uses sequence numbers to ensure that all packets sent by an application on one device are read in the correct order by an application on another device. The packets might not be received at the transport layer in the correct order, but TCP will sequence them in their original order before passing them to the application layer.

➤ **Provides buffer management** Any time two devices are communicating, the possibility exists that one device can send data faster than the other can accept it. Initially, the receiving device will put the extra packets into a buffer and read them when it gets a chance. However, when this data overflow persists, the buffer eventually is filled and packets begin to drop. TCP performs some preventive maintenance called *flow control* to avoid this scenario.

➤ **Initiates connection with three-way handshake** TCP uses the concept of the three-way handshake to initiate a connection between two devices. Figure 7.2 illustrates this procedure. A TCP connection begins with device A by sending SYN a request to synchronize sequence numbers and initiate a connection (a SYN). Device B receives the message and sends a SYN message in response with the sequence number incremented by one. Device A responds with a response to a SYN indicating that the device received the sequence number it expected (an ACK) to device B indicating that it received SYN message requesting a TCP connection.

➤ **Performs error and duplication checking** TCP uses a checksum to identify packets that have changed during transport. If a device receives a packet with a bad checksum, it drops the packet and does not send an acknowledgment for it. Thus, the sending device then resends the packet (hopefully, it will not change during transport this time). In addition, any time TCP receives a duplicate packet it will drop it.

➤ **Performs acknowledgment windowing to increase efficiency of bandwidth use** Anytime a TCP device sends data to another device, it must wait for the acknowledgment that this data was received. Figure 7.3 illustrates TCP communication between two devices with a window size

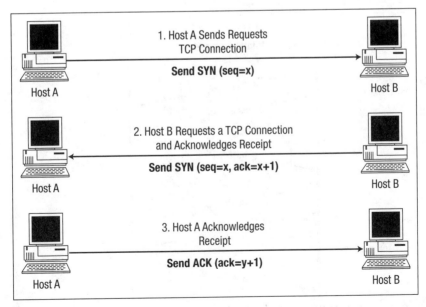

Figure 7.2 TCP three-way handshake.

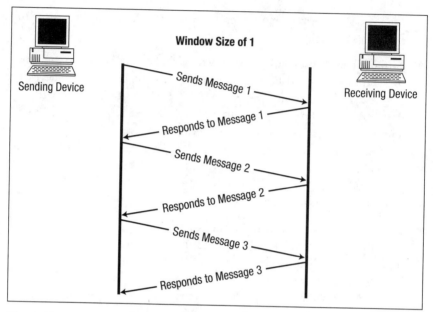

Figure 7.3 TCP communication with window size of 1.

of 1. To increase the efficiency in utilizing the bandwidth, TCP can change the window size. If the window size is increased to 2, as shown in Figure 7.4, then the sending device requires only one acknowledgment

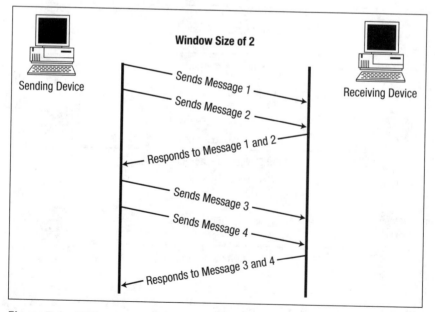

Figure 7.4 TCP communication with window size of 2.

for every two packets sent. TCP dynamically sets the window size during a connection, allowing either device involved in the communication to slow down the sending data rate based on the other device's capacity. This process is often referred to as *sliding windows* because of TCP's ability to change the window size dynamically.

TCP Header Format

The TCP header is designed to support all the functions mentioned previously and much more. The TCP header, illustrated in Figure 7.5, is 20 bytes and encapsulated in an IP packet during transport.

The purpose of each of the fields in the TCP header is as follows:

➤ **Source port** Identifies the sending application for the data. It is interesting to note that the combination of the source and destination IP

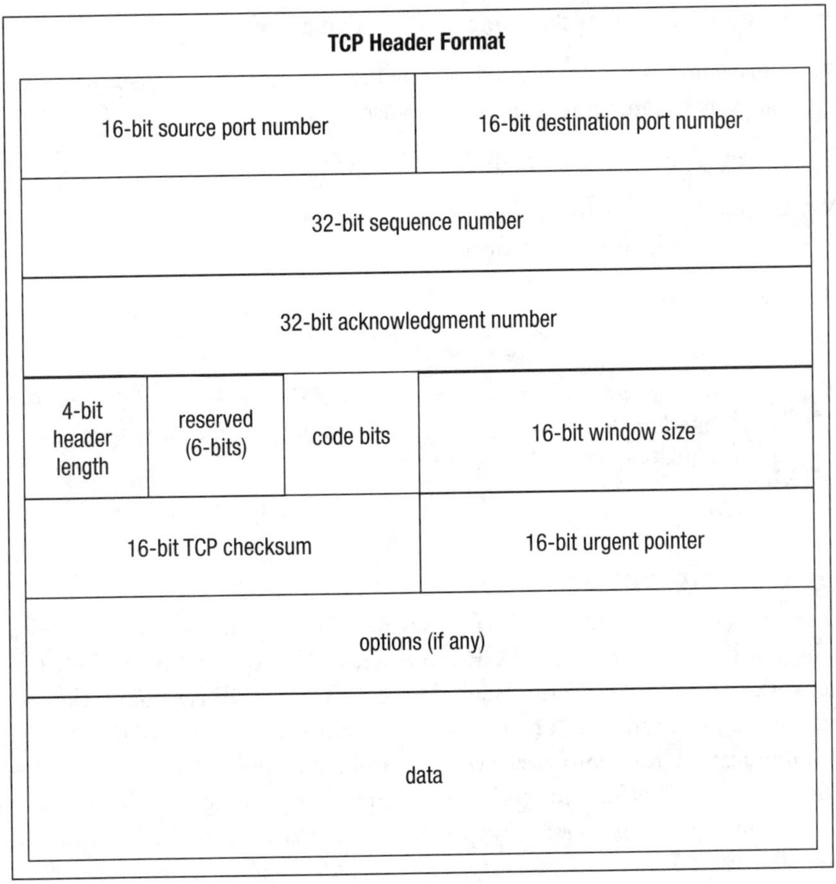

TCP Header Format

16-bit source port number		16-bit destination port number	
32-bit sequence number			
32-bit acknowledgment number			
4-bit header length	reserved (6-bits)	code bits	16-bit window size
16-bit TCP checksum		16-bit urgent pointer	
options (if any)			
data			

Figure 7.5   TCP header format.

addresses and ports uniquely identifies all TCP connections. This combination is often referred to as a *socket*.

➤ **Destination port** Identifies the destination application for the data.

➤ **Sequence number** Allows the receiving device to order data correctly before passing it to an application.

➤ **Acknowledgment number** Identifies which TCP octet is expected next.

➤ **Header length** Gives the length of the header in 32-bit words. This is necessary because the TCP header can have optional fields in it that can extend the header.

➤ **Reserved** Reserved for later use. Always set to zero.

➤ **Code bits** Identify what type of segment is being sent. For example, the code bit can designate a SYN or ACK segment type.

➤ **Window** Identifies the number of bits that a device is willing to accept.

➤ **Checksum** A field that is verified by the receiving device to ensure that data was not manipulated during transport.

➤ **Urgent pointer** Indicates the end of urgent data.

➤ **Option** Identifies the maximum TCP segment size. This is the only option that is currently defined.

➤ **Data** The payload.

 It is not important to memorize all of the fields in the TCP or IP headers. However, it is important to understand the overall capabilities of the TCP and IP header.

User Datagram Protocol

User Datagram Protocol (*UDP*) is a transport layer protocol that provides a subset of the functionality of TCP. However, UDP requires considerably less network resources to perform its job than does TCP. UDP is a connectionless protocol because it does not require acknowledgments or sequence numbers to communicate. UDP simply receives data from the application layer and applies the proper header and sends the datagram on its merry way. This is why UDP is referred to as a *best-effort protocol*. A comparison to TCP is provided below in Table 7.2.

Table 7.2	Functional comparison of TCP and UDP application layer services.	
Function	**UDP**	**TCP**
Data segmentation	Every datagram is the same size	Dynamically assigns datagram size for efficiency.
Reliability	Best effort only	Sequence numbers, acknowledgments, and three-way handshake
Flow control	None	Provides buffer management to avoid overflow and lost packets. Uses sliding windows to maximize bandwidth efficiency.
Error checking	Checksum	Checksum

UDP Header Format

The UDP header requires only eight bytes for all its information. In comparison to TCP's 20-byte header, the UDP header is very small and requires minimal bandwidth. Figure 7.6 illustrates the UDP header format.

The purpose of each of the fields in the UDP header follows:

➤ **Source port** Identifies the sending application for the data.

➤ **Destination port** Identifies the destination application for the data.

➤ **Checksum** A checksum that covers the UDP header and data.

➤ **Header Length** The length of the UDP and the UDP in bytes.

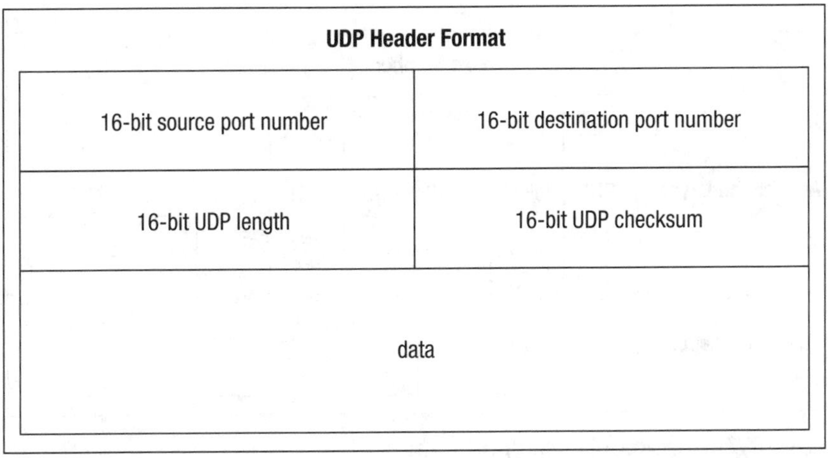

UDP Header Format	
16-bit source port number	16-bit destination port number
16-bit UDP length	16-bit UDP checksum
data	

Figure 7.6 UDP header format.

Ports And Sockets

We have mentioned the purpose of ports and sockets in our explanation for TCP and UDP. This section provides a little more detailed look at ports and sockets. A port number identifies a sending or destination application. Every application running on a host uses certain ports or ranges of ports to communicate with applications running on other hosts. It is by these port numbers that TCP or UDP determines which application to pass the data to in the application layer. A total of 65,535 ports exists; however, only a subset of these ports is most commonly used and referred to as the *well-known ports*.

The well-known ports have a value between 0–1,023. Therefore, when an application on one device wants to communicate with an application on another device, it must specify the address of the device (IP address) and identify the application (port number). The combination of the sending and destination port numbers and the sending and destination IP addresses defines a *socket*. A socket can be used to uniquely define any UDP or TCP connection. Figure 7.7 illustrates some of the most commonly used ports and their associated applications. Notice that each port number is assigned to either UDP or TCP. All of the well-known port numbers are defined in RFC 1700.

Network Layer

The *network layer* is responsible for path determination and packet switching. The network layer utilizes a logical addressing scheme to make intelligent decisions regarding path determination and packet switching. TCP/IP uses the IP addressing scheme that is explained in detail in Chapter 8. The network layer performs the actual relay of packets from an originating network to a destination network in an efficient manner.

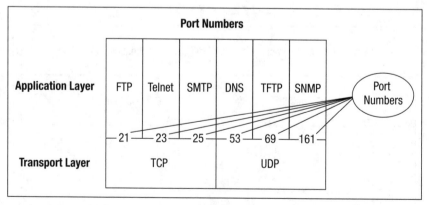

Figure 7.7 Commonly used port numbers.

Internet Protocol

Internet Protocol (*IP*) is the transport for TCP, UDP, and Internet Control Message Protocol (ICMP) data. TCP and UDP have been previously explained in detail and ICMP will be discussed shortly. IP provides an unreliable service; it lets the upper layer protocols such as TCP or application specific devices worry about reliability. In addition, IP performs as a connectionless service because it handles each datagram as an independent entity. IP performs packet switching and path determination by maintaining tables that indicate where to send a packet based on its IP address. The format of the IP packet header is provided in Figure 7.8.

The purpose of each of the fields in the IP header is as follows:

➤ **Bit version** Identifies the current version of IP. The current IP version is 4 or Ipv4.

➤ **Header length** The number of 32-bit words in the header.

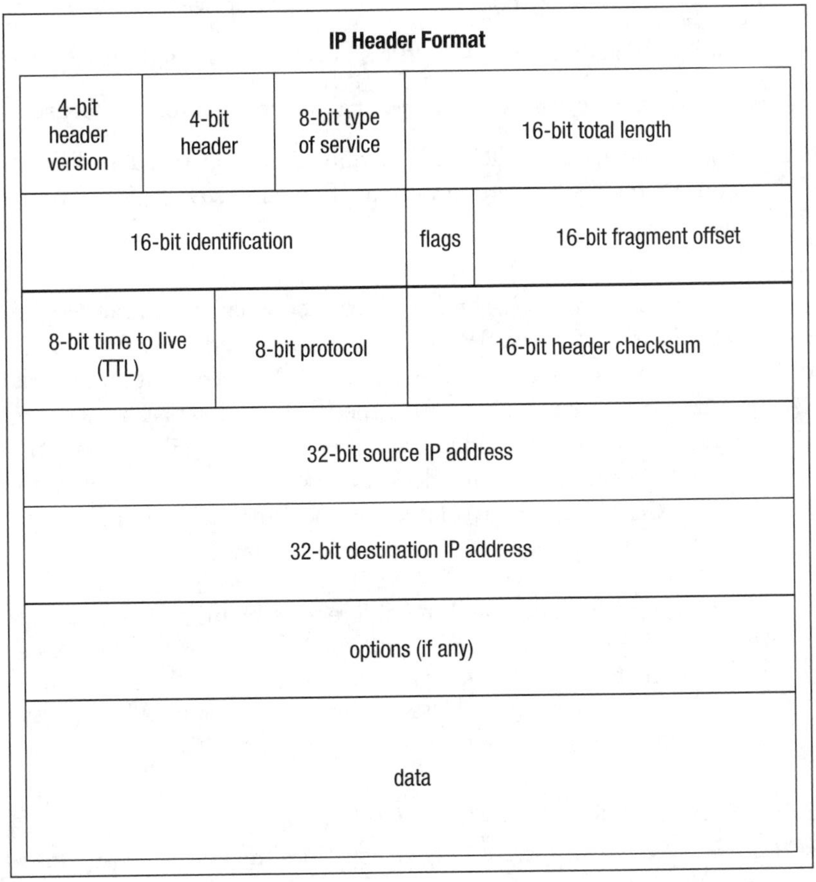

IP Header Format			
4-bit header version	4-bit header	8-bit type of service	16-bit total length
16-bit identification		flags	16-bit fragment offset
8-bit time to live (TTL)		8-bit protocol	16-bit header checksum
32-bit source IP address			
32-bit destination IP address			
options (if any)			
data			

Figure 7.8 IP header format.

➤ **TOS** The type-of-service field is broken into a 3-bit precedence bit and four type-of-service bits. This field is used to provide quality of service for IP data transport.

➤ **Total length** Provides the total length of the IP datagram in bytes.

➤ **Identification** Uniquely identifies every packet from the sending device. This field, along with the flags and fragment offset fields, is used for packet fragmentation and reassembly.

➤ **Time to live (TTL)** This field sets an upper limit on the number of routers that can switch the packet. It is used to drop packets that are in routing loops.

➤ **Protocol field** Identifies the protocol to pass the packet to upstream. For example, this protocol could be TCP, UDP, ICMP, or IGMP.

➤ **Checksum** A cyclical redundancy check of the IP header only.

➤ **Source IP address** The IP address of the sending device.

➤ **Destination IP address** The IP address of the destination device.

➤ **Options** A variable-length list of optional information for the packet.

Chapter 8 provides more detailed information on IP and IP addressing. In addition, you can find a complete account of IP in RFC 791.

Address Resolution Protocol

Address Resolution Protocol (ARP) bridges the gap between physical and logical addressing by mapping a known IP address to a physical address. Therefore, if two devices want to communicate, the first device can send out a broadcast ARP requesting the physical address for a specified IP address. The receiving device will respond with its IP address, and the first device will maintain this entry in its ARP cache. If a device does not exist on the same subnet, the sending device will address the resolution protocol for the default gateway's physical address and send the packet to the default gateway.

 It is vital to understand the difference scenarios when ARP versus RARP is applicable. One rule of thumb is that diskless machines use RARP and typically all other machines will use ARP. This is due to diskless machines not having an IP address during the boot sequence.

Reverse Address Resolution Protocol

Reverse Address Resolution Protocol (RARP) provides the exact opposite mapping from ARP. RARP maps a known physical address to a logical address.

Diskless machines that do not have a configured IP address when started typically use RARP. These devices send a broadcast requesting an IP address. In these scenarios, a device on the same LAN is designed to respond to this broadcast request and supply the IP address for that physical address. Table 7.3 defines both ARP and RARP.

Internet Control Message Protocol

Internet Control Message Protocol (*ICMP*) communicates error messages and control messages between devices. Thirteen different types of ICMP messages are defined. The ICMP protocol allows devices to check the status of other devices, query the current time, and perform other functions. The most used function of ICMP is the ping utility. This utility is illustrated in Chapter 8. The most common ICMP messages are:

➤ **Destination unreachable** Indicates that a certain device cannot be contacted.

➤ **Time exceeded** Indicates that a certain device could not be reached within a specified time limit.

➤ **Echo** This is a request for an echo reply to determine device reachability.

➤ **Echo reply** This is a reply to an echo request indicating that a host is reachable.

The ping command is extremely useful in troubleshooting network problems. An extended ping command is also available in Cisco IOS. An extended ping is performed by simply using the IP ping command. After executing this command, you will be given the option to alter many of the variables in the ping command. Some example variables include the number of attempts and the size of the packet.

Table 7.3 ARP and RARP.

Protocol	Action	Purpose
ARP	Maps a known IP address to a physical address.	Used to identify the physical address of another workstation.
RARP	Maps a known physical address to an IP address.	Used in diskless environments so machines can determine their IP address from another device on the same LAN.

Network Interface Layer

This layer provides access to the local area network. The physical addressing and network specific protocols exist at this layer. Token ring, Ethernet, and FDDI are some examples of network interface layer protocols.

Practice Questions

Question 1

Which of the following terms does not identify a layer of the TCP/IP model?

O a. Application

O b. Transport

O c. Presentation

O d. Network

O e. Network interface

Answer c is correct. The presentation layer is only used by the OSI model, and therefore, it does not identify a layer of the TCP/IP model. Answers a, b, d, and e all identify separate layers of the TCP/IP model.

Question 2

Which of the following services exist at the application layer of the TCP/IP model? [Choose the three best answers]

❑ a. SMTP

❑ b. FTP

❑ c. ICMP

❑ d. ARP

❑ e. TFTP

Answers a, b, and e are correct. SMTP, FTP, and TFTP all exist at the application layer of the TCP/IP model. Answer c is incorrect because ICMP exists at the Internet layer of the TCP/IP model. Answer d is incorrect because ARP exists at the network interface layer of the TCP/IP model.

Question 3

Which of the following services is used to copy files between Cisco routers?

○ a. SMTP

○ b. SMNP

○ c. TFTP

○ d. RARP

○ e. HTTP

Answer c is correct. The TFTP protocol is used by Cisco routers to copy configuration and software files between clients and servers. Chapter 5 covers this command in more detail. Answer a is incorrect because SMTP is used to pass email messages between devices. Answer b is incorrect because SMNP is used to monitor devices. Answer d is incorrect because RARP is used to determine an IP address, given the MAC address. Finally, HTTP, answer e, is used to browse the Web.

Question 4

Which of the following services is used to translate word-based addresses into IP addresses?

○ a. SNMP

○ b. SMTP

○ c. IP

○ d. UDP

○ e. DNS

Answer e is correct. DNS is used to translate word-based addresses into IP addresses or vice versa. SNMP and SMTP are TCP/IP application layer services, but do not perform address translation. Therefore, answers a, b, and c are incorrect. SNMP is used to monitor remote devices and SMTP is used to send email between devices. IP is not a service, but a protocol used for addressing. Finally, UDP is a transport layer protocol used for packet sequencing. Therefore, answer d is incorrect.

Question 5

Which of the following functions is not performed by TCP?

○ a. Flow control

○ b. Sequencing

○ c. Error checking

○ d. Subnetting

Answer d is correct. Subnetting is not a function performed by TCP; it is a process used to create more networks out of classful IP addresses. Answer a is incorrect because TCP does indeed provide flow control in the form of sliding windows and buffer management. Answer b is incorrect because TCP provides sequencing to ensure datagrams are read in the correct order on the receiving side. Finally, answer c is incorrect because TCP provides error checking by applying a checksum to the TCP header and encapsulated data.

Question 6

Which of the following functions do UDP and TCP both perform? [Choose the two best answers]

❑ a. Provide destination and source port numbers

❑ b. Flow control

❑ c. Dynamic datagram size allocation

❑ d. Checksum

❑ e. Acknowledgments of datagram receipt

Answers a and d are correct. Answer a is correct because the destination and source port numbers are provided in both the UDP and TCP headers. In addition, answer d is correct because both TCP and UDP provide for a checksum in the header to verify accurate delivery. However, answer b is incorrect because only TCP performs flow control type activities in the form of buffer management and sliding windows. Answer c is incorrect because UDP does not dynamically set datagram sizes, but assigns each datagram the same size. Finally, only TCP provides reliability in its data transport. Therefore, answer e is incorrect because UDP does not generate acknowledgments for the receipt of datagrams.

Question 7

Which of the following are functions of the network layer? [Choose the two best answers]

❑ a. Path determination

❑ b. Packet switching

❑ c. Code formatting

❑ d. Reliability

❑ e. Physical addressing

Answers a and b are correct. Answer a is correct because the network layer uses the logical address of a packet to determine the best path to take in route to a destination. In addition, the network layer uses the logical address to make packet switching decisions. Therefore, answer b is correct. Answer c is incorrect because code formatting would be performed by the TCP/IP application layer, not the network layer. Answer d is incorrect because the network layer does not provide reliability, but relies on the TCP/IP transport and application layers to provide the reliability. Answer d is incorrect because physical addressing is a function of the TCP/IP interface layer.

Question 8

Which of the following are characteristics of the protocol ARP? [Choose the two best answers]

❑ a. It resides at the network layer.

❑ b. It resides at the network interface layer.

❑ c. It maps a known IP address to MAC address.

❑ d. It maps a known MAC address to IP address.

Answers a and c are correct. Answer a is correct because the protocols ARP, RARP, ICMP, and IP exist at the network layer. Answer c is correct because devices use ARP to determine the physical address (MAC address) for a known IP address. Answer b is incorrect because LAN protocols such as token ring, Ethernet, and FDDI exist at this layer. Answer d is incorrect because the process of mapping a known MAC address to an unknown IP address is accomplished by the protocol RARP.

Question 9

> Which transmission layer protocol provides connectionless services?
>
> ○ a. UDP
>
> ○ b. TCP
>
> ○ c. ICMP
>
> ○ d. IP
>
> ○ e. FTP

Answer a is correct. UDP is a transport layer protocol that provides a best-effort connectionless service. Answer b is incorrect because TCP provides a connection-oriented transport layer service through the use of acknowledgments and sequence numbers. Answer c is incorrect because ICMP is a network layer protocol used for control messaging. Answer d is incorrect because IP is a network layer protocol used for addressing and path determination. Answer e is incorrect because FTP is an application layer protocol used for transferring files between two devices.

Need To Know More?

 Chappell, Laura: *Introduction to Cisco Router Configuration*. Cisco Systems Inc., Macmillan Publishing Company, 1998. ISBN 0-7645-3186-7. The first three chapters cover some great OSI material.

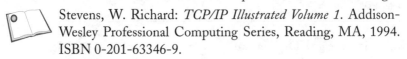 Lammle, Todd, Donald Porter, and James Chellis: *CCNA Cisco Certified Network Associate*. Sybex Network Press, Alameda, CA, 1999. ISBN 0-7821-2381-3. Chapter 4 covers IP addressing.

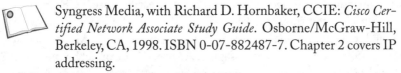 Stevens, W. Richard: *TCP/IP Illustrated Volume 1*. Addison-Wesley Professional Computing Series, Reading, MA, 1994. ISBN 0-201-63346-9.

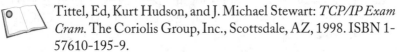 Syngress Media, with Richard D. Hornbaker, CCIE: *Cisco Certified Network Associate Study Guide*. Osborne/McGraw-Hill, Berkeley, CA, 1998. ISBN 0-07-882487-7. Chapter 2 covers IP addressing.

Tittel, Ed, Kurt Hudson, and J. Michael Stewart: *TCP/IP Exam Cram*. The Coriolis Group, Inc., Scottsdale, AZ, 1998. ISBN 1-57610-195-9.

Internet Protocol

8

Terms you'll need to understand:

√ Dotted decimal notation

√ Classful addressing

√ Subnetting

√ Subnet mask

√ Logical AND

√ Variable Length Subnet Masking (VLSM)

√ Classless Interdomain Routing (CIDR)

√ Ping

√ Traceroute

Techniques you'll need to master:

√ Describing the two parts of IP network addressing

√ Identifying the different classes of IP addressing

√ Developing an IP addressing scheme with subnetting

√ Configuring IP addressing on a Cisco router

√ Verifying IP addressing on a Cisco router

√ Monitoring IP addressing on a Cisco router

The proliferation of the Internet into many aspects of our lives has increased the importance of *Internet Protocol*, or *IP*, drastically. The building blocks of the Internet are wires, switches, and routers, but the glue that keeps it together is IP. The secret password into the Internet is a registered IP address. IP has been chosen as the protocol of choice for the Internet. This means that vendors, corporations, and consultants work feverishly to develop, utilize, and implement this protocol. This also means that the amount of products that utilize the IP are increasing, which ensures the longevity of its importance.

This chapter focuses on explaining the fundamentals of IP addressing. We will explain IP in its binary and decimal forms. The ability to understand IP in both these forms is expected of beginning engineers. In addition, this chapter explains classful addressing and identifies the differences among the various classes of IP addresses. After providing a foundation, we'll introduce and explain the concept of subnetting. We will also cover the steps to configure, verify, and monitor IP on a Cisco router.

IP Addressing

The purpose of an IP address is to uniquely identify a device to the rest of the digital world. IP addresses have two parts: a *network ID* and a *host ID*, and each plays an important role in uniquely identifying a device. Figure 8.1 illustrates an IP address in binary format divided into its network ID and host ID parts.

The purpose of having two distinct parts of an address is to simplify the process of finding any individual host in a sea of networks. Computers use the network ID to quickly route data to the gateway device of the network. The gateway device of that network then uses the host ID part of the IP address to uniquely identify a device on that network. The division of the IP address into two parts allows a quick and accurate method for isolating a host's network first, then identifying the host. The concepts of *classful addressing* and *subnetting* increase the complexities of IP addressing a little bit; nevertheless, it is an interesting topic that is a staple of networking. However, before these topics are tackled, it is important to understand the format of an IP address in more detail.

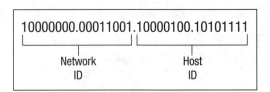

Figure 8.1   An IP address that is a two part network address.

Dotted Decimal Notation

IP addresses are typically shown in *dotted decimal notation*. This was developed so humans could more easily read and write IP addresses. An IP address in its native form is binary. Figure 8.2 illustrates the same Binary IP address used in Figure 8.1; however, the address is now displayed in dotted decimal notation. An IP address under IP Version 4 (IPv4) is comprised of 32 bits that have been divided into 8-bit groups referred to as *octets* or *bytes*. An IP address in dotted decimal notation specifies the decimal value of each of the four octets separated by dots. Each octet can have a decimal value between 0 and 255. Why? The total number of possible values for a binary number with 8 bits can be written mathematically as 2^8. Although 2^8 has a total value of 256, IP addresses begin with the number 0; therefore, the decimal range starts at 0 and ends with 255 for a total of 256 possible values.

The ability to convert IP addresses between binary and decimal is very important to becoming effective in using IP addressing. The difference between the decimal and binary number systems is the number of digits they use. The decimal system uses 10 digits: 0, 1, 2, 3, 4, 5, 6, 7, 8, and 9. The 'dec' in the name 'decimal' refers to the 10 digits. The binary number system uses two digits: 0 and 1. The 'bi' in the name 'binary' refers to the two digits. When a decimal number is higher than nine, the proper procedure is to increment the number of digits that are used to represent the number. The first time you increment the number of digits, you indicate this by putting the number 1 to the left of a new character with the value of 0.

Binary is just the same, except it only uses two values. When a binary value is higher than 1, the proper procedure is to increment the number of digits that are used to represent the number by one. The first time you increment the number of digits, you indicate this by putting the number 1 to the left of a new number with the value of 0. Because this binary number equals the same number of increments as the decimal number 2, it is said to have a decimal value of 2. Adding the decimal value of every bit in the octet together derives the total decimal value of an octet. The total decimal value of an octet is displayed in an IP address in dotted decimal notation. Table 8.1 contains a sample of a binary to decimal conversion table.

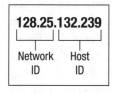

Figure 8.2 An IP address in dotted decimal notation.

Table 8.1	Binary to decimal conversion.	
Binary Value	Bit Conversion	Decimal Value
00000001	1	1
00000010	2 + 0	2
00000110	4 + 2 + 0	6
11110000	128 + 64 + 32 + 16 + 0 + 0 + 0 +0	240
11111111	128 + 64 + 32 + 16 + 8 + 4 + 2 +1	255

Classful Addressing

The number of bits assigned to the network ID and the host ID depends on the number of hosts required on a given network and the number of networks required in an environment. Before the idea of classful addressing was in place, it was the network administrator's responsibility to determine which bits in the 32-bit address to assign to the network ID and which bits to assign to the host ID. If the number of hosts required on a given network was enormous, then a network administrator would assign a large portion of the 32 bits available to host IDs and use a small portion for network IDs. If a large number of networks were required with only a few hosts per network, the network administrator would use a small portion of the bits for host IDs and a large number for network IDs.

This method of allocating address space was inefficient, often giving small organizations the right to a large number of IP address spaces. Therefore, IP address space was divided into three classes in the attempt to meet the needs of large and small organizations. (Actually, the IP address was divided into five classes, however, we will focus on the three main classes used by the Internet community.) With the class system, it is possible to assign a corporation address space based on the number of hosts and networks that it requires. This system is referred to as *classful addressing*. Classful addressing divides the 2^{32} (4,294,967,296) possible IP addresses into five different classes.

A class A, B, or C IP address can be determined by looking at the first two bits of the address. Figure 8.3 illustrates the relationship between the first two bits of an IP address and its class. Also, note the range in the decimal value for each class. Once you understand IP addressing it is only necessary to look at the first octet of an IP address in decimal format to determine its class. The class of an IP address governs the number of bits that can be used for network IDs and the number of bits that can be used for host IDs. For example, an organization that is allocated a class B address must use 16 bits to identify its network ID and 16 bits to identify its host IDs. It is important to note that this strict rule can be avoided and most often is through a process known as *subnetting*.

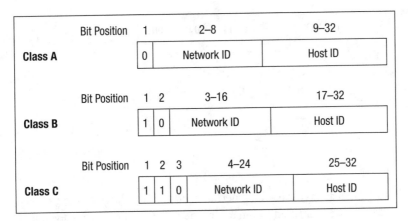

Figure 8.3   Class addressing.

Class A

Class A addresses are typically assigned to very large organizations, universities, or the military. It is extremely difficult—if not impossible—to get a class A address today. These addresses are identified in binary by the first bit having a value of 0 or in decimal by having a value between 1 and 126. Class A addresses use the first 8 bits to specify the network ID and the last 24 bits to designate the host ID. We will see later that the 24 bits used for the host ID can also be used as network IDs by using the process of subnetting. However, for now it is only important to understand the division of bits for network and host IDs.

Class A addresses have a maximum of 126 network IDs. This value is arrived at by taking the number of bits used for the network ID to the power of 2. In this case, 2^7 equals a total of 128. However, the network ID 0.0.0.0 is reserved for the default route and the network ID 127.0.0.0 is reserved for the loopback function. Therefore, the range of possible class A network IDs in decimal is 1 to 126.

Each class A network ID can support a total of $2^{24}-2$ (16,777,214) host IDs. The purpose of subtracting two from the possible number of hosts is to remove two special host IDs. Any time every bit in the host ID portion of an IP address has a value of 1, it is considered a broadcast IP address. Therefore, all hosts should read a message sent to this address. Obviously, no device should have an address that is used for broadcasting information. The second consideration is when every bit in the host ID's binary value is 0. This value is used to uniquely distinguish a network from a network and host ID. Figure 8.4 illustrates a class A address in decimal and binary formats, highlighting the network and host portions of the address.

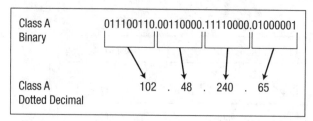

Figure 8.4   A class A IP address.

Class B

Class B addresses are typically assigned to medium and large organizations. These addresses are identified in binary by the first two bits having a value of 10 or in decimal by having a value between 128 and 191. Class B addresses use the first 16 bits to specify the network ID and the last 16 bits to designate the host IDs. However, because the first two bits of all class B addresses are always 10, only 14 bits are available to use for network IDs. This allows a total of 2^{14} (16,384) class B network addresses. Each network ID supports a total of $2^{16}-2$ (65,534) host IDs. Figure 8.5 illustrates a class B address in decimal and binary formats, highlighting the network and host portions of the address.

Class C

Class C addresses are typically assigned to small to medium organizations. These addresses are identified in binary by the first three bits having a value of 110 or in decimal by having a value between 192 and 223. Class C addresses use the first 24 bits to specify the network ID and the last 8 bits to designate the host IDs. However, because the first 3 bits of a class C address are 110, only 21 bits are available to use for network IDs. This allows a total of 2^{21} (2,097,152) class C network addresses. Each network ID supports a total of $2^{8}-2$ (254) host IDs. Figure 8.6 illustrates a class C address in decimal and binary formats, highlighting the network and host portions of the address.

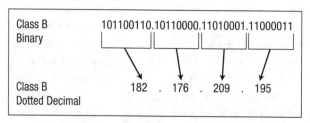

Figure 8.5   A class B IP address.

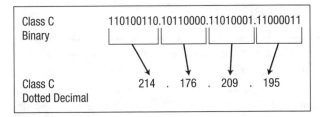

Figure 8.6 Class C IP address.

Note: *It is important to be able to quickly identify the class of an IP address by looking at its decimal or binary value. This skill will serve you well for the exam and your career.*

Other Classes

Two other classes of addresses are available in the IPv4 address space. These classes are not used as public address space, but have been reserved for specific functions. Class D addresses are identified in binary by the first four bits having a value of 1110 or in decimal by having a value between 224 and 239. Class D addresses have been reserved to support IP *multicasting*, which is the process of using one address to send a message to a group of people. Class E addresses are identified in binary by the first 4 bits having a value of 1111 or in decimal by having a value between 240 and 247. Class E addresses have been reserved for experimental or research use.

Summary Of Classful Addressing

The purpose of assigning classes to the IP address space was to provide a mechanism to efficiently assign address space to public and commercial organizations. This allocation scheme had a fundamental problem, however, it occurred because organizations typically have more than one network. It was inefficient to have to assign a company an entire class B address for every separate network in its organization. This would lead to a huge waste of address space.

For example, if XYZ corporation required enough address space to support two networks that have 5,000 and 1,000 users respectively, it would be extremely inefficient to assign them two class B addresses. XYZ has a requirement of only 6,000 total addresses for its organization today. One class B provides a total of $2^{16}-2$ (65,534) addresses. If XYZ were given two class B addresses, it would only be using 6,000 out of 131,068 total possible addresses. Furthermore, if it wanted to add another network, this problem would be compounded. This is a grossly inefficient allocation mechanism. Subnetting is the solution to this problem.

Subnetting

Subnetting creates multiple IP networks from a single allocated class A, B, or C IP network. Subnetting divides a single class A, B, or C network into smaller subnetworks. One of the major goals of allocating IP addresses to organizations based on their size was to have to only allocate one class A, B, or C address to any given organization. Therefore, only one routing entry would have to be maintained per organization. However, organizations had the need for multiple subnetworks within their network. Subnetting allowed the InterNIC to allocate only a single class A, B, or C network and for organizations to have multiple networks.

Internet routers need to maintain only one classful network entry per organization because each organization is assigned only one class A, B, or C IP address. (Organizations are typically assigned only one class address; however, this is not always true thanks to subnetting.) Even though organizations divide their IP address into multiple networks, they still look like only one class A, B, or C IP address to the rest of the world. Organizations accomplish this by performing route summarization at the boundary of their network and any other network. Figure 8.7 illustrates this point.

Default Mask

A *default mask* is a 32-bit number divided into four octets just like an IP address. A default mask indicates the number of bits that are used to identify the network ID and is implied with all class A, B, and C addresses. Class A addresses imply an 8-bit default mask because the first 8 bits in their addresses designate the network ID. Therefore, the default mask (the number of bits that indicate the network ID) can be represented in decimal as 255.0.0.0. Table 8.2 illustrates the default masks for class A, B, and C addresses in binary and decimal. Note that the default mask represents the number of bits used to identify the network ID.

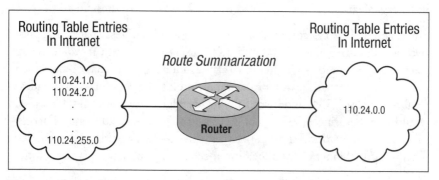

Figure 8.7 Class C IP address summarization.

Table 8.2	Default masks of class A, B, and C addresses.	
Class	Binary Notation	Dotted Decimal Notation
A	11111111.00000000.00000000.00000000	255.0.0.0
B	11111111.11111111.00000000.00000000	255.255.0.0
C	11111111.11111111.11111111.00000000	255.255.255.0

After viewing Table 8.2, it is easy to see that a default mask indicates which bits are used to identify the network ID versus the host ID. Why do we need a default mask if we can already determine this by the class of the IP address? As mentioned earlier, organizations often have the need to increase the number of networks in their intranet. However, they are only assigned one IP address and can advertise only one IP address to the Internet. An organization can get around this by using some of the host ID bits as network ID bits. The organization can indicate that it has used some of the host ID bits as network ID bits by providing a subnet mask.

Subnet Mask

A *subnet mask* is an extension to the default mask. It indicates the number of bits in addition to the default mask that should be used to identify network IDs. What does this do for an organization? It increases the number of networks an organization can create from one class A, B, or C network ID.

For example, if an organization has a registered class C address and needs to create two networks, it somehow must get more network IDs. The organization can accomplish this by using some of the bits designated as host IDs as network IDs. However, the organization must indicate that this class C no longer is using the default 24 bits as a network ID. The organization can indicate this by applying a subnet mask to represent the additional bits that are to be used as network IDs versus host IDs. The subnet mask can be represented in various ways; in this chapter, we will refer to the subnet mask as the default mask plus any additional bits used for network IDs.

Logical AND

How should the subnet mask be used to determine what the network ID is for an IP address? To determine the network ID and the host ID for an IP address, it is necessary to perform a process known as the *logical AND*. This indicates which bits to use as network bits and which bits to use as host bits when deciphering an IP address. When applying the subnet mask to an IP address, each bit starting from the most significant bit to the least significant bit is compared between the IP address and the subnet mask. For example, the first bit of the first octet of the IP address is compared to the first bit of the first octet of the subnet mask. The resulting value from this bit-by-bit comparison is the network ID. The rule set to apply is listed as follows:

➤ If the subnet mask and the IP address both have values of 1, then the resulting network ID bit is 1.

➤ If the subnet mask has a value of 1 and the IP address has a value of 0, then the resulting network ID bit is 0.

➤ If the subnet mask has a value of 0, then the resulting network ID bit is 0.

Table 8.3 illustrates the logical AND process. Note in Table 8.3 the only difference between the dotted decimal IP address and the dotted decimal network ID is in the last two octets. The difference between the values in the octet is due to the co-mingling of network and host bits in the same octet. The logical AND process drops all the host IDs and retains the network IDs. Therefore, in Table 8.3 we determine that the host 129.253.235.252 is actually part of the network 129.253.232.0.

A computer performs the logical AND process every time it sends a message to another computer. To send a message, a PC must determine whether it should send it to a device on its local network using its MAC address or send it to a default gateway to be forwarded to another network. A PC performs a logical AND on the destination IP address to determine if the message is local or remote. If the result of the logical AND indicates that the destination device is on the same network, the PC looks in its ARP cache for the corresponding MAC address for the destination address. If the MAC address is found, the PC sends the message using the MAC address to the destination. If the MAC address is not found in the ARP cache, the PC performs an ARP to get the corresponding MAC address.

Table 8.4 illustrates another example of the logical AND process, but this time uses a class C address. Note that with a class C address the only difference in the

Table 8.3   The logical AND process.

Binary IP Address	Dotted Decimal IP Address
10000001.11111101.11101011.11111010	129.253.235.250

Binary Subnet Mask	Dotted Decimal Subnet Mask
11111111.11111111.11111000.00000000	255.255.248.0

Binary Network ID	Dotted Decimal Network ID
10000001.11111101.11101000.00000000	129.253.232.0

Table 8.4 The logical AND process.	
Binary IP Address	**Dotted Decimal IP Address**
11000001.11011101.10101011.00111010	193.221.17758
Binary Subnet Mask	**Dotted Decimal Subnet Mask**
11111111.11111111.11111111.11100000	255.255.255.224
Binary Network ID	**Dotted Decimal Network ID**
11000001.11011111.11111111.11100000	193.221.177.32

IP address occurs in the last octet. The reason that the differences are isolated to the last octet is that in a class C address only the last octet contains bits assigned to host IDs and therefore, only these bits are available for subnetting.

So far, we have learned that IP addresses are divided into classes to efficiently allocate the IP address space to varying sizes of organizations. Efficient allocation of address space also minimizes the number of entries that need to be maintained in the routing tables of Internet routers. However, organizations required more networks than the InterNIC believed reasonable to assign due to wasted IP address space. The solution was the creation of a subnet mask, which gave organizations a tool for increasing the number of networks they had by borrowing bits from the host IDs of their assigned IP address space. A subnet mask uses the logical AND process to distinguish between the network ID and host ID of an IP address.

Next we'll discuss some of the items to consider in determining the number of bits to use for the subnet mask. A bad decision on a subnet mask can place constraints on an organization's future addressing choices.

Subnetting Consideration

Remember that the purpose of the subnet mask is to give an organization the flexibility to increase the number of networks in its environment. So, one might think that an organization should give itself the maximum number of networks possible with its assigned IP address space. However, anytime a bit is added to the network ID, a bit is removed from the host ID. Therefore, if the number of networks is increased, the number of host IDs available per network is decreased. Table 8.5 illustrates this fact by presenting the number of network and host IDs for class B IP addresses with different subnet masks.

Organizations need to determine the happy medium between sufficient host IDs and network IDs for their specific needs. The cost of changing the subnet mask on thousands of computers because of a scaling issue is not a welcome

Table 8.5 Class B networks with various subnet masks.

Subnet Mask	Bits In Subnet Mask	Network IDs	Host IDs
255.255.255.0	24	$2^8-2= 254$	$2^8-2 = 254$
255.255.255.128	25	$2^9-2= 510$	$2^7-2 = 126$
255.255.255.192	26	$2^{10}-2= 1022$	$2^6-2 = 64$
255.255.255.224	27	$2^{11}-2= 2046$	$2^5-2 = 30$
255.255.255.240	28	$2^{12}-2= 4094$	$2^4-2 = 14$
255.255.255.248	29	$2^{13}-2= 8190$	$2^3-2 = 6$

thought for network administrators. Some of the questions that must be asked before developing a subnet addressing scheme are:

➤ What is the total number of network IDs that my organization needs today?

➤ What is the total number of host IDs that my largest network requires today?

➤ What is the total number of network IDs that my organization will need in the future?

➤ What is the total number of host IDs that my largest network will require in the future?

The answers to these questions will determine how an organization subnets its assigned IP address space. The purpose of asking about today's and future requirements is to get an understanding of what is absolutely needed today and what should be planned for in the future. To illustrate the process of classful IP addressing, subnetting, the logical AND, and IP addressing considerations, examples using class A and B addresses are provided in the following sections.

Class A Network Example

This example uses a fictitious company named DGR Inc. to illustrate the process of determining the proper subnetting for an organization. DGR Inc. has been allocated the class A IP address 114.0.0.0 by the InterNIC. DGR Inc. must determine the proper way to use this IP address space to support its current and future needs. To determine these needs, we must answer the four preceding questions. These questions are repeated below, along with DGR Inc.'s responses to them:

➤ What is the total number of network IDs that DGR Inc. needs today? Answer: 5,000.

➤ What is the total number of network IDs that DGR Inc. will need in the future? Answer: 9,000.

➤ What is the total number of host IDs that DGR Inc. requires on its largest network today? Answer: 1,000.

➤ What is the total number of host IDs that DGR Inc. requires on its largest network in the future? Answer: 2,000.

DGR Inc. has been assigned only one network; however, it requires several more to support its current and future requirements. DGR Inc. plans to use subnetting to create more networks IDs. As mentioned earlier, by default 24 bits have been allocated for host IDs with class A IP address space. We know that the DGR organization requires 5,000 networks today and 9,000 in the future. Therefore, to create enough network IDs, bits have to be taken from the host IDs and used for network IDs. How many bits have to be taken from the host ID bits to provide 5,000 network IDs?

DGR Inc. requires a total of 13 bits to provide 5,000 network IDs. The number of bits required can be determined by taking 2^{13} (8,192 possible networks). A subnet mask of 255.255.248.0 is used to represent the 13 bits of subnetting. However, 13 bits only provides 8,192 total possible networks, which is not enough to support DGR Inc.'s expected growth. A total of 14 bits is required to ensure that 9,000+ networks can be supported in the future. If DGR uses 14 bits as the subnet mask (a subnet mask of 255.255.252.0), it has a total of 2^{14} (16,384) possibilities for network IDs. Therefore, the DGR organization would prefer to use 14 bits of the host ID to subnet the current 114.0.0.0 Class A address; however, taking 13 bits from the host ID would provide a sufficient number of network IDs (subnets) to provide for today's needs. Table 8.6 illustrates the number of bits required to provide 5,000 and 9,000+ network IDs.

DGR Inc. must determine if enough bits still remain to provide an adequate number of host IDs. The DGR organization requires 1,000 host IDs today and expects to need 2,000 host IDs in the future. How many bits are required to provide 1,000 host IDs? How about 2,000 host IDs? How many bits are still available to be used as host IDs?

Table 8.6   The number of bits required for 5,000 and 9,000+ network IDs.

IP Address	Subnet Mask	Network IDs	Host IDs
114.0.0.0	255.255.248.0	$2^{13} = 8192$	$2^{11} - 2 = 2046$
114.0.0.0	255.255.252.0	$2^{14} = 16384$	$2^{10} - 2 = 1022$

The number of bits required for 1,000 host IDs is 10, which provides a total combination of 1022 (2^{10-2}). Remember that we subtract 2 to represent the broadcast (all 1s) and the zero (all 0s) value in each network. However, DGR Inc. requires 11 bits to provide sufficient host IDs to support its future requirement of 2,000 hosts. Table 8.7 illustrates the number of bits required to provide 1,000 and 2,000 host IDs.

DGR only has 24 bits of host IDs in its class A 114.0.0.0 IP address to use for both hosts and networks. However, to get enough host IDs for 2,000 users per network and 9,000+ network IDs, it would take 14 network ID and 11 host ID bits for a total of 25 bits. DGR Inc. is shy one bit, so it has to decide whether to limit the number of hosts or networks that it will have available in the future. In this case, DGR would probably opt to use only 13 bits (8,192 networks) for network IDs and 11 bits for host IDs (2,046 host IDs per network). However, the decision can become more difficult when an organization doesn't have the luxury of owning an entire class A IP address.

Class C Network Example

In this example, we will define the actual subnets and host IDs. If an organization named CMN Inc. has been assigned the IP address space 210.14.12.0, it has been assigned a class C address with a default mask of 255.255.255.0. This organization requires five networks today and expects to need eight in the future. In addition, CMN Inc. expects the largest number of hosts on a given network now and in the future to be 30 users.

CMN Inc. requires more networks and must subnet the eight bits allocated to host IDs to provide these networks. To do so, CMN Inc. must subnet Three bits to provide eight more networks (2^3). The subnet mask of this IP address is now 255.255.255.224. The value of the last octet has changed to represent the three bits (128 + 64 + 32 = 224) that are now used to identify networks instead of hosts. However, CMN Inc. must make sure that it will have enough host IDs left to identify all 30 devices on its largest network. CMN Inc. has five bits remaining for host IDs, giving CMN a total of 30 (2^5-2) host IDs per network.

CMN Inc. has a total of eight subnets; these are listed on Table 8.7 along with the range of host IDs available for each subnet. A total of 30 host IDs exist for each subnet because the All 0s and the All 1s host IDs have not been included. Once again, the All 1s host ID is reserved for the broadcast of information. For example, for subnet 210.14.12.64, host ID 210.14.12.95 is the broadcast address because every bit used for determining the host ID is set to 1.

Table 8.7	Subnets and host IDs for IP address 210.14.12.0 255.255.255.224.			
Subnet	Lowest Host ID	Highest Host ID	All 1s Host ID	All 0s Host ID
210.14.12.0	210.14.12.1	210.14.12.30	210.14.12.31	210.14.12.0
210.14.12.32	210.14.12.33	210.14.12.62	210.14.12.63	210.14.12.32
210.14.12.64	210.14.12.65	210.14.12.94	210.14.12.95	210.14.12.64
210.14.12.96	210.14.12.97	210.14.12.126	210.14.12.127	210.14.12.96
210.14.12.128	210.14.12.129	210.14.12.158	210.14.12.159	210.14.12.128
210.14.12.160	210.14.12.161	210.14.12.190	210.14.12.191	210.14.12.160
210.14.12.192	210.14.12.193	210.14.12.222	210.14.12.223	210.14.12.192
210.14.12.224	210.14.12.225	210.14.12.254	210.14.12.255	210.14.12.224

Summary Of Subnetting

We have seen that flexibility has been built into IP addressing via a process known as subnetting, which allows organizations to divide up a classful network ID into a number of other networks. Any device can determine how the IP address was divided by looking at the IP address's subnet mask; this mask indicates which bits have been used for subnetting and which bits are still being used to identify hosts. Of course, each class of IP address has a default mask. Furthermore, we identified some important questions when setting up an addressing scheme. Specifically, we need to know the number of hosts and networks an organization requires in the present and the future.

The ability to decipher subnet masks and classes of IP addresses for the CCNA exam is crucial.

The good news is that this ability is also crucial to being proficient at networking in general. So, feel good about spending a significant amount of time practicing the art of subnetting.

Variable Length Subnet Masking (VLSM)

One of the main problems faced with IP addressing is the amount of wasted IP addresses that occur on the networks of organizations. As we demonstrated earlier, if an organization requires 30 hosts for its largest network, then all networks end up having to be able to support 30 hosts. Therefore, if a network has only 2 hosts, it wastes a total of 28 host IDs that could have been used somewhere else. This problem was recognized and the solution is *Variable Length Subnet Masking (VLSM)*.

A network is considered to be using VLSM when more than one subnet mask exists for the entire network. The limiting factor in the past was the ability of routing protocols to decipher between IP addresses with different subnet masks. This led to packets getting routed down the wrong path or in loops. However, many of the newer protocols support VLSM and require that the number of bits used for subnetting be forwarded with route. Therefore, the router can determine if a packet is destined for a particular destination.

Classless Interdomain Routing (CIDR)

Classless Interdomain Routing is a partial solution to the rapid depletion of IP address space in the Internet. CIDR provides a more efficient method of allocating IP address space by removing the concept of classes, such as A, B, and C. CIDR is not constrained by the 8-bit, 16-bit, and 24-bit class boundaries applied in classful addressing. Instead, CIDR associates a value (bit mask) with each IP address that identifies the number of bits used to identify the network portion of the IP address. This method does not waste bits for hosts or networks; additionally, the exact number of bits can be used to identify networks and hosts.

In addition, CIDR reduces the number of routing entries required through *route aggregation*, in which a single routing entry represents IP address space across traditional classful bit boundaries. Therefore, Internet routers can summarize IP address space to other routers, thus minimizing the number of entries required. In the past, every classful address would require an entry in the routing table.

Configure And Verify IP Addresses

We have spent a significant amount of time explaining IP addressing. We focused on topics such as classful addressing, subnetting, VLSM, and CIDR. Because of the volume of information presented in these areas, you might think that it is extremely difficult to configure a Cisco router with an IP address. Wrong. The process of configuring a Cisco router with an IP address and subnet mask is very simple. Once you have determined your IP addressing scheme, the actual process of configuring the router only takes a few moments. Enter the IP address at the configuration mode of the interface that is being addressed. The actual commands are shown in Listing 8.1.

Listing 8.1   Configuring an Ethernet interface with an
IP address.

```
Router#configure terminal
Router(config)#interface ethernet 0
Router(config-if)#IP Address 172.16.24.12 255.255.255.0
Router(config-if)#exit
Router(config)#
```

In the previous example, Ethernet interface 0 was configured with the class B address 172.16.12. A subnet mask of eight bits was used as indicated by the mask of 255.255.255.0.

IP Host Names

With Cisco routers, it is possible to map a literal host name to a numeric IP address. This can often make it easier to navigate around a complex network. For example, if we wanted to map the host name "Coriolis" with the IP address 172.16.30.12, we would perform the following set of commands:

```
Router(config)#ip host coriolis 172.16.30.12
Router(config)#exit
```

Now an administrator can use the literal "Coriolis" in place of the numeric IP address when configuring the router and navigating around the network.

Verifying IP Addresses

The process of verifying IP addressing is one that you will perform countless times during your career as a network professional. Knowing how to use the many different tools for verifying IP addresses will save you an enormous amount of time in the long run. The three tools that are vital to know for the CCNA exam are ping, Telnet, and traceroute.

Ping

The ping test is used to test *IP connectivity* between two devices. IP connectivity means that both devices have the ability to send IP packets to each other. Ping tests layer 3 connectivity between two devices. The **ping** command sends ICMP echo packets to the destination device. The destination device then responds with ICMP echo reply packets if it receives the message. If the message does not reach its destination, the last hop sends an ICMP host unreachable packet back to the sending device. An example of a ping between two devices on different networks is shown in Listing 8.2.

Listing 8.2   Pinging between two devices.

```
Router>ping 172.16.29.3
Type escape sequence to abort.
Sending 5, 100-byte ICMP echos to 172.16.29.3,
Timeout is 5 seconds
!!!!!
Success rate is 100%, round-trip min/avg/max = 2/4/8 ms
Router>
```

The preceding messages indicate that five ICMP echo requests were sent to host 172.16.29.3. If these messages did not reach their destination in five seconds, they would be dropped. An exclamation point is written to the screen each time an ICMP echo reply packet was received by the sending device. Therefore, the sending device received all five ICMP echo requests. A number of variations to the ping test allow the user to extract more detailed information. We encourage you to explore this tool.

Telnet

The Telnet application can be used to test application layer connectivity between two hosts. The Telnet protocol is explained in more detail in Chapter 7. The Telnet application is used to gain remote access of a host device; therefore, it must travel across all layers of the OSI model to reach its destination. It is the fact that it passes through all seven layers of both the source and destination devices that make it an effective tool. If we can open a Telnet session, we know that all layers of the OSI model are functioning properly.

Traceroute

The **traceroute** command is a useful command to determine the actual path a packet takes between its source and destination. The traceroute command uses ICMP and the time-to-live (TTL) field in the IP header to map the typical course a packet would take between two destinations. The TTL field's original purpose was to identify transient packets that are caught in routing loops. This is accomplished by setting the TTL field to some value (usually 255) and subtracting one from the value each time the packet reaches a router. When the TTL field reaches a value of 0, a router will drop the packet. The traceroute program capitalizes on the fact that routers drop IP packets with a value of 0. Whenever a router decrements a TTL packet to a value of zero, it sends an ICMP TTL exceeded message back to the sending device. It is this ICMP message that the traceroute program uses to gather information about each hop between two devices.

For example, if a user sends an ICMP packet to the destination with the TTL field set to 1, the first router in the path to the destination receives the packet and decrements the value of the TTL field. The value of the TTL field is now 0, so the router drops the packet and sends an ICMP host unreachable message back to the sending device. The sending device then sends an ICMP packet with the TTL field set to 2. The first router receives the packet and decrements the TTL field, but this time forwards the packet because it still has a TTL of 1. The second router decrements the TTL field to 0 and drops the packet. However, it still sends an ICMP host unreachable message back to the sending device. The sending device continues this process until the destination device receives the ICMP packet. An example of a traceroute between two devices is shown in Listing 8.3.

Listing 8.3 Traceroute between two devices.

```
Router#traceroute 172.16.19.2
Type escape sequence to abort.
Tracing the route to 172.16.19.2

1 172.16.14.254 100 msec 10 msec 4 msec
2 172.16.13.254 100 msec 10 msec 5 msec
3.172.16.63.250 110 msec 12 msec 8 msec
4 172.16.19.2 140 msec *
```

Monitoring IP

The functioning of IP in a router can be monitored in many ways. However, three of the best and most useful commands are the **show ip protocol, show ip interface**, and the **show ip route** commands. Although these three commands do not provide a 100 percent comprehensive view of IP, they will provide enough information for the majority of inquiries.

Show IP Interface

The **show ip interface** command contains a vast amount of information about any interface using the IP protocol. An example of the **show ip interface command** is illustrated in Listing 8.4. The first line of the command distinguishes whether the interface has data-link connectivity and is administratively active. From an IP perspective, the command illustrates the IP interface is using an IP address of 172.16.52.10 with a 24-bit default mask. In addition, the MTU size of all IP packets has been set to 1,500 bytes. A wealth of information is provided in this command. I encourage you to explore this command and identify key information that can be retrieved with it.

Listing 8.4 The **show ip interface** command.

```
Router#sh ip int e0
Ethernet0 is up, line protocol is up
  Internet address is 172.16.52.10/24
  Broadcast address is 255.255.255.255
  Address determined by non-volatile memory
  MTU is 1500 bytes
  Helper address is not set
  Directed broadcast forwarding is enabled
  Outgoing access list is not set
  Inbound  access list is not set
  Proxy ARP is enabled
  Security level is default
  Split horizon is enabled
  ICMP redirects are always sent
  ICMP unreachables are always sent
  ICMP mask replies are never sent
  IP fast switching is enabled
  IP fast switching on the same interface is disabled
  IP multicast fast switching is enabled
  Router Discovery is disabled
  IP output packet accounting is disabled
  IP access violation accounting is disabled
  TCP/IP header compression is disabled
  Probe proxy name replies are disabled
  Gateway Discovery is disabled
  Policy routing is disabled
  Network address translation is disabled
```

Show IP Protocol

The **show ip protocol** command is used to determine which protocols are performing routing for IP. The command displays the protocol name, the frequency of protocol updates, gateways, and identifies the IP networks that are routing is being performed on. An example of the **show ip protocol** command is provided in Listing 8.5.

Listing 8.5 The **show ip protocol** command.

```
Router#sh ip prot
Routing Protocol is "eigrp 33"
  Outgoing update filter list for all interfaces is not set
  Incoming update filter list for all interfaces is not set
  Default networks flagged in outgoing updates
  Default networks accepted from incoming updates
  EIGRP metric weight K1=1, K2=0, K3=1, K4=0, K5=0
```

```
EIGRP maximum hop count 100
EIGRP maximum metric variance 1
Redistributing: static, eigrp 33
Automatic network summarization is in effect
Routing for Networks:
  172.16.25.0
Passive Interface(s):
  Serial0
  Serial1
  Serial2
  Serial3
  Serial4
  Serial5
  Serial6
  Serial7
Routing Information Sources:
  Gateway         Distance      Last Update
  Gateway         Distance      Last Update
  148.171.63.2          90      0:00:00
  148.171.63.3          90      0:00:02
  148.171.63.4          90      0:00:02
  148.171.63.11         90      0:00:02
  148.171.63.126        90      0:00:00
Distance: internal 90 external 170
```

Show IP Route

The **show ip route** command displays the routing table that the router uses to forward packets. The command also displays how it learned of the route (static, connected, IGRP, etc.). This command can be used to understand why a packet follows a certain path when traveling between two devices. An example of the **show ip route** command is provided in Listing 8.6.

Listing 8.6   The **show ip route** command.

```
Router#sh ip route
Codes: C - connected, S - static, I - IGRP, R - RIP, M - mobile,
       B - BGP
       D - EIGRP, EX - EIGRP external, O - OSPF,
       IA - OSPF inter area
       N1 - OSPF NSSA external type 1, N2 - OSPF NSSA
       external type 2
       E1 - OSPF external type 1, E2 - OSPF external type 2,
       E - EGP
       i - IS-IS, L1 - IS-IS level-1, L2 - IS-IS level-2,
       * - candidate default
       U - per-user static route, o - ODR
```

Gateway of last resort is 172.16.50.1 to network 0.0.0.0

```
C       172.16.50.0 is directly connected, Ethernet0
C       172.16.51.0 is directly connected, Ethernet1
S     140.71.0.0/16 [1/0] via 172.16.50.3
S*    0.0.0.0/0 [1/0] via 172.16.50.1
E     172.16.29.0/16 via 172.16.50.1
```

Practice Questions

Question 1

> An IP address is listed below in dotted decimal format. Please indicate the corresponding binary value of this IP address.
>
> 112.14.12.8
>
> ○ a. 01100000.00110000.01101111.10110111
>
> ○ b. 0.11.0.11
>
> ○ c. 01110000.00001110.00001100.00001000
>
> ○ d. 01110000.00001110.11000000.00110011

Answer c is correct. The conversion of these binary bits yields a decimal value of 112.14.12.8. Answer a can be identified as incorrect quickly by noting that the fourth octet begins with a 1, but its value is not greater than 128. Answer b can immediately be eliminated, because it is not in the format of a binary IP address. Answer d could be determined to be incorrect by determining the decimal value of either the third or fourth octet. It is important to note that it was not necessary to convert each one of the answers above into decimal format. It is much quicker to eliminate the obviously wrong answers (like b) and then isolate reasons to remove other answers before converting any values.

Question 2

> How many of the following addresses are class B addresses? [Choose the two best answers]
>
> ❑ a. 130.15.130.254
>
> ❑ b. 10100000.11000000.11111111.11110000
>
> ❑ c. 11010001.11001100.10101010.00001111
>
> ❑ d. 127.0.0.0

Answers a and b are correct. The first octet of answer a has a decimal value of 130. The first octet of all class B addresses must be in the range of 128-191; therefore, this is a correct answer. Answer b's first two bits are 10, which is also a characteristic of a binary class B address. Answer c is incorrect because the value of its first two bits is 11. This is not a characteristic of a class B address. Finally, answer d has the decimal value of a loopback address, not a class B address.

Question 3

How many of the following characteristics describe this IP address and subnet mask? [Choose the two best answers]

194.122.14.5 255.255.255.0

❑ a. It has a host ID of 14.5.

❑ b. It has a class C address.

❑ c. It has a network ID of 194.122.14.

❑ d. It is a class B address.

❑ e. It has a network ID of 194.122.

Answers b and c are correct. The IP address 194.122.14.5 is a class C address, so answer b is correct and answer d is incorrect. This can be determined by noting that the decimal value of the first octet is in the range of 192 and 223. Also, if this IP address were converted to binary, the three bits would have a value of 110. Class C addresses by default use the first three octets to represent the network ID and the last octet to represent the host ID. Therefore, the network prefix is 194.122.14 and the host ID is 5. Answer a is incorrect because the default mask of a class C IP address is 24 bits, so the bits in the third octet are used for the network ID not the host ID. Likewise, answer e is incorrect because it should include the third octet as part of the network ID.

Question 4

How many of the following characteristics describe this IP address? [Choose the two best answers]

10001000.00011000.00011000.00001111

❑ a. It is a class A address.

❑ b. It is a class B address.

❑ c. It has a host ID of 24.15.

❑ d. It has a host ID of 24.24.15.

❑ e. It has a host ID of 24.16.

Answers b and c are correct. The first step in solving this problem is to convert the IP address into decimal. If you fail in this conversion, you are probably going to miss the question. Therefore, make sure you are proficient at the binary to decimal conversion. However, you could determine that this was a class B address without the conversion by looking at the two leading bits, 10. Also, this tells you that only the last 16 bits need to be converted in order to determine the host ID. These types of techniques will save you valuable time on the exam. Answer a is incorrect because the address is not a class A address. Answer d is incorrect because the second octet would not be used to identify a host ID. Finally, answer e is incorrect because the dotted decimal value of the fourth octet is 15, not 16.

Question 5

Which of the following is not true when deciphering a subnet ID from an IP address and subnet mask?

- O a. If the subnet mask and the IP address both have values of 1, the resulting network ID bit is 1.
- O b. If the subnet mask has a value of 1 and the IP address has a value of 1, the resulting network ID bit is 0.
- O c. If the subnet mask has a value of 1 and the IP address has a value of 0, the resulting network ID bit is 0.
- O d. If the subnet mask has a value of 0, the resulting network ID bit is 0.

Answer b is correct. It specifies that a network ID bit of zero is the result when comparing a subnet mask bit with a value of 1 and a IP address with a value of 1. This is not one of the rules used to decipher network IDs and therefore is the correct answer. Answers a, c, and d are the three rules presented in the chapter for deciphering network IDs from an IP address with a subnet mask, so these answers are incorrect.

Question 6

A subnet mask can have a value of 255.0.255.128.

- O a. True
- O b. False

Answer b is correct, False. A subnet mask must use contiguous bits when masking an IP address. Thus, the 0 in the second octet is not a valid value for a subnet mask.

Question 7

Which of the following tools can be utilized to test IP connectivity between two devices? [Choose the three best answers]

❑ a. Ping

❑ b. Telnet

❑ c. Traceroute

❑ d. Show IP interface

❑ e. Show IP protocol

Answers a, b, and c are correct. These answers are all different tools mentioned in this chapter for testing IP connectivity between two devices. Answers d and e are used to monitor IP addresses and the functioning of IP within a local router.

Question 8

Which of the following tools will identify the address of intermediate hops between two destinations?

○ a. Traceroute

○ b. Telnet

○ c. Ping

○ d. Rlogin

○ e. TCP

Answer a is correct. The **traceroute** command can be used to identify the address of every intermediate hop between two locations. Answer b is incorrect because the **telnet** command is used to obtain remote control of a destination device. Answer c is incorrect because the **ping** command only tells the user if he or she has IP connectivity. Answer d is a command used for remote access on Unix machines. Finally, answer e is incorrect because TCP is a layer 4 protocol that is not used for testing IP connectivity.

Question 9

Which of the following commands will show the MTU size used by the interface?

○ a. **show ip route**

○ b. **show ip interface**

○ c. **show ip protocol**

Answer b is correct. The **show ip interface** command displays a wealth of information regarding the interface specified, including the MTU size. Answers a and c are incorrect because neither of these commands displays information regarding the MTU size of an interface.

Question 10

The default mask of a class A IP address is which of the following?

○ a. 255.0.0.255

○ b. 255.255.0.0

○ c. 255.0.0.0

○ d. 255.255.255.0

Answer c is correct. Class A addresses have a default mask of eight bits or 255.0.0.0. Answer a is incorrect because all default masks are contiguous bits. Answer b is the default mask of a class B IP address and not a class A IP address. Answer d is incorrect because it is the default mask of a class C IP address and not a class A IP address.

Need To Know More?

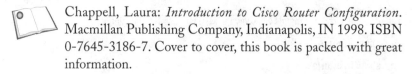

Chappell, Laura: *Introduction to Cisco Router Configuration.* Macmillan Publishing Company, Indianapolis, IN 1998. ISBN 0-7645-3186-7. Cover to cover, this book is packed with great information.

Lammle, Todd, Donald Porter, and James Chellis: *CCNA Cisco Certified Network Associate.* Sybex Network Press, Alameda, CA, 1999. ISBN 0-7821-2381-3. Chapter 4 covers IP addressing.

Stevens, W. Richard: *TCP/IP Illustrated Volume 1 Visit.* Addison-Wesley Professional Computing Series, Reading, MA, 1996. ISBN 0-201-63346-9. A great resource for TCP/IP information.

Syngress Media, with Richard D. Hornbaker, CCIE: *Cisco Certified Network Associate Study Guide.* Osborne/McGraw-Hill, Berkeley, CA, 1998. ISBN 0-07-882487-7. Chapter 2 covers IP addressing.

Tittel, Ed, Kurt Hudson, and J. Michael Stewart: *TCP/IP Exam Cram.* The Coriolis Group, Inc., Scottsdale, AZ, 1997. ISBN 1-57610-195-9. This book is also packed with great information on TCP/IP.

IPX

Terms you'll need to understand:

√ NetWare

√ Internet Packet Exchange (IPX)

√ Network Operating System (NOS)

√ Netwrk Basic Input/Output System (NetBIOS)

√ NetWare shell

√ NetWare Core Protocol (NCP)

√ Sequence Packet Exchange (SPX)

√ Routing Information Protocol (RIP)

√ Network Interface Card (NIC)

√ Service Advertisment Protocols (SAP)

√ Encapsulation

√ Ticks

√ Hop count

√ NetWare Link State Protocol (NLSP)

Techniques you'll need to master:

√ Describing the Novell IPX protocol stack

√ Listing key features and characteristics of Novell IPX

√ Understanding IPX addressing

√ Describing IPX encapsulation types

√ Explaining IPX SAPs

√ Configuring the IPX protocol on a router

√ Monitoring IPX status and activity on a router

√ Troubleshooting IPX activity on a router

This chapter introduces *NetWare* and the *Internet Packet Exchange* (*IPX*) protocol. Like Internet Protocol, IPX resides at the network layer of the OSI model. This chapter also describes how the NetWare protocol suite maps to the OSI model and covers IPX addressing, encapsulation, and Service Advertisment Protocols (*SAPs*). It also lists IPX commands for configuring, monitoring, and troubleshooting IPX.

In the early 1980s, Novell, Inc. created a new proprietary suite of protocols for LANs entitled *NetWare*. Derived from Xerox Network Systems, NetWare defines protocols for the upper five layers of the OSI model. It is considered a *Network Operating System* (*NOS*) and provides support for file sharing, printing, database access, and various applications. Like other NOSs, NetWare is based upon a client-server architecture where clients (such as PCs) request services from different servers (such as printers).

NetWare Protocol Suite

Figure 9.1 shows the relationship between the OSI model and the NetWare protocol suite.

Upper Layer

NetWare supports many applications, such as email and other industry-standard protocols. For example, NetWare includes emulation software that supports

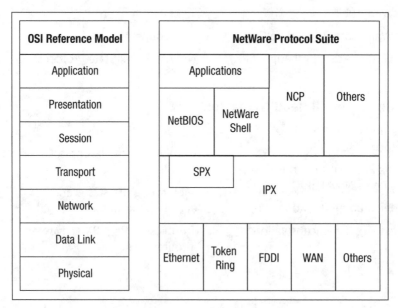

Figure 9.1 NetWare protocol suite.

Network Basic Input/Output System (*NetBIOS*) application interfaces. NetBIOS is a common session-layer interface specification from IBM and Microsoft. Also, NetWare provides an additional service, a *NetWare shell*, which determines whether application calls require network services. The NetWare shell interrogates the calls and sends them to lower-layer protocols for additional network services, if necessary. The *NetWare Core Protocol* (*NCP*) is a collection of server routines that satisfies requests from other applications, like a NetWare shell.

Transport Layer

Sequenced Packet Exchange (*SPX*) is the transport protocol used within NetWare. Similar to other transport protocols, SPX provides reliable, connection-oriented services that supplement NetWare's network layer protocol.

Network Layer

NetWare uses IPX as its network layer protocol. Like other network protocols, IPX supports the routing of information from a source network, through any intermediate networks, to the destination network. Also, IPX does not require acknowledgment of each packet it transmits—SPX provides that capability. IPX relies upon *Routing Information Protocol* (*RIP*) to exchange network routing information.

Data Link And Physical Layers

NetWare supports several different media access protocols and physical media types. NetWare can run over an Ethernet or Token Ring LAN. It can also operate in several WAN environments, including Integrated Services Digital Network (ISDN), Point-to-Point Protocol (PPP), and Frame Relay (Chapters 11 and 12 discuss WAN protocols in detail).

IPX Addressing

Similar to addressing within an IP network, an IPX logical address contains a network number and a node number. Although an IPX logical address can contain up to 80-bits, a network administrator defines the IPX network number, which can contain a maximum of 32-bits. The node number is provided by the MAC address of the *network interface card* (*NIC*) and can be up to a maximum of 48-bits. Since MAC addresses are virtually unique, it is nearly impossible for two devices within the same network to possess the same node number. Also, using the MAC address as the node's logical address eliminates the need for ARP to determine the physical address. Figure 9.2 depicts a router connected to four IPX networks.

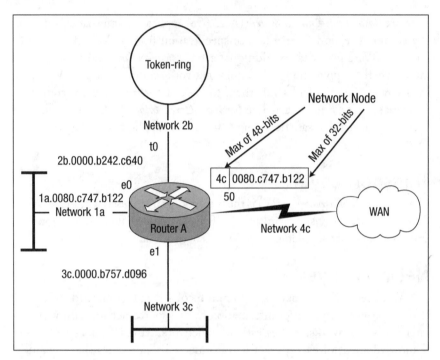

Figure 9.2 IPX network and node addressing.

Note: Serial interfaces do not have physical MAC addresses. In that event, IPX uses the MAC address of another interface.

 An IPX address consists of a network number and a node number, which is the node's MAC address. For example, if a node's MAC address is "0080.c729.b112" and it resides on IPX network "1a", the IPX address for that node would be "1a.0080.c729.b112".

IPX Encapsulation

Novell's IPX supports various encapsulation types; several of those can be configured on a single router interface. As IPX packets are passed to the data link layer, the packets are encapsulated into one of several framing types supported by NetWare. However, you need to assign each encapsulation type to a unique network number on the router's interface. (The encapsulation type you select depends on the router's interface.) Table 9.1 lists the four Ethernet encapsulation types.

Even though a single interface can support multiple encapsulation types, clients and servers that use different encapsulation types cannot communicate directly, but do so instead via the router.

Table 9.1 IPX Ethernet encapsulation framing types.	
IPX Name	**Usage**
Ethernet II	With TCP/IP and DECnet
Ethernet 802.2	With NetWare version 4.x and OSI routing
Ethernet SNAP	With TCP/IP and AppleTalk
Ethernet 802.3	With NetWare versions 2.x and 3.x

Table 9.2 lists the IPX encapsulation names and the corresponding Cisco IOS names that you will need to use when configuring the router.

The default encapsulation types for Cisco routers are:

➤ **Ethernet** novell-ether

➤ **Token Ring** snap

➤ **FDDI** snap

IPX Routing

Routing Information Protocol (RIP), the routing protocol used by IPX, is a distance vector routing protocol and (in version 2 of RIP) relies upon ticks and hop count as its metrics. A *tick* is a measure of delay time—about 1/18th second. In RIP version 2, ticks serve as the primary value used in determining best path. If two or more network paths have the same tick value, RIP then uses *hop count* (the number of routers the packet must traverse) to break the tie. Should multiple network paths have equal tick values and hop counts, RIP either uses a user-defined tiebreaker or loads balance across the paths. Refer to Chapter 6 for additional information on RIP.

Table 9.2 IPX encapsulation names.	
IPX Name	**Usage**
Ethernet_II	arpa
Ethernet_802.2	sap
Ethernet _SNAP	snap
Ethernet_802.3	novell-ether
Token ring	token
Token-Ring_SNAP	snap

Note: *Although IPX uses RIP as its default, two other routing protocol choices exist: Novell's link-state routing protocol, dubbed NetWare Link Services Protocol (NLSP) and Cisco's Enhanced Interior Gateway Protocol (EIGRP).*

IPX Service Advertisement

In an IPX network, servers *advertise* (that is, broadcast the services they offer and their addresses) across the network. These advertisements are defined within the *Service Advertisement Protocol* (*SAP*) and are supported by all versions of NetWare. Clients learn of services that are being provided by issuing SAP broadcast queries and receiving SAP responses. SAP broadcasts traverse the network on a regular basis, every 60 seconds by default. Routers also receive SAP broadcasts, learn of services offered, and store the information in SAP tables. However, routers do not forward SAP broadcasts; they share SAP table information with other routers. Like SAP broadcasts, SAP table information is forwarded every 60 seconds by default. Figure 9.3 illustrates SAP broadcasts within an IPX network.

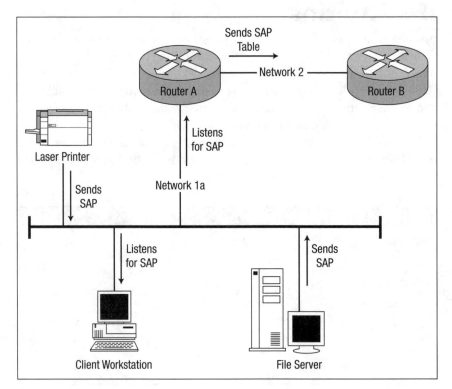

Figure 9.3 SAP broadcasts.

Table 9.3 Common SAP services.	
Hex Number	**SAP Description**
0004	NetWare file server
0007	Print server
0024	Router
039B	Lotus Notes server

A unique hexadecimal number identifies the services within a SAP broadcast. Table 9.3 lists some common SAP services.

One example of a SAP broadcast involves a *Get Nearest Server* (*GNS*) request. Figure 9.4 presents the GNS process. A client workstation typically issues this type of request when it needs to log in to the network. The client broadcasts the GNS request across the network, and both the NetWare file server and the router receive the request. If a file server resides on the network, it replies with a *Give Nearest Server* SAP. If no file server responds and the router knows of another file server, the router will respond with information from its SAP table.

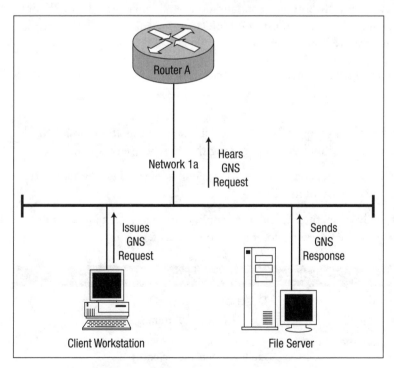

Figure 9.4 A Get Nearest Server.

Key features of IPX include:

➤ The logical address is 80 bits (network.node).

➤ The interface MAC address is the node address.

➤ A router interface can support multiple encapsulation protocols.

➤ RIP is the default routing protocol.

➤ Servers advertise their services in SAP packets.

Configuring IPX

Configuring Novell IPX on a router requires that both global and interface parameters be set. Global configuration includes starting the IPX routing process and enabling load balancing. Interface configuration includes assigning unique network numbers and defining encapsulation settings.

Table 9.4 lists the global configuration commands necessary to enable IPX routing. These commands must be executed from the global configuration prompt.

The following lists the interface configuration command required for IPX routing on an interface. You must configure this command for each interface connected to an IPX network:

```
ipx network number [encapsulation encapsulation-type] [secondary]
```

where:

number indicates a unique IPX network number; **encapsulation** *encapsulation-type* is optional and indicates the framing that will be used (sap, snap, etc.).

secondary is optional and indicates whether an additional encapsulation type exists on the current interface.

To further illustrate, the IPX network configuration as depicted in Figure 9.2 would require the following commands to be executed:

Table 9.4 IPX global configuration commands.	
Command	Description
ipx routing [node]	Enables Novell IPX routing.
ipx maximum-paths paths	Enables round robin load balancing across multiple equal metric paths.

```
RouterA (config)#
RouterA (config)# ipx routing
RouterA (config)# ipx maximum-paths 2
RouterA (config)# interface ethernet 0
RouterA (config-if)# ipx network 1a encapsulation sap
RouterA (config-if)# exit
RouterA (config)# interface tokenring 0
RouterA (config-if)# ipx network 2b encapsulation snap
RouterA (config-if)# exit
RouterA (config)# interface ethernet 1
RouterA (config-if)# ipx network 3c encapsulation sap
RouterA (config-if)# exit
RouterA (config)# interface serial 0
RouterA (config-if)# ipx network 4d encapsulation snap
RouterA (config-if)# exit
RouterA (config)#
```

Monitoring IPX

After configuring IPX on the router, the commands listed in this section enable you to monitor IPX activity.

The **show ipx interface** command displays IPX status and parameters configured on each interface. Sample output from this command is shown in Listing 9.1.

Listing 9.1   The **show ipx interface** command.

```
Ethernet0 is up, line protocol is up
  IPX address is 1A.00e0.b055.28e1,SAP [up] line-up,
      RIPPQ:0,SAPPQ:0
  Delay of this IPX network,
      in ticks is 1 throughput 0 link delay 0
  IPXWAN processing not enabled on this interface.
  IPX SAP update interval is 1 minute(s)
  IPX type 20 propagation packet forwarding is disabled
  Outgoing access list is not set
  IPX Helper access list is not set
  SAP GNS processing enabled,delay 0 ms,output filter list not set
  SAP Input filter list is not set
  SAP Output filter list is not set
  SAP Router filter list is not set
  Input filter list is not set
  Output filter list is not set
  Router filter list is not set
  Netbios Input host access list is not set
  Netbios Input bytes access list is not set
  Netbios Output host access list is not set
  Netbios Output bytes access list is not set
```

```
Updates each 60 seconds, aging multiples RIP: 3 SAP: 3
SAP interpacket delay is 5 ms, maximum size is 480 bytes
RIP interpacket delay is 5 ms, maximum size is 432 bytes
IPX accounting is disabled
IPX fast switching is configured (enabled)
RIP packets received 25913, RIP packets sent 4
SAP packets received 122226, SAP packets sent 3
```

This interface has been configured for IPX network 1a with encapsulation type SAP. It sends SAP broadcasts every 60 seconds.

Listing 9.2 shows the **show ipx route** command output. This command displays the contents of the IPX routing table.

Listing 9.2   The **show ipx route** command.

```
Codes:C-Connected primary network,c-Connected secondary network
      S-Static,F-Floating static,L-Local (internal),W-IPXWAN
      R-RIP,E-EIGRP,N-NLSP,X-External,s-seconds,u-uses

4 Total IPX routes. Up to 2 parallel paths and 16 hops allowed.

No default route known.

C    1A (SAP),          Et0
R       1002 [02/01] via 1A.00aa.0047.5aa6,   45s, Et0
R    361FB7A0 [02/01] via 1A.0080.5f65.abbd,  51s, Et0
R    5F78776E [21/01] via 1A.0080.5f78.776e,   1s, Et0
```

This router can reach four IPX networks. It is directly connected to network 1a and has "learned"—via RIP—of three other IPX networks that it can reach via its Ethernet 0 interface.

The **show ipx servers** command displays the IPX server list stored in the SAP table. Sample output from the command is shown in Listing 9.3.

Listing 9.3   The **show ipx server** command.

```
Codes: S - Static, P - Periodic, E - EIGRP, N - NLSP,
       H - Holddown, + = detail
22 Total IPX Servers
Table ordering is based on routing and server info
  Type Name                 Net      Address       Port Route Hops Itf
  P   4 HOUSTON_FS_01     361FB7A0.0000.0000.0001:0451  2/01 1  Et0
  P   7 HOUSTON_PS_01     10008022.0080.c780.d9c7:0451  2/01 1  Et0
  P  2C BKUPEXECv7_01     361FB7A0.0000.0000.0001:400D  2/01 1  Et0
  P 107 HOUSTON_FS_01     361FB7A0.0000.0000.0001:8104  2/01 1  Et0
  P 23F HOUSTON_FS_01     361FB7A0.0000.0000.0001:907B  2/01 1  Et0
```

```
P 26B HOUSTON_____  361FB7A0.0000.0000.0001:0005  2/01 1  Et0
P 278 HOUSTON_____  361FB7A0.0000.0000.0001:4006  2/01 1  Et0
P 30C 0060B00294C400CG  10008022.0060.b002.94c4:400C  1/00 1  Et0
P 30C 0060B096AB7910C4  10008022.0060.b096.ab79:400C  1/00 1  Et0
P 30C 0060B096AB7920C4  10008022.0060.b096.ab79:401C  1/00 1  Et0
P 30C 0060B096AB79B0C4  10008022.0060.b096.ab79:402C  1/00 1  Et0
P 30C 0060B0CC836B10C4  10008022.0060.b0cc.836b:400C  1/00 1  Et0
P 30C 0060B0CC836BA0C4  10008022.0060.b0cc.836b:401C  1/00 1  Et0
P 30C 0060B0CC836BB0C4  10008022.0060.b0cc.836b:402C  1/00 1  Et0
P 30C 0800098A09E400CE  10008022.0800.098a.09e4:400C  1/00 1  Et0
P 355 00202055777_APPS  10008022.00a0.c959.91d2:6000  1/00 1  Et0
P 39B 002020HOUSTONNOT  10008022.0080.5f78.776e:6000  1/00 1  Et0
P 535 PS_CLR_03         10008022.0800.1104.175a:5005  1/00 1  Et0
P 640 IWEARPOLLY        10008022.0080.c780.e9c1:E885  1/00 1  Et0
P 640 HOUSTON_APPS_01   10008022.00a0.c959.91d2:E885  1/00 1  Et0
P 64E HOUSTON_APPS_01A  10008022.00a0.c959.91d2:4068  1/00 1  Et0
P 82B HOUSTON_FS_01     361FB7A0.0000.0000.0001:400D  2/01 1  Et0
```

This router has received SAPs from several different types of servers.

Listing 9.4 gives the **show ipx traffic** command output. This command displays the number and type of IPX packets transmitted and received by the router.

Listing 9.4   The **show ipx traffic** command.

```
System Traffic for 0.0000.0000.0001 System-Name: RouterA
Rcvd:    165726 total, 37463 format errors,
         0 checksum errors, 0 bad hop count,
         15539 packets pitched, 155441 local destination,
         0 multicast
Bcast:   155405 received, 6 sent
Sent:    7 generated, 0 forwarded
         0 encapsulation failed, 0 no route
SAP:     17409 SAP requests, 0 SAP replies, 22 servers
         104725 SAP advertisements received, 0 sent
         0 SAP flash updates sent, 112 SAP format errors,
         last seen from 0.0000.0
         000.0000
RIP:     8284 RIP requests, 1 RIP replies, 4 routes
         17633 RIP advertisements received, 0 sent
         0 RIP flash updates sent, 0 RIP format errors
Echo:    Rcvd 0 requests, 0 replies
         Sent 0 requests, 0 replies
         2024 unknown: 0 no socket, 0 filtered, 2024 no helper
         0 SAPs throttled, freed NDB len 0
Watchdog:
         0 packets received, 0 replies spoofed
Queue lengths:
         IPX input: 0, SAP 0, RIP 0, GNS 0
```

```
       SAP throttling length: 0/(no limit),
       0 nets pending lost route reply
       Delayed process creation: 0
EIGRP:  Total received 0, sent 0
       Updates received 0, sent 0
       Queries received 0, sent 0
       Replies received 0, sent 0
       SAPs received 0, sent 0
NLSP:   Level-1 Hellos received 0, sent 0
       PTP Hello received 0, sent 0
       Level-1 LSPs received 0, sent 0
       LSP Retransmissions: 0
       LSP checksum errors received: 0
       LSP HT=0 checksum errors received: 0
       Level-1 CSNPs received 0, sent 0
       Level-1 PSNPs received 0, sent 0
       Level-1 DR Elections: 0
       Level-1 SPF Calculations: 0
       Level-1 Partial Route Calculations: 0
```

This router has received more than 100,000 SAP advertisements from various servers.

> *Note:*   *Given the high number of SAP advertisements that are broadcast through an IPX network, IPX is considered "chatty."*

Troubleshooting IPX

The commands listed in this section provide information to assist you in diagnosing problems with IPX.

 You must be connected to the router's console or configure log messages to be displayed to your terminal session before you will be able to view any debug messages.

The **debug ipx routing activity** command displays IPX routing update information:

```
IPX routing debugging is on

IPXRIP: posting full update to 1A.ffff.ffff.ffff
        via Ethernet0 (broadcast)
IPXRIP: suppressing null update to 1A.ffff.ffff.ffff
```

The **debug ipx sap activity** command displays IPX SAP packet information:

```
IPX service debugging is on

IPXSAP: posting update to 1A.ffff.ffff.ffff
        via Ethernet0 (broadcast) (full)
IPXSAP: posting update to 1A.ffff.ffff.ffff
        via Ethernet0 (broadcast) (full)
IPXSAP: posting update to 1A.ffff.ffff.ffff
        via Ethernet0 (broadcast) (full)
```

 The **no debug all** command quickly turns off any debug commands that are active.

 You can use the following commands to monitor and troubleshoot IPX activity:

➤ **show ipx interface**

➤ **show ipx route**

➤ **show ipx server**

➤ **show ipx traffic**

➤ **debug ipx routing activity**

➤ **debug ipx sap activity**

Practice Questions

Question 1

Which of the following protocols is used within the transport layer of the NetWare protocol suite?

○ a. Ethernet

○ b. UDP

○ c. SPX

○ d. ARP

Answer c is correct. SPX is the transport layer protocol used within NetWare's protocol suite. Answer a is incorrect because Ethernet is data link layer protocol that supports NetWare. UDP is a transport layer protocol, but it is used within the TCP/IP suite, so answer b is incorrect. Answer d is incorrect because ARP resides at the network layer within the TCP/IP suite.

Question 2

Which of the following is a valid and complete IPX logical address?

○ a. 0080.c747.b122

○ b. 1a.0080.c747.b122

○ c. 1a.172.16.101.123

○ d. 1a

Answer b is correct. It is a complete IPX logical address for network 1a and node 0080.c747.b122. Answer a is incorrect because it is a node address (MAC address) and is incomplete. Answer c contains an IPX network number (1a), but also includes an IP address, so it is incorrect. Answer d is incomplete because it is only the IPX network number; therefore, it is incorrect.

Question 3

Which of the following is the default routing protocol within an IPX network?

○ a. RIP

○ b. NLSP

○ c. EIGRP

○ d. IGRP

Answer a is correct. RIP is the default routing protocol within an IPX network. Although NLSP and EIGRP can be used as the routing protocol for IPX, they are not the default. Therefore, answers b and c are incorrect. IGRP is incorrect because it is not supported within IPX. Therefore, answer d is incorrect.

Question 4

IPX RIP version 2 uses which of the following metrics to determine the best path? [Choose the two best answers]

❑ a. Bandwidth

❑ b. Hop count

❑ c. Load

❑ d. Ticks

Answers b and d are correct. Hop count and ticks (delay) are the two metrics used within IPX RIP version 2. Bandwidth and load are not used in RIP, but in more sophisticated routing protocols, such as EIGRP and OSPF. Therefore answers a and c are incorrect.

Question 5

Which of the following are Cisco names for standard IPX encapsulation types? [Choose the five best answers]

❑ a. arpa

❑ b. sap

❑ c. ethernet

❑ d. token

❑ e. snap

❑ f. novell-ether

❑ g. novell

Answers a, b, d, e, and f are correct. Cisco's encapsulation name for Ethernet II is arpa; for Ethernet_802.2, its sap; for Ethernet_SNAP and Token Ring_SNAP, its snap; for Ethernet_802.3, its novell-ether; and for Token-Ring, its token. Ethernet and novell are not IPX encapsulation types; therefore, answers c and g are incorrect.

Question 6

Which configuration command must be executed for each interface supporting IPX?

○ a. **ipx routing**

○ b. **ipx protocol**

○ c. **ipx interface**

○ d. **ipx network**

Answer d is correct. The **ipx network** command assigns a network number to a router interface. This command must be repeated for each IPX network that the router must support. The **ipx routing** command enables IPX routing within the router. Therefore, answer a is incorrect. Answers b and c are also incorrect because the **ipx protocol** and **ipx interface** commands are not valid commands.

Question 7

Which of the following statements is a feature of an IPX environment? [Choose the answers that best apply]

- ❑ a. A logical address is 80 bits (network.node).
- ❑ b. Interface MAC address is the node address.
- ❑ c. A router interface can support multiple encapsulation protocols.
- ❑ d. RIP is the default routing protocol.
- ❑ e. Servers advertise their services in SAP packets.

Answers a, b, c, d, and e are correct. They are all features of an IPX environment.

Question 8

Which router command displays the contents of the router's SAP table?

- ○ a. **show ipx traffic**
- ○ b. **show ipx route**
- ○ c. **show ipx server**
- ○ d. **show ipx interface**

Answer c is correct. The **show ipx server** command displays the information learned through SAP advertisements. Answer a is incorrect because the **show ipx traffic** command displays the number and type of IPX packets transmitted and received by the router. The **show ipx route** command displays the contents of the IPX routing table, so answer b is incorrect. The **show ipx interface** command displays IPX status and parameters configured on each interface; therefore, answer d is incorrect.

Question 9

SNAP is the default IPX encapsulation type for which type of LAN interface? [Choose the two best answers]

- ❑ a. Ethernet
- ❑ b. Token Ring
- ❑ c. FDDI
- ❑ d. Serial

Answers b and c are correct. SNAP is the default encapsulation type for both Token Ring and FDDI. The default encapsulation type for Ethernet is "novell-ether". Therefore, answer a is incorrect. Because a serial interface is a WAN interface, it does not have a default encapsulation type; therefore, answer d is incorrect.

Question 10

Which of the following reside within the upper layers of the NetWare protocol suite? [Choose the three best answers]

- ❑ a. NCP
- ❑ b. NetBIOS emulation
- ❑ c. NOS
- ❑ d. A NetWare shell

Answers a, b, and d are correct. NCP is a collection of server routines that interfaces with other applications. NetBIOS is a common session-layer interface specification from IBM and Microsoft. A NetWare shell determines whether application calls require network services. Answer c is incorrect because NetWare itself is considered a NOS and cannot be a protocol within NetWare.

Need To Know More?

 Chappell, Laura, *Novell's Guide to LAN/WAN Analysis: IPX/SPX*. IDG Books Worldwide, 1998. ISBN 0-76454-508-6. This book provides additional information on IPX, SPX, RIP, and NCP. It also introduces techniques for performing network analysis, troubleshooting, and optimization within a NetWare environment. The book includes a CD-ROM, which contains a demonstration version of LAN analyzer software.

 Cisco Systems, *Cisco IOS Solutions for Network Protocols, IPX, APP Vol 2*. ISBN 1-57870-050-7. This book provides exhaustive information on implementing and troubleshooting IPX within a network utilizing Cisco IOS.

 Using Cisco's documentation CD, you can immediately access Cisco's entire library of end-user documentation, selected product news, bug databases, and related information. The documentation CD-ROM is produced monthly.

 The official Cisco Web site, **www.cisco.com**, contains several Cisco white papers on topics such as connecting Novell LANs to the Internet and NLSP route aggregation when you search for "Novell IPX".

IP And IPX
Access Lists

Terms you'll need to understand:

√ IP standard access list

√ IP extended access list

√ Service Advertisement Protocol (SAP)

√ IPX standard access list

√ IPX extended access list

√ IPX SAP filter

Techniques you'll need to master:

√ Configuring standard access lists for IP

√ Configuring extended access lists for IP

√ Configuring standard access lists for IPX

√ Configuring extended access lists for IPX

√ Configuring IPX SAP filters

√ Monitoring access list operations on the router

√ Verifying access list operations on the router

This chapter will cover access lists for IP and IPX traffic. *Access lists* allow network administrators to restrict access to certain networks, devices, and services. They provide an effective means of applying security within an organization; they also permit or deny specific types of traffic to pass through an interface. The types of IP traffic they filter can be based on source or destination address or address range, protocol, precedence, type of service, **icmp-type, icmp-code, icmp-message, igmp-type,** port, or state of the TCP connection. These filtered types can also be based on source or destination address, sockets, protocol number, and SAP type. In addition, other IPX access lists restrict other types of traffic, however, we will not cover these additional categories because they are beyond the scope of the CCNA exam. However, a full list of access lists is provided in Table 10.1.

Access lists provide a powerful set of tools that can deny and permit users to access specific applications or hosts. However, the trade-off for using access lists is that they require processing power to compare packets entering or exiting an interface to the entries in the list. Figure 10.1 illustrates how routers filter packets to restrict network access.

A wide variety of access lists can be applied to a router interface. Table 10.1 lists the different types of available access lists. This chapter will focus only on the IP standard and extended access lists, IPX SAP access lists, and IPX standard and extended access lists.

IP Access Lists

IP access lists are used to deny or permit specific traffic into or out of an interface on a router. They filter IP source and destination addresses and protocol

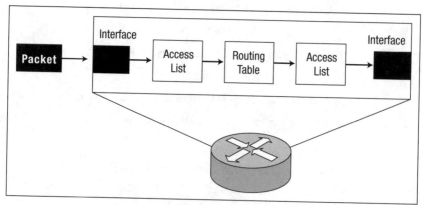

Figure 10.1   Access list architecture.

Table 10.1 Types of access lists.	
Numeric Range	**Description**
1 through 99	IP standard access list
100 through 199	IP extended access list
200 through 299	Protocol type-code access list
300 through 399	DECnet access list
600 through 699	AppleTalk access list
700 through 799	48-bit MAC address access list
800 through 899	IPX standard access list
900 through 999	IPX extended access list
1,000 through 1,099	SAP access list

or service specific traffic. IP access lists are of two types: *standard* and *extended*. The difference between the two is the preciseness by which each can filter IP traffic.

IP Standard Access Lists

IP standard access lists filter traffic based on the source IP address or address range. Therefore, administrators can use this tool to restrict access to specific users and allow access to others. The lists are applied to the interface of a router where traffic is to be filtered, and they restrict access into or out of the interface. The direction in which traffic is restricted is determined by the Cisco command used to apply the access list to the interface.

IP Standard Access List Commands

Creating and applying an access list to an interface consists of two steps, both of which are performed in configuration mode. First, the access list must be created. A single access list can consist of many access list *statements*. An access list *number* identifies an individual access group that can consist of many access list *entries*. In addition, the order in which access list entries are created plays an important role in the behavior of the access list. When traffic passes through the interface, it is compared to each access list entry in the order in which the entry was created. If the traffic matches an access list entry, the indicated function (permit or deny) of the access list entry is performed on the traffic. When a packet is permitted entry, the router caches the entry and any subsequent packets in this session are granted access without being applied against the access list. All access lists have an implicit **deny all** statement at the end of the list. Thus, if the traffic does not match any entry, it is denied access into or out of the interface. The command to create an access list is as follows:

```
access-list access-list-number {deny|permit} source [source-wildcard]
```

The format of this previous command listing is typical of Cisco commands. The listing can be interpreted as follows. The bold words should be written exactly as shown. In this case, the "|" indicates that either **deny** or **permit** should be written, but not both. The italicized words indicate that a character string must be written in this field. In this case, the character string would be a number. The square brackets indicate that a field is optional. A brief description of each field is provided in Table 10.2.

The source-wildcard field, referred to as a *wildcard mask*, is used to identify bits in an IP address that have meaning and bits that can be ignored. In this case, the wildcard mask is referred to as a *source-wildcard*, indicating that it is a wildcard mask of the source IP address. A source wildcard mask is applied to a source IP address to determine a range of addresses to permit or deny.

At first, the best way to learn wildcard masks is to convert the mask from decimal to binary. The wildcard mask is applied by comparing the IP address bits to the corresponding IP wildcard bits. A "1" bit in the wildcard mask indicates that the corresponding bit in the IP address can be ignored. Thus, the IP address bit can be either a "1" or "0." A "0" in the wildcard mask indicates that the corresponding bit in the IP address must be strictly followed. Thus, the value must be exactly the same as specified in the IP address. Tables 10.3 and 10.4 illustrate applying a source wildcard to a source address to determine a range of addresses.

Tables 10.3 and 10.4 illustrate that the first three octets must be strictly followed; therefore, the values of these octets must be 172.16.16 to be a match. However, the 1 bits in the fourth octet indicate that any value between 0 and

Table 10.2	IP standard access list command field descriptions.
Identifier	**Description**
Access-list-number	A dotted decimal number between 1 and 99.
Deny	Denies access if condition is matched.
Permit	Permits access if condition is matched.
Source	Number of the network or host from which the packet is being sent.
Source-wildcard	Wildcard bits to be applied to the source.

Table 10.3   Applying a source-wildcard to a source IP address in binary.

Source Address In Bits	Binary
Source address	10101100.00010000.00010000.00000000
Source-wildcard	00000000.00000000.00000000.11111111
Result	10101100.00010000.00010000.any

Table 10.4   Applying a source-wildcard to a source IP address in decimal.

Source Address In Bits	Binary
Source address	172.16.16.0
Source-wildcard	0.0.0.255
Result	172.16.16.any

255 will result in a match. Therefore, any host with the IP address of 172.16.16.0 through 172.16.16.255 would be a match for this source IP address and source-wildcard mask.

The next step is to apply the access list to an interface. The syntax for doing so is as follows:

```
ip access-group access-list-number {in|out}
```

The *access-list-number* is the number used to identify the access list. This number must be the same as specified in the **access-list** command used to create the previously shown entries. The **in|out** option indicates whether this list is to filter on inbound or outbound traffic through the interface. It is important to remember that the access list is being applied to a specific interface on a router, rather than to all the interfaces of the router.

Creating And Applying An IP Standard Access List

The network in Figure 10.2 will be used to further illustrate IP standard access lists.

In this example, suppose we want permit the following devices to have access to the network 172.16.4.0:

➤ Any device on network 172.16.14.0

➤ Any device on network 172.16.3.0 except 172.16.3.5

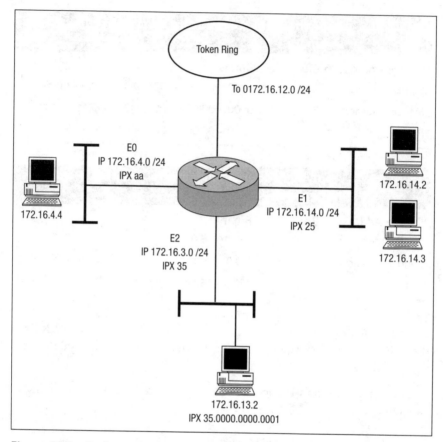

Figure 10.2 Basic network used to explain access lists.

➤ Only the device with the IP address of 172.16.12.4 on network
   172.16.12.0

As mentioned previously, applying an IP standard access list to a router interface involves two steps. The first step, creating the access list, indicates all the
source addresses that are permitted or denied access. The second step is applying the access list to the interface on which we are restricting either outbound
or inbound traffic. By applying the **access-group** command to interface Ethernet
0, we can restrict access to network 172.16.4.0. The commands to create this
access list are:

```
Router#configure terminal
Router(config)#access-list 5 permit 172.16.14.0 0.0.0.255
Router(config)#access-list 5 deny 172.16.3.5 0.0.0.0
Router(config)#access-list 5 permit 172.16.3.0 0.0.0.255
Router(config)#access-list 5 permit 172.16.12.4 0.0.0.0
Router(config)#access-list 5 deny 0.0.0.0 255.255.255.255
```

These commands restrict and permit the traffic that we detailed in our requirements. The first **access-list** entry permits access to all users from network 172.16.14.0 to pass through the access list on Ethernet 0. Note that the source-wildcard of 0.0.0.255 indicates that every host ID in the last octet can be ignored, thus allowing all IP addresses between 172.16.14.0 and 172.16.14.255. The second **access-list** command denies host ID 172.16.3.5 to pass through the access list. Note that the source-wildcard of 0.0.0.0 indicates that only the source address (172.16.3.5) specified is denied access. The third **access-list** command permits all users on network 172.16.3.0 to pass through the access list. Note that host ID 172.16.3.5 will still not be allowed to pass through the access list, because any traffic from this host was dropped by the previous **deny** command. The order in which a **permit** or **deny** command is placed in an access list is extremely important.

 When adding new entries to existing access lists, it is sometimes necessary to reorder the access list so that it will filter traffic correctly. Often, the best way to reorder the entries is to copy all the entries into a text file, to add or remove the required entries, and to reorder them in that text file. After you have them correctly ordered, add them all to the router configuration.

The fourth **access-list** entry permits only user 172.16.12.4 to pass through the access list. Finally, the last **access-list** command in italics is implicit whenever an access list is created. Therefore, any packet not generated by the router with the access list that does not match one of the permit entries will be dropped. You would not have to configure this **deny** all entry.

Before these access list entries can filter traffic, they must be applied to the interface as an access group. We are going to apply access list to outbound packets on Ethernet 0. Therefore, any packet attempting to travel out interface Ethernet 0 must match one of the entries in access group 5. The steps to configure an outbound access list on Ethernet 0 are as follows:

```
Router#config t
Enter configuration commands, one per line. End with CNTL/Z.
Router(config)#interface ethernet 0
Router(config-if)#ip access-group 5 out
```

We have applied **access-group 5** to the outbound Ethernet 0 interface. Now, every packet that is sent out the Ethernet 0 interface will be checked to see if it matches. More complicated scenarios for restricting access through an interface exist. As we have seen earlier, sometimes a network administrator will want only to permit a range of IP addresses through an access list. However, it is more complicated to permit access to a range of IP addresses that do not fall exactly on octet bit boundaries. A second example follows to illustrate this scenario.

Standard Access List Example 2

For this example, we will again use the network provided in Figure 10.2. However, in this case we want to allow the following devices to have access only to the network 172.16.4.0. Therefore, we want to permit any device with the IP address between 172.16.3.32 through 172.16.3.39.

For this scenario, we must determine the proper source wildcard mask to apply to allow devices in the IP address range 172.16.3.32 through 172.16.3.39. We start with the IP address 172.16.3.32 to create this access list. Next, we apply a network mask that allows eight incremental bits in the fourth octet. Table 10.5 illustrates the proper source IP address and source wildcard mask in binary and decimal for this example.

Table 10.5 illustrates that by applying the source wildcard mask of 0.0.0.7, we have allowed a range of IP addresses that do not fall on an octet boundary. Each permitted address is determined by taking the bits indicated as "ignored bits" by the source wildcard mask and listing the possible permutations. A few good rules to know are as follows:

➤ When grouping IP addresses the group size will always be a power of 2 (2, 4, 8, 16, …).

Table 10.5	Applying a source-wildcard to a source IP address in binary.	
Source Address In Bits	**Binary**	**Decimal**
Source address	10101100.00010000.00000011.00100000	172.16.3.32
Source-wildcard	00000000.00000000.00000000.00000111	0.0.0.7
Permitted address 1	10101100.00010000.00010000.00100000	172.16.3.32
Permitted address 2	10101100.00010000.00010000.00100001	172.16.3.33
Permitted address 3	10101100.00010000.00010000.00100010	172.16.3.34
Permitted address 4	10101100.00010000.00010000.00100011	172.16.3.35
Permitted address 5	10101100.00010000.00010000.00100100	172.16.3.36
Permitted address 6	10101100.00010000.00010000.00100101	172.16.3.37
Permitted address 7	10101100.00010000.00010000.00100110	172.16.3.38
Permitted address 8	10101100.00010000.00010000.00100111	172.16.3.39

➤ Anytime IP addresses are grouped together, the first IP address in the group will be divisible by the size of the group. For example, a group of eight IP addresses can start only on multiples of eight (0, 8, 16, 24, …).

➤ The wildcard mask is always one less than the group size. For example, a group of eight has a wildcard mask of seven. A group of 64 has a wildcard mask of 63.

Whereas IP standard access lists provide a powerful set of tools for restricting access, they can only restrict access based on the source IP address. Extended IP access lists increase the variables that we can use to restrict access through an interface.

IP Extended Access Lists

IP standard access lists filter traffic based on the source IP address only; therefore, administrators can use this tool to restrict access to specific users only. This tool was created because administrators wanted more control of the traffic that could travel through interfaces. Cisco responded with IP extended access lists, which perform the same basic function as standard access lists (permitting and denying IP packets through an interface), except they extend the types of IP traffic that can be filtered. Consequently, IP extended access lists allow for more precise filtering of IP traffic. Whereas IP standard access lists allow only source IP address filtering, IP extended access lists provide source and destination IP address filtering. In addition, IP extended access lists filter on layer 4 protocol (TCP, UDP, etc.), look into the TCP or UDP header, and allow filtering on TCP/UDP port numbers. Table 10.6 provides a listing of some of the most common layer 4 protocols and TCP port numbers that are filtered using IP extended access lists.

Table 10.6	Common port numbers filtered using IP extended access lists.	
Protocol	**Port Number**	**Protocol Name**
TCP	21	File Transfer Protocol (FTP)
TCP	23	Telnet
TCP	25	Simple Mail Transfer Protocol (SMTP)
UDP	53	Domain Name System (DNS)
UDP	69	Trivial File Transfer Protocol (TFTP)
UDP	80	Hypertext Transfer Protocol (HTTP)
UDP	162	Simple Network Management Protocol (SNMP)

Memorizing these TCP and UDP port numbers is a good move for the CCNA exam. While there are many other port numbers, these are the port number that are most important for the exam.

In addition, IP extended access lists allow filtering based on the **IP precedence** field, **TOS** field, **ICMP-type**, **ICMP-code**, **ICMP-message**, **IGMP-type**, and TCP established connections. This book will only cover source and destination address, IP protocol, and TCP/UDP port numbers.

IP Extended Access List Commands

The steps for creating and applying an IP extended access list are the same as an IP standard access list. First, you create the access list entries. Second, you apply the access list group to the interface where you want to filter traffic.

It is still important to enter IP extended access list entries in the correct order. Also, an implicit deny all traffic is still at the end of every IP extended access list.

The command to create an IP extended access list is very similar to the command used to create an IP standard access list. However, the additional filtering capabilities require some additional fields in the command. The command to create an access-list is as follows:

```
access-list access-list-number {deny|permit} protocol source
source-wildcard [operator port [port]]  destination [destination-
wildcard] [operator port [port]]
```

We covered how to read the command listing in the IP standard access list section. We will discuss only the additional fields here. The first noticeable difference is the addition of the protocol field. This field will typically be filled with either TCP or UDP (other possibilities exist, but these are beyond the scope of this book and the CCNA exam). The **operator port [port]** field is used to indicate the TCP/UDP port or range of ports for the **source** and **source-wildcard** field. In addition, the **destination** and **destination-wildcard** fields are added with their corresponding **operator port [port]** field. Basically, we have added the necessary fields to filter traffic on source and destination address, IP protocol (TCP or UDP), and port numbers. In addition, the **access-list number** field now must be a number between 100 and 199, as indicated in Table 10.1. A complete listing of all the fields in the IP extended access list command is provided in Table 10.7.

Table 10.7   Access list command field descriptions.

Access List Command	Description
Access list-number	Identifies the access list for which it belongs.
Deny	Denies access if condition is matched.
Permit	Permits access if condition is matched.
Protocol	Name or number of the IP protocol.
Source	Number of the network or host from which the packet is being sent.
Source-wildcard	Wildcard bits to be applied to the source.
Destination	Number of the network or host from which the packet originated.
Destination-wildcard	Wildcard bits to be applied to the destination.
Precedence	Filter packets by precedence level.
Tos	Filter packets by type of service.
Icmp-type	Filter packets by icmp-type.
Icmp-code	Filter packets by icmp-code.
Icmp-message	Filter packets by icmp-message.
Igmp-type	Filter packets by igmp-type.
Operator	Compares source or destination ports.
Port	Decimal value or name of a TCP or UDP port.
Established	Indicates an established connection.
Log	Causes an information logging entry.

To apply an IP extended access list, use the same IP access group command used for standard access lists. Simply apply the access list to the interface where you want to filter traffic.

Creating And Applying An IP Extended Access List

To illustrate the use of the IP extended functionality, we will continue to use the network in Figure 10.2. In this example, we will extend the types of traffic we filter. Suppose we want to permit the following traffic to pass through our access list:

➤ Any device on network 172.16.14.0 is permitted to communicate with any device on network 172.16.4.0 using the IP, TCP and the port number 23 (Telnet).

- ► Device 172.16.14.2 is permitted to communicate with device 172.16.4.4 using the IP, UDP and the UDP port number 69 (TFTP).

- ► Device 172.16.14.3 is permitted to communicate with any device on any network using IP and TCP for any port number.

The following commands create this access list:

```
Router#configure terminal
Router(config)#access-list 105 permit tcp 172.16.14.0 0.0.0.255
172.16.4.0 0.0.0.255 eq 23
Router(config)#access-list 105 permit udp host 172.16.14.2
host 172.16.4.4 eq 69
Router(config)#access-list 105 permit tcp host 172.16.14.3 any any
Router(config)#access-list 105 deny any any
```

Let's discuss these access list entries. The last entry in italics is the implicit **deny** statement. It is not necessary to add this entry, because it is always there. The first entry performs the extended functionality by indicating that we are permitting only TCP traffic from any device on network 172.16.14.0 (indicated by the source-wildcard of 0.0.0.255) to communicate with 172.16.4.0 (indicated by the destination-wildcard of 0.0.0.255) using the TCP port number (indicated by the operator **eq** and the port number 23). The operator **eq** stands for equal to. A subset of the different possible operators is supplied in Table 10.8.

The second entry introduces the word "host" into the command; this is a short way of indicating the wildcard mask 0.0.0.0. However, the "host" word precedes the IP address, versus the traditional trailing wildcard mask. So in this entry, we have allowed only the device with the IP address of 172.16.14.2 to communicate with only the device 172.16.4.4, using the protocol UDP for the port number 69 (TFTP).

The third entry introduces the word "any" into the command. Similar to the word "host" in the preceding condition, the "any" word is a short way of indicating any source or destination address with the wildcard mask of 255.255.255.255. This mask indicates that all IP addresses are being described, and therefore, it does not matter what source or destination IP address is specified. In this case, we have described all destination addresses. So in this entry, we have allowed the device with the IP address of 172.16.14.3 to communicate with any device using the TCP protocol for any port number.

The second step is applying the access list to the interface that we are restricting. Once again we will specify whether we are filtering outbound or inbound traffic by adding the key word "out" or "in" to the end of the command. In this

Table 10.8 Extended access list command field descriptions.

Operator	Meaning
eq	Match only packets on a given port number.
lt	Match only packets with a lower port number.
gt	Match only packets with a greater port number.
range	Match only packets in the range of port numbers.

example, we will apply the access list to Ethernet 1 to illustrate the ability of IP extended access lists to filter traffic based on destination address as well as source address. The command to apply the access-group to the interface is as follows:

```
Router#config t
Enter configuration commands, one per line. End with CNTL/Z.
Router(config)#interface ethernet 1
Router(config-if)#ip access-group 105 in
```

In summary, extended access lists use increases the preciseness of our filtering. The steps performed to create and apply access lists do not change. Next, we will discuss IPX access lists.

IPX Access Lists

The same basic concepts apply to IPX access lists that applied to IP standard and extended access lists. The main difference is that these lists filter IPX addresses or other IPX-related items. Four types of IPX access lists exist; see Table 10.9.

Table 10.9 Types of IPX access lists.

Name	Function
Standard IPX access list	Restricts access based on IPX source and destination address.
Extended IPX access list	Restricts access based on IPX source and destination address, IPX protocol, and source and destination sockets.
SAP access list	Restricts access based on IPX Service Advertisement Protocol (SAP).
IPX NetBIOS access list	Restricts IPX NetBIOS traffic based on NetBIOS names.

This book will not cover IPX NetBIOS access lists, because they are beyond the scope of the CCNA exam. Before proceeding, refer to Table 10.1 to memorize the access list number ranges for these IPX access lists.

 It is vital to know the numbers associated with each type of access list. This will save you time on the CCNA exam, because you will be able to rule out possible answers quickly.

Standard IPX Access Lists

The standard IPX access list follows the same rules as IP access lists. The general rules to remember are:

➤ The order in which access list entries are configured determines the order in which traffic is checked.

➤ The implicit **deny everything** statement exists at the bottom of every IPX access list.

The **access-list** command is used to create a standard IPX access list. Because this is the same command used when creating the IP standard access list, the router uses the access list number to delineate between IP and IPX standard access lists. The command format is as follows:

```
access-list access-list-number {deny|permit} source-
network[.source-node [source-node-mask]] [destination-
network[.destination-node [destination-node-mask]]]
```

To illustrate IPX access lists, we are going to use the network shown in Figure 10.2.

Creating And Applying A Standard IPX Access List

In this example, we are going to deny IPX network 25 access to IPX network aa, but allow IPX network 35 to access IPX network aa. The first step is to create the access lists:

```
Router#configure terminal
Router(config)#access-list 805 deny 25 aa
Router(config)#access-list 805 permit 35 aa
```

In the above example, the deny statement is not actually required because of the implicit deny all at the end of all access lists. We provided it here just to illustrate our example. Although it was not shown in this example, we could have used source- and destination-wildcard masks to specify ranges of addresses. Refer to the standard and extended IP access lists previously shown for the steps to apply wildcard masks. The next step is to apply the access list to an interface. Once again, this step is the same as for IP standard and extended access lists: We simply pick the appropriate interface where we want to filter the traffic and assign the access list to that interface. The command to perform this step is as follows:

```
Router#config t
Enter configuration commands, one per line. End with CNTL/Z.
Router(config)#interface ethernet 0
Router(config-if)#ipx access-group 805 out
```

Note that the command changed from **ip access-group** to **ipx access-group**. Otherwise, it is exactly the same command.

 Spend most of your time really understanding IP access lists. After you have mastered this skill, understanding IPX access lists is trivial, because the only real difference is the type of logical address being used.

We introduced the concept of using the word "any" to represent all addresses when we explained IP standard and extended access lists. IPX standard and extended access lists use the number "-1" to perform the same function. For example, suppose we wanted to allow any network address to access IPX network aa except IPX network 25. We would have created our access list entries as follows:

```
Router#configure terminal
Router(config)#access-list 805 deny 25 aa
Router(config)#access-list 805 permit -1 -1
```

In this example, we denied IPX network 25 access to IPX network aa first. We must perform this command first, because all traffic is compared to the access list in the order in which the entries are configured. Therefore, any traffic from IPX network 25 is denied based on our first entry and all other IPX network traffic is allowed to pass through, because it matches our second entry.

Extended IPX Access Lists

Extended IPX access lists increase the preciseness in which IPX traffic can be filtered. Extended IPX access lists allow filtering on source and destination addresses, IPX protocol, and source and destination sockets. The command format for an IPX extended access list is as follows:

```
access list access-list-number {deny|permit} protocol source
[source-wildcard] source-socket destination [destination-wildcard]
destination-socket
```

The preceding command extended the IPX standard access list functionality by adding the **protocol** and the **source** and **destination socket** fields. The **protocol** field is used to describe IPX protocols, such as SPX or SAP. The **socket** field is similar to the **port** field used with IP extended access lists. It uses a number to identify a specific service.

We will continue to use our example network in Figure 10.2 to illustrate IPX extended access lists. Suppose we want to allow all IPX networks except 35 to use all IPX protocols and sockets to use the services of IPX network 15. The commands to configure this scenario would be as follows:

```
Router#configure terminal
Router(config)#access-list 905 deny -1 35 0 15 0 0
Router(config)#access-list 905 permit -1 -1 0 0 15 0 0
```

Note that we have indicated all IPX protocols (indicated by the "-1") and all IPX sockets (indicated by the "0") in both entries. However, we explicitly identified that IPX network 35 cannot access IPX network 15 in our first entry. In our second entry, we identified all networks as being allowed to use all services on the destination network 15. The IPX access list can be applied to interface Ethernet 0 as follows:

```
Router#config t
Enter configuration commands, one per line. End with CNTL/Z.
Router(config)#interface ethernet 0
Router(config-if)#ipx access-group 905 out
```

IPX SAP Filters

As explained in Chapter 9, Service Advertisement Protocol (SAP) messages are a common source of traffic on IPX networks. Typically, Novell servers generate SAP advertisements to communicate the different services that they offer. Administrators often want to filter what advertisements are delivered to specific networks, so they create IPX SAP filters and apply them to the appropriate interfaces. The command to create an IPX SAP filter is as follows:

```
access-list access-list-number {deny|permit} source [source-
wildcard] [service-type [server-name]]
```

To illustrate an IPX SAP filter, suppose we would like to filter all SAP type 4 (file server) messages from IPX server 35.0000.0000.0001 from reaching IPX network aa. First we must create the access list entry using the following commands:

```
Router#configure terminal
Router(config)#access-list 1005 deny 35.0000.0000.0001 4
Router(config)#access-list 1005 permit -1
```

In the previous example, we denied the specific server 35.0000.0000.0001 from sending SAP type 4 and permitted every other address to send any SAP type. Once again, remember that an implicit **deny all** is on every access list. The command to apply it to an interface is as follows:

```
ipx output-sap-filter access-list number
ipx input-sap-filter access-list number
ipx router-sap-filter access-list-number
```

IPX designates the direction of traffic to filter by using the keyword "output", "input", or "router" in the command. This is different from an IP access list that designated the direction in which to filter traffic by adding the word "out" or "in" to the end of the command. Therefore, to apply our example to an interface, we simply perform the following command:

```
Router#config t
Enter configuration commands, one per line. End with CNTL/Z.
Router(config)#interface ethernet 0
Router(config-if)#ipx output-sap-filter 1005
```

Monitor And Verify Access Lists

After you have configured all your access lists, it is important to be able to review your entries and to determine that you are filtering traffic in the manner intended. Many different methods exist to monitor and verify access lists. For the scope of this book and the CCNA exam, we will illustrate only two of the more basic methods. Please refer to the *Cisco Command Reference* to identify some of the other methods for monitoring access lists. To determine which access lists you have applied to specific interfaces, use the **show ip interface** command as follows:

```
Router# show ip interface
Ethernet 0 is up, line protocol is up
        Internet address is 172.16.4.4, subnet mask is 255.255.255.0
        Broadcast address is 255.255.255.255
```

```
                Address determined by non-volatile memory
                No helper address
                No secondary address
                Outgoing access list 5 is set
                Inbound access list is not set
                Proxy ARP is enabled
                Security level is default
                Split horizon is enabled
                ICMP redirects are always sent
                ICMP unreachables are always sent
                ICMP mask replies are never sent
                IP fast switching is enabled
                Gateway Discovery is disabled
                IP accounting is disabled
                TCP/IP header compression is disabled
Router#
```

The entry identifying the outbound access list is highlighted. To get a more detailed look at the type of access lists that you have applied, use the **show access-lists** command as follows:

```
Router>show access-lists
Standard IP access list 5
permit 172.16.14.0, wildcard bits 0.0.0.255
deny 172.16.3.5, wildcard bits 0.0.0.0
permit 172.16.4.0, wildcard bits 0.0.0.255
permit 172.16.12.4, wildcard bits 0.0.0.0
Extended IP access list 105
permit tcp 172.16.14.0 0.0.0.255 172.16.4.0 eq 23
permit udp host 172.16.14.2 host 172.16.4.4 eq 69
permit tcp host 172.16.14.3 any any
deny 0.0.0.0 255.255.255.255
Router>
```

Practice Questions

Question 1

> Which of the following commands identifies an IP standard access list?
>
> ○ a. **ip access-group 204 in**
>
> ○ b. **ip access group 110**
>
> ○ c. **ip access-group 45 out**
>
> ○ d. **ip access-group 105 out**
>
> ○ e. **ipx access-group 805 in**

Answer c is correct. The command in answer c identifies an IP standard access list by the access list number 45, which is the proper numeric range for identifying an IP standard access list. Answer a is incorrect because it uses the access list number 204, which is reserved for protocol type access lists not IP standard access lists. Answer b is incorrect because the command is not in the correct format. In addition, it should specify whether the access-group is being applied against inward or outward packets with the "in" or "out" identifiers. The command should be **ip access-group**, not **ip access group**. Answer d is incorrect because it identifies an IP extended access list (access list number 105), not an IP standard access list. Answer e is incorrect because it identifies an IPX standard access list, not an IP extended access list.

Question 2

> Which of the following can be used to permit or deny traffic with IP standard access lists? [Choose the two best answers]
>
> ❑ a. Source IP address
>
> ❑ b. A range of source IP addresses
>
> ❑ c. Destination IP address
>
> ❑ d. A range of destination IP addresses

Answers a and b are correct. IP standard access lists allow IP traffic to be filtered based on source IP addresses; they also allow both individual as well as a range of IP addresses to be specified. Answers c and d are incorrect because IP standard access lists do not filter traffic based on individual or on ranges of destination IP addresses.

Question 3

For an IP standard access list, which source IP address and source-wildcard would indicate all IP addresses from IP network 172.16.23.0 /24?

○ a. 172.16.23.4 0.0.0.0

○ b. 172.16.23.0 0

○ c. 172.16.23.0 0.0.0.255

○ d. 172.16.23.0 0.0.255.0

Answer c is correct, because it uses a wildcard mask of 0.0.0.255 to identify any bit combination in the fourth octet. Therefore, any source IP address with the value of 172.16.23.0 through 172.16.23.255 is identified. Answer a is incorrect because it identifies only the IP address 172.16.23.4. All the bits in every octet must be strictly followed as indicated by the source-wildcard of 0.0.0.0. Answer b is incorrect because it only identifies the source IP address of 172.16.23.0. Answer d is incorrect because the source-wildcard of 0.0.255.0 indicates that any combination of bits in the third octet is identified; however, the fourth octet must be strictly followed. This source IP address and source wildcard combination indicates that the third octet can be any value, but the fourth must be 0.

Question 4

Which of the following commands identifies an IP extended access list?

○ a. **ip access-group 204 in**

○ b. **ip access group 110**

○ c. **ip access-group 115 out**

○ d. **ip access-group 95 out**

○ e. **ipx access-group 805 in**

Answer c is correct. The command in answer c identifies an IP extended access list by the correct numeric range of 100 through 199 for IP extended access lists. Answer a is incorrect because it uses the access list number 204, which is reserved for protocol type access lists. Answer b is incorrect because the command is not in the correct format; it should be **ip access-group**, not **ip access group**. In addition, the command should specify whether the access-group is being applied to inward or outward packets with the "in" or "out" identifiers.

Answer d is incorrect because it identifies an IP standard access list (access list number 95), not an IP extended access list. Answer e is incorrect because it identifies an IPX standard access list, not an IP extended access list.

Question 5

Which of the following can be used to permit or deny traffic with IP extended access lists? [Choose the three best answers]

❑ a. Source IP addresses

❑ b. Destination IP address

❑ c. IP sequence number

❑ d. TCP or UDP port numbers

Answers a, b, and d are correct. Answers a and b are correct because IP extended access lists allow traffic to be filtered based on both source and destination IP addresses. Answer d is correct because IP extended access lists allow traffic to be filtered based on TCP or UDP port number. Please refer to Table 10.6 to see a list of the different items the IP extended access lists can use to filter traffic. Answer c is incorrect because IP extended access lists do not filter traffic based on IP sequence number.

Question 6

What is the valid range for an IP extended access list?

○ a. 1 through 99

○ b. 100 through 199

○ c. 800 through 899

○ d. 900 through 999

Answer b is correct. IP extended access lists are identified by the numeric range of 100 through 199. Answer a is incorrect because the numeric range of 0 through 99 identifies IP standard access lists. Answer c is incorrect because the numeric range of 800 through 899 identifies IPX standard access lists. Answer d is incorrect because the numeric range of 900 through 999 identifies IPX extended access lists.

Question 7

Which of the following commands identifies an IPX extended access list?

O a. **ipx access-group 899 in**

O b. **ipx access-group 905 in**

O c. **ipx access-list 910 out**

O d. **ipx access-group 105 out**

Answer b is correct. The numeric range for an IPX extended access list is from 900 through 999. Answer a is incorrect because an access group number of 899 would refer to an IPX standard access list, not an IPX extended access list. Answer c is incorrect because the command format of **ip access-list 910 out** is incorrect; the correct format is **IPX access-group**, not **access-list**. Answer d is incorrect because the number 105 is not in the correct range for an IPX extended access list. The number 105 identifies an extended access list.

Question 8

Which of the following IP standard access lists would deny the host 172.16.23.2? [Choose the two best answers]

❏ a. **access-list** 5 deny 172.16.23.0 0.0.0.255

❏ b. **access-list** 105 deny host 172.16.23.2

❏ c. **access-list** 25 deny host 172.16.23.2

❏ d. **access-list** 5 deny 172.16.24.2 0.0.0.255

Answers a and c are correct. Answer a would deny traffic with the source address between 172.16.23.0 and 172.16.23.255. The source-wildcard of 0.0.0.255 for answer a indicates that all bit combinations in the fourth octet are identified. Answer c would deny only traffic with the source IP address of 172.16.23.2. Answer b is incorrect because the access list number is 105, which identifies an IP extended access list, not an IP standard access list. Answer d is incorrect because it identifies that source IP addresses 172.16.24.0 through 172.16.24.255 are denied access, which does not include source IP address 172.16.23.2.

Question 9

Which of the following IP extended access list entries would permit Telnet (TCP port # 23) from IP source address of 172.16.29.0 through 172.16.29.255 to access any destination address?

○ a. **access-list** 105 permit tcp 172.16.29.0 0.0.0.255 any eq 23

○ b. **access-list** 105 permit tcp 172.16.29.0 0.0.0.255 172.16.0.0
      0.0.255.255 eq 23

○ c. **access-list** 105 permit tcp host 172.16.29.10 any eq 23

○ d. **access-list** 105 permit udp 172.16.29.0 0.0.0.255 any eq 23

Answer a is correct. Answer a specifies that TCP traffic with the IP port number of 23 should be permitted from IP source addresses of 172.16.29.0 through 172.16.29.255 to any destination IP address. Answer b is incorrect because this access list permits TCP traffic with the IP port number of 23 from source IP address of 172.16.29.0 through 172.16.29.255 to only the destination IP addresses of 172.16.0.0 through 172.16.255.255. Answer c is incorrect because it only permits the host 172.16.29.0. Answer d is incorrect because it permits UDP traffic, not TCP traffic.

Question 10

Which of the following commands can be used to show access lists? [Choose the three best answers]

❏ a. **show ip interfaces**

❏ b. **show ipx interfaces**

❏ c. **show access-lists**

❏ d. **show access lists**

Answers a, b, and c are correct, because they all will show configured access lists. Answer d is incorrect because the command format is wrong; it should be **show access-lists**, not **show access lists**.

Need To Know More?

Chappell, Laura: *Introduction to Cisco Router Configuration*. Cisco Systems Inc., Macmillan Publishing Company, 1998. ISBN 0-7645-3186-7. This book is a great reference for introductory material on Cisco router configuration.

Lammle, Todd, Donald Porter, and James Chellis: *CCNA Cisco Certified Network Associate*. Sybex Network Press, Alameda, CA, 1999. ISBN 0-7821-2381-3. Chapter 4 covers IP addressing.

Syngress Media, with Richard D. Hornbaker, CCIE: *Cisco Certified Network Associate Study Guide*. Osborne/McGraw-Hill, Berkeley, CA, 1998. ISBN 0-07-882487-7. Chapter 2 covers IP addressing.

Internetworking technology overview. Chapter 19 Configuring Novell IPX. Cisco Systems Inc.

Wide Area Networking

Terms you'll need to understand:

√ Data terminal equipment (DTE)

√ Data communication equipment (DCE)

√ Frame Relay

√ Integrated Services Digital Network (ISDN)

√ High-level Data Link Control (HDLC)

√ Point-to-point protocol (PPP)

√ Frame check sequence

√ Discard eligibility bit

√ Permanent virtual circuits (PVC)

√ Data link connection identifier (DLCI)

√ Local Management Information (LMI)

√ Subinterface

√ Nonbroadcast mulitaccess (NBMA)

Techniques you'll need to master:

√ Differentiating between the following WAN services: Frame Relay, ISDN, HDLC, and PPP

√ Recognizing key Frame Relay terms and features

√ Listing commands to configure Frame Relay LMIs, maps, and subinterfaces

√ Listing commands to monitor Frame Relay activity in a router

This chapter provides an overview of wide area network (WAN) protocols and services. It introduces four common protocols, then delves into one of them—Frame Relay. It also discusses Frame Relay configuration and monitoring commands.

WAN Services

WANs differ from LANs, because a WAN covers long distances. An organization also typically owns all components of its LAN, whereas an organization subscribes to an outside provider for WAN services. These services (usually telephone and data) are routed from an interface at one end of the customer's network through the provider's network to the other end of the customer's network. Figure 11.1 illustrates a WAN service provider's network cloud.

Table 11.1 defines the commonly used terms presented in Figure 11.1.

It is the provider's responsibility to provide the customer with the parameters necessary to connect to their network. The WAN provider's network appears as a "cloud" to the customer, who simply makes a point-to-point connection to the remote site.

The main interface between the customer network and provider network occurs between the *data terminal equipment* (*DTE*) and the *data communication equipment* (*DCE*). The customer's router usually serves as the DTE device and performs the packet switching function. Sometimes, DTE devices are bridges or terminals. The DCE attaches to the DTE and provides clocking, converts

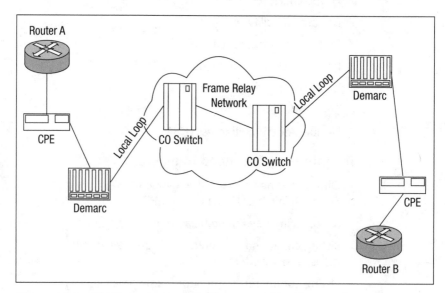

Figure 11.1   WAN service provider's network cloud.

Table 11.1 Common WAN service provider terms.	
Term	**Description**
Customer premise equipment (CPE)	Devices that are physically located on the subscriber's premises. These devices are either owned by the customer or leased from the WAN service provider.
Demarcation (Demarc)	The point where the CPE ends and the local loop begins—usually in the customer's main data closet.
Local loop (last mile)	Cabling that extends from the Demarc into the service provider's central office.
Central office (CO)	The WAN service provider's switching facility that provides the nearest point of presence (POP) for the service. The CO is also referred to as the service provider's POP.

the data into a suitable format, and switches the data across the provider's network. DCE devices include modems, *channel service unit/data service unit* (*CSU/DSU*), or *terminal adapter/network termination 1* (*TA/NT1*). Figure 11.2 depicts DTE devices (routers) and DCE devices within a WAN.

The DTE/DCE interface serves as the boundary where responsibility for the network traffic shifts between the customer's network and the WAN provider's network. It can support several common types of WAN service connections when the DTE is a Cisco router. The first type involves switched services.

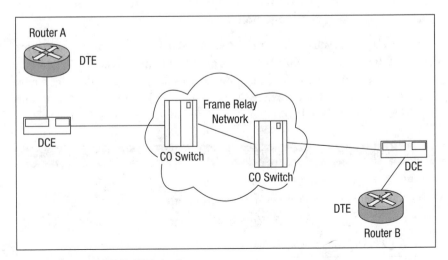

Figure 11.2   DTE/DCE interface.

Switches within the provider's network transmit data from one customer DTE to that customer's other DTEs. *Frame Relay* and *integrated services digital network* (*ISDN*) are examples of packet-switched and circuit-switched services respectively.

The second type involves connecting remote devices to a central mainframe. *Synchronous data link control* (*SDLC*) is the protocol used in these types of point-to-point or point-to-multipoint connections. SDLC is a bit-synchronous data-link protocol that supports legacy IBM networks.

A third type involves connecting peer devices. *High-level data link control* (*HDLC*) and *point-to-point protocol* (*PPP*) can be used to encapsulate the data for transmission to peer DTE devices. *Dial-on-demand routing* (*DDR*) can be used to trigger a Cisco router to initiate the WAN connection. Table 11.2 lists the types of connectivity of common WAN services, and Figure 11.3 highlights common types of connections and services supported by Cisco routers.

Frame Relay

Frame Relay is a high-speed, packet switching WAN protocol. Packet switching protocols enable devices to share the available network bandwidth. Like its name implies, Frame Relay operates at layer 2 of the OSI model and runs on nearly any type of serial interface. Frame Relay encapsulates packets from the upper layers of the OSI model and switches them through the provider's network. Figure 11.4 provides a quick comparison of Frame Relay and the OSI model.

Frame Relay services have been streamlined to gain more throughput. Services such as flow control, robust congestion management, and error checking are left to upper layer protocols like TCP. However, Frame Relay does include some error checking and congestion management.

Frame Relay uses cyclic redundancy checking (CRC) to quickly perform error checks. CRC produces a *frame check sequence* (*FCS*), which is appended to each frame that is transmitted. When a node receives the frame, it calculates a new FCS (based on the data portion of the frame) and compares it to the one contained in the frame. If the values are different, the frame is dropped.

Table 11.2 Connectivity of common WAN services.	
Type	**Connects To**
Frame Relay, ISDN	A device in a WAN service provider's network.
SDLC	An IBM enterprise data center computer (mainframe hosts).
HDLC, PPP, DDR	A peer device on the WAN.

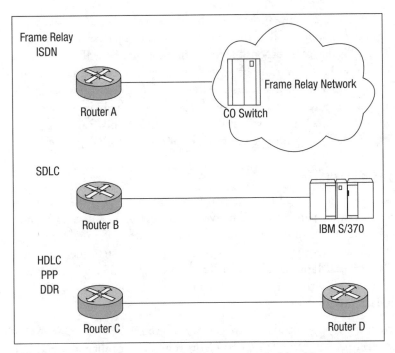

Figure 11.3   Common WAN services supported by Cisco routers.

OSI Reference Model	Frame Relay
Application	0
Presentation	0
Session	0
Transport	0
Network	0
Data Link	Frame Relay
Physical	Physical

Figure 11.4   The OSI reference model and Frame Relay.

Frame Relay manages congestion through the use of a *discard eligibility bit*. This bit is set to a value of 1 if the frame has lower importance than other frames; the DTE device is responsible for setting the bit and will set the bit to 1 for frames that have lower importance than other frames. Switches within the WAN provider's network may discard frames to manage congestion. However, the switches only discard frames with the discard eligibility bit set to 1; frames with their bits set to 0 will still be transmitted. This feature protects against critical data being dropped during periods of network congestion.

Virtual Circuits

Communication in a Frame Relay network is connection-oriented and a defined communication path must exist between each pair of DTE devices. Virtual circuits provide the bi-directional communication within Frame Relay networks. In essence, a virtual circuit is a logical connection established between two DTE devices. Many virtual circuits can be multiplexed into one physical circuit, and a single virtual circuit can cross multiple DCE devices within the Frame Relay network.

Virtual circuits can be grouped into two categories: *switched virtual circuits* (*SVC*) and *permanent virtual circuits* (*PVC*). SVCs are temporary connections and can be used when only sporadic data communication is necessary between DTE devices. SVCs require the connection to be set up and terminated for each session. Conversely, PVCs are permanent connections. They support frequent and consistent data communications across a Frame Relay network. Once the PVC is established, DTE devices can begin transmitting data when they are ready. PVCs are much more widely used in Frame Relay networks than SVCs.

Data Link Connection Identifier

A *data link connection identifier (DLCI)* serves as the addressing scheme within a Frame Relay network. The service provider assigns a DLCI for each PVC, and it is locally significant within the network. In other words, the DLCI may not be unique within the network (like an IP address). Two DTE devices that have a PVC established between them may or may not use the same DLCI value. Figure 11.5 illustrates how PVCs and DLCIs appear within a Frame Relay network. Table 11.3 clarifies how each router maps its ports to DLCI numbers.

Local Management Information

Local Management Information (*LMI*) is a set of enhancements to the Frame Relay protocol specifications. Developed in 1990 by four companies (nicknamed the "gang of four"), LMI extensions offer several features for better

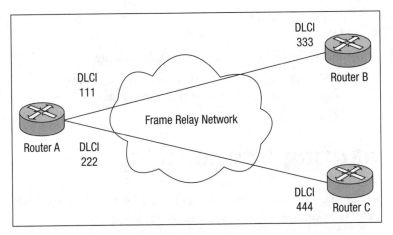

Figure 11.5 PVCs with DLCIs.

Table 11.3	DLCI mapping.	
From Router	**To Router**	**Use DLCI**
A	B	111
A	C	222
B	A	333
C	A	444

management of complex Frame Relay networks. These extensions include global addressing, virtual circuit status messaging, and multicasting.

Note: The "gang of four" includes Cisco Systems, StrataCom, Northern Telecom, and Digital Equipment Corporation.

The LMI global addressing extension enables a DLCI to have global instead of local significance. With LMI, DLCI values are unique within a Frame Relay network and standard address resolution protocols, such as ARP, reverse ARP (or inverse ARP), and discovery protocols can be used to identify nodes within the network. Virtual circuit status messaging improves the communication and synchronization between DTE and DCE devices. The status messages, which are similar to hello packets, report on the status of PVCs. LMI multicasting enables multicast groups to be assigned. Multicasting reduces overhead by allowing route updates and address resolution messages to be sent to specific groups of DTE devices.

Cisco supports the following Frame Relay LMI protocol variations:

➤ **ANSI** American National Standards Institute

➤ **ITU-I (q933a)** International Telecommunication Union - Telecommunication Standardization Sector

➤ **Cisco** "Gang of four"

Configuring Frame Relay

Configuring a Cisco router to serve as a DTE within a Frame Relay network involves configuring interfaces on the router. Table 11.4 lists the commands you must execute to configure Frame Relay on an interface.

In configurations where inverse-ARP is not used to dynamically discover network protocol addresses on the virtual circuit, the **frame-relay map** command must be used to map the layer 3 protocol address to the layer 2 DLCI. You must configure the **frame-relay map** command as follows:

```
Frame-relay map protocol protocol-address dlci [broadcast]
[cisco | ietf]
```

In this example, *protocol* is a supported protocol such as IP or IPX. *Protocol-address* is the destination protocol address. Dlci is the DLCI number used to connect to the specified protocol address on the interface. *Broadcast* (optional) forwards broadcasts to this address—this is optional but usually a good idea to include it. *Ietf* (optional) uses the IETF form of Frame Relay encapsulation; use this parameter when the router or access server is connected to another vendor's equipment across a Frame Relay network. *Cisco* (optional) is the Cisco encapsulation method.

Nonbroadcast Multiaccess

Because Frame Relay connections are established by direct PVCs. Frame Relay cannot support broadcast transmissions. If broadcast services are required, a router

Table 11.4 Frame Relay basic configuration.	
Command	**Description**
encapsulation frame-relay [cisco | ietf]	Enables Frame Relay encapsulation—the default setting is "cisco" and "ietf" (RFC1490) enables connections to non-Cisco equipment.
frame-relay lmi-type [ansi | cisco | q933a]	Sets the LMI type—the default setting is "cisco".

must copy the broadcast, then transmit it on each of its PVCs. A term that describes this behavior is called *nonbroadcast multiaccess* (*NBMA*). NBMA simply describes any multiaccess layer 2 protocol which does not provide a mechanism for broadcasting messages (such as route updates between routers). In order for broadcast messages to be communicated in an NBMA network, each router within the network serves as a peer and is part of the same subnet. In a Frame Relay network, broadcast messages must be duplicated and then sent out each PVC to each peer.

Subinterfaces

A single physical serial interface can be configured with several virtual interfaces called *subinterfaces*. These subinterfaces can be configured on a serial line; different information is sent and received on each of its subinterfaces. Using subinterfaces, a single router can support PVCs to several other routers. Figure 11.6 depicts a simple Frame Relay network with subinterfaces.

Before configuring a subinterface for Frame Relay, the Frame Relay configuration on the physical interface must be complete. Execute the following command to create a subinterface and assign it a DLCI value:

```
Interface type .subinterface point-to-point
Frame-relay interface-dlci DLCI [broadcast]
```

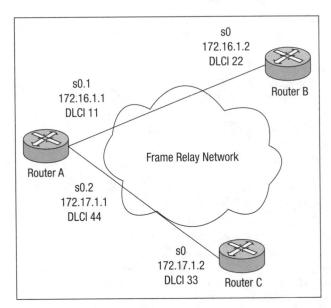

Figure 11.6 Frame Relay network using subinterfaces.

In this command **type** is the physical serial interface number; **subinterface** is the subinterface number; **dlci** is the DLCI number used to connect to the specified protocol address on the interface; and **broadcast** (optional) forwards broadcasts to this address.

The proper syntax for creating and accessing a subinterface is the interface number followed by a period (.), followed by the subinterface number. For example, serial 0.11 indicates the subinterface 11 on serial interface 0.

A common practice in choosing subinterface numbers is to use the same number as the DLCI value.

Monitoring Frame Relay

After the Frame Relay configuration is complete, you can use the **show interface** and **debug frame-relay** commands to monitor and troubleshoot the configuration. Listing 11.1 shows the output from the **show interface** command.

Listing 11.1   Showing Frame Relay interfaces.

```
Router# show interface serial 0
  Serial0 is up, line protocol is up
  Hardware is MCI Serial
  Internet address is 172.59.1.1,
    subnet mask is 255.255.255.252
  MTU 1500 bytes, BW 1544 Kbit, DLY 20000 usec, rely 249/255,
    load 1/255
  Encapsulation FRAME-RELAY, loopback not set,
    keepalive set (10 sec)
  LMI enq sent  4, LMI stat recvd 0, LMI upd recvd 0,
    DTE LMI UP
  LMI enq recvd 268, LMI stat sent  264, LMI upd sent  0
  LMI DLCI 1023  LMI type is CISCO  frame relay DTE
  Last input 0:00:09, output 0:00:07, output hang never
  Last clearing of "show interface" counters 0:44:57
  Output queue 0/40, 0 drops; input queue 0/75, 0 drops
  Five minute input rate 0 bits/sec, 0 packets/sec
Five minute output rate 0 bits/sec, 0 packets/sec
     309 packets input, 6641 bytes, 0 no buffer
     Received 0 broadcasts, 0 runts, 0 giants
     0 input errors, 0 CRC, 0 frame, 0 overrun,
     0 ignored, 0 abort
```

```
0 input packets with dribble condition detected
268 packets output, 3836 bytes, 0 underruns
0 output errors, 0 collisions, 2 interface resets,
0 restarts
180 carrier transitions
```

Note: *The encapsulation type, DLCI, LMI type, and the router status as DTE are displayed.*

Use the **show frame-relay pvc** command to display the status of the virtual circuit:

```
RouterA#show frame-relay pvc

PVC Statistics for interface Serial0 (Frame Relay DTE)

DLCI = 222, DLCI USAGE = LOCAL, PVC STATUS = ACTIVE, INTERFACE =
Serial0

  input pkts 50          output pkts 20        in bytes 11431
  out bytes 1474         dropped pkts 2        in FECN pkts 0
  in BECN pkts 0         out FECN pkts 0       out BECN pkts 0
  in DE pkts 0           out DE pkts 0
  pvc create time 04:14:12, last time pvc status changed 00:39:06
RouterA#
```

Note: *No packets have had their discard eligibility bits set.*

Use the **show frame-relay lmi** command to display whether LMI is being transmitted successfully:

```
RouterA#show frame-relay lmi

LMI Statistics for interface Serial0 (Frame Relay DTE) LMI TYPE =
CISCO
  Invalid Unnumbered info 0      Invalid Prot Disc 0
  Invalid dummy Call Ref 0       Invalid Msg Type 0
  Invalid Status Message 0       Invalid Lock Shift 0
  Invalid Information ID 0        Invalid Report IE Len 0
  Invalid Report Request 0       Invalid Keep IE Len 0
  Num Status Enq. Sent 292       Num Status msgs Rcvd 292
  Num Update Status Rcvd 0       Num Status Timeouts 0
RouterA#
```

Note: *No LMI status messages have been lost.*

Use the **show frame-relay map** command to display mappings among protocol, protocol address, and DLCI:

```
RouterA#show frame-relay map
Serial0 (up): ip 172.59.1.1 dlci 222(0xDE,0x34E0), dynamic,
              broadcast,, status defined, active
RouterA#
```

> *Note:* *IP address 172.59.1.1 is mapped to DLCI 222, and the PVC is active.*

The **debug frame-relay** command enables you to closely monitor the Frame Relay activity. Table 11.5 shows the different debug frame-relay options.

The **debug frame-relay lmi** command enables you to closely monitor LMI activity on a router. Listing 11.2 shows sample output from the **debug frame-relay lmi** command.

Listing 11.2   Debugging Frame Relay LMI.

```
RouterA#debug frame-relay lmi
Frame Relay LMI debugging is on

RouterA#
Serial0(out): StEnq, myseq 20, yourseen 67, DTE up
 datagramstart = 0x23A3820, datagramsize = 13

 FR encap = 0xFCF10309
00 75 01 01 01 03 02 14 43
```

Table 11.5	Debugging Frame Relay LMI.
Option	**Description**
autoinstall	Autoinstall over Frame Relay
dlsw	Frame Relay dlsw
events	Important Frame Relay packet events
ip	Frame Relay Internet Protocol
llc2	Frame Relay llc2
lmi	LMI packet exchanges with service provider
packet	Frame Relay packets
rsrb	Frame Relay rsrb
verbose	Frame Relay

```
Serial0(in): Status, myseq 20
RT IE 1, length 1, type 1
KA IE 3, length 2, yourseq 68, myseq 20
RouterA#
Serial0(out): StEnq, myseq 21, yourseen 68, DTE up
 datagramstart = 0x23A3820, datagramsize = 13
```

Note: *The sequence counters for the LMI transmission are being incremented properly.*

Enabling a single debug command on a router does not use much of the router's system resources; however, enabling several debug commands may severely impact the router's ability to perform its functions. The **no debug all** command quickly disables all debug commands on a router.

Practice Questions

Question 1

> Which of the following commands will display Frame Relay information about serial interface 0?
>
> ○ a. **sh frame-relay s0**
>
> ○ b. **sh frame-relay interface s0**
>
> ○ c. **sh interface s0**
>
> ○ d. **sh ip interface brief**

Answer c is correct. **sh interface** displays the configuration and statistics for the serial 0 interface on the router. The **sh frame-relay s0** and **sh frame-relay s0** interface commands are invalid, so answers a and b are incorrect. The **sh ip interface brief** command displays IP addressing and status information for all interfaces, so answer d is incorrect.

Question 2

> Frame Relay operates at which layer of the OSI model?
>
> ○ a. Transport
>
> ○ b. Network
>
> ○ c. Data link
>
> ○ d. Physical

Answer c is correct. Frame Relay operates with the data link. Answers a and b are incorrect because Frame Relay does not include any specifications for layer 4 (transport) or layer 3 (network). Although Frame Relay can operate on several different physical media, it does not include specifications for layer 1 (physical); therefore, answer d is also incorrect.

Question 3

Which of the following devices can serve as a DTE? [Choose the two best answers]

❑ a. router

❑ b. terminal

❑ c. modem

❑ d. CSU

Answers a and b are correct. Routers and terminals can be configured to act as DTEs. Modems and CSUs cannot be configured as DTEs—they can be configured as DCEs; therefore, answers c and d are incorrect.

Question 4

Which of the following are common WAN services supported by Cisco? [Choose the best answers that apply]

❑ a. ISDN

❑ b. Frame Relay

❑ c. PPP

❑ d. BGP

❑ e. HDLC

❑ f. SDLC

Answers a, b, c, e, and f are correct. ISDN, Frame Relay, PPP, HDLC, and SDLC are all WAN services supported by Cisco equipment. Although BGP is supported by Cisco equipment, it is an exterior routing protocol, so answer d is incorrect.

Question 5

Which of the following can be used to establish bi-directional communication between two DTE devices? [Choose the two best answers]

❑ a. CVC

❑ b. DVC

❑ c. PVC

❑ d. SVC

Answers c and d are correct. A permanent virtual circuit (PVC) remains established between two DTE devices, even when data is not being transmitted. A switched virtual circuit (SVC) is established only when two DTEs need to transmit data. It is disconnected once the transmission is over. CVC and DVC are not related to virtual circuits between DTEs, so answers a and b are incorrect.

Question 6

Which of the following serves as the addressing scheme within a Frame Relay network?

○ a. DLCI

○ b. LMI

○ c. NBMA

○ d. SVC

Answer a is correct. A DLCI number serves as the addressing scheme and is assigned to each PVC. LMI provides several enhancements to Frame Relay specifications, so answer b is incorrect. Answer c is incorrect because NBMA describes how a router must send broadcasts within a Frame Relay network. An SVC is established to enable DTE to communicate; therefore, answer d is incorrect.

Question 7

Cisco supports which of the following Frame Relay LMI protocol variations? [Choose the three best answers]

☐ a. IETF

☐ b. ANSI

☐ c. Q933A

☐ d. Cisco

Answers b, c, and d are correct. Cisco supports LMI extensions from American National Standards Institute (ANSI), International Telecommunication Union–Telecommunication Standardization Sector (Q933A), and the "Gang of Four" (Cisco). Answer a is incorrect because the IETF is a type of frame encapsulation supported by Cisco that enables Cisco devices to communicate with non-Cisco devices across a Frame Relay network.

Question 8

Frame Relay uses what mechanism to perform error checking?

○ a. CRC

○ b. LMI

○ c. TA/NT1

○ d. inverse ARP

Answer a is correct. Frame Relay uses CRC to derive the FCS, which is a calculated value based on the data portion of each frame. If a device calculates an FCS value that is different from the FCS value it receives, the frame is dropped. LMI is communicated between DTE and DCE devices and contains the status of the virtual circuit, so answer b is incorrect. Answer c is incorrect because a TA/NT1 is a DCE device and has nothing to do with error checking. Answer d is also incorrect, because inverse ARP is the method by which DTE devices discover layer 3 protocol address information about each other.

Question 9

DCEs provide which of the following functions? [Choose the best answers that apply]

❑ a. Provides clock to the DTE.

❑ b. Converts the data into a suitable format.

❑ c. Switches the data across the provider's network.

❑ d. All of the above.

Answer d is correct. Answers a, b, and c are all functions of DCEs.

Question 10

Which of the following commands allow you to closely monitor Frame Relay activity? [Choose the two best answers]

❑ a. **debug frame-relay lmi**

❑ b. **debug frame-relay activity**

❑ c. **debug frame-relay all**

❑ d. **debug frame-relay verbose**

Answers a and d are correct. The **debug frame-relay lmi** command monitors link information between the DCE and DTE devices. The **debug frame-relay verbose** command displays detailed information. Answers b and c are incorrect because the commands are not valid.

Need To Know More?

 Reed, Kenneth: *Data Network Handbook*. Van Nostrand Reinhold Publishing, 1996. ISBN 0-442-02299-9. Chapter 11 provides more information on voice and data telecommunications.

 Syngress Media, with Richard D. Hornbaker, CCIE: *Cisco Certified Network Associate Study Guide*. Osborne/McGraw-Hill, Berkeley, CA, 1998. ISBN 0-07-882487-7. This book is a great study guide to reference when preparing for the CCNA exam.

 The official Cisco Web site, **www.cisco.com**, contains several Cisco white papers on topics such as Frame Relay configuration and troubleshooting.

 The Computer and Information Science web site at Ohio State University, **www.cis.ohio-state.edu/hypertext/information/ rfc.html**, provides detailed specifications on Frame Relay (RFC 2427).

 Using Cisco's documentation CD, you can immediately access Cisco's entire library of end user documentation, selected product news, bug databases, and related information. The documentation CD-ROM is produced monthly.

Wide Area Networking (Additional Information)

12

Terms you'll need to understand:

√ Point-to-point protocol (PPP)

√ Password Authentication Protocol (PAP)

√ Challenge Handshake Authentication Protocol (CHAP)

√ Netware Core Protocol (NCP)

√ Link Control Protocol (LCP)

√ Integrated Services Digital Network (ISDN)

√ Basic rate interface (BRI)

√ Primary rate interface (PRI)

√ Functions

√ Reference points

√ Dial-on-demand routing (DDR)

Techniques you'll need to master:

√ Identifying PPP operations to encapsulate WAN data on Cisco routers

√ Stating a relevant use and context for ISDN networking

√ Identifying ISDN protocols, function groups, reference points, and channels

√ Describing Cisco's implementation of ISDN BRI

This chapter continues the overview of wide area network (WAN) protocols and services. It discusses PPP components and operations; it also presents the configuration and monitoring commands, and discusses the use and context for ISDN networking. Finally, it addresses ISDN components, and configuration and monitoring commands.

PPP Overview

Point-to-point protocol (PPP) encapsulates network layer information for transmission over point-to-point links. It was designed by developers on the Internet and is described by a series of documents called Request for Comments (RFC), namely, 1661, 1331, and 2153. Figure 12.1 shows how PPP's layered architecture relates to the OSI model.

 PPP consists of three main components:

➤ **High-level Data Link Control (HDLC)** As a basis for encapsulating datagrams over point-to-point links.

➤ **Link Control Protocol (LCP)** Establishes, configures, and tests the connection.

➤ **Network Control Programs (NCP)** Configure many different network layer protocols.

PPP Physical Layer

PPP can operate on a variety of Data terminal equipment (DTE)/Data communications equipment (DCE) physical interfaces, including:

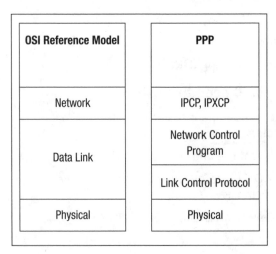

OSI Reference Model	PPP
Network	IPCP, IPXCP
Data Link	Network Control Program
	Link Control Protocol
Physical	Physical

Figure 12.1 The OSI reference model and PPP.

➤ Asychrononous serial

➤ Synchronous serial

➤ High speed serial interface (HSSI)

➤ Integrated services digital network (ISDN)

Other than what is required by a particular physical interface, PPP makes no special transmission rate requirements.

PPP Connections

It is the responsibility of the *Link Control Protocol (LCP)* within PPP to establish, configure, test, maintain, and terminate the point-to-point connection. Four phases occur during the LCP process:

➤ Link establishment

➤ Link quality determination

➤ Network-layer protocol negotiation

➤ Link termination

During the first phase, link establishment, LCP opens the connection and negotiates configuration parameters. Acknowledgment frames must be sent and received before this phase can be considered completed successfully.

The link quality determination phase involves testing the connection to determine whether the line quality is sufficient to support the network-layer protocols. Although this phase seems very important, it is optional.

In the third phase, the appropriate network-layer protocols are configured. *Network Control Programs (NCP)* configure PPP to support different network-layer protocols, including IP, IPX, and AppleTalk. The PPP devices transmit NCP packets to select and configure one or more network-layer protocols. After each selected network-layer protocol has been configured, data can begin being transmitted across the link. Should the LCP terminate a link, it notifies the NCP, which then takes appropriate action.

The final phase, link termination, can be initiated by the LCP at any time. Link termination can occur from events such as a user request, loss of carrier, or the expiration of a timeout parameter.

PPP Authentication

PPP authentication occurs during the link quality determination phase; therefore, authentication is optional. The caller (or calling side of the link) must transmit information to ensure that the caller is authorized to establish the connection; this is accomplished by a series of authentication messages being sent between the routers. PPP supports two types of authentication: *Password Authentication Protocol* (*PAP*) and *Challenge Handshake Authentication Protocol* (*CHAP*).

PAP

PAP uses a two-way handshake to allow remote hosts to identify themselves. After the link has been established, PAP performs the following steps after the link establishment phase is complete:

1. The remote host initiates the call and sends a username and password to the local host and continues to send the information until it is either accepted or rejected.

2. The local host receives the call and either accepts or rejects the username and password information. If the local host rejects the information, the connection is terminated.

CHAP

CHAP uses a three-way handshake to force remote hosts to identify themselves after the link establishment phase. CHAP performs the following steps after the link establishment phase is complete:

1. The local router that received the call sends a challenge packet to the remote host that initiated the call. The challenge packet consists of an ID, a random number, and either the name of the local host performing the authentication or a username on the remote host.

2. The remote host must respond with its encrypted unique ID, a one-way encrypted password, the remote host name or a username, and a random number.

3. The local router performs its own calculation on what the expected response values. It accepts or rejects the authentication request based on whether the value it received from the remote host matches the value it calculated.

Like PAP, CHAP terminates the connection immediately if the local host rejects the authentication request.

During the PAP process, the username and password information is sent from the remote host in clear text, so PAP is not a strong protocol. It offers no protection from a network analyzer capturing the information and using it. Because CHAP uses secret, encrypted passwords and unique IDs, it is a much stronger protocol than PAP. You can only choose one type of authentication, so CHAP is definitely recommended. (However, PAP is still better than no authentication at all.)

LCP Configuration Options

Cisco routers support several configuration options for LCP:

➤ Authentication options include PAP and CHAP.

➤ By reducing the amount of data that must be transmitted, data compressions increase the throughput on a network link. The data is compressed as it is sent and decompressed as it is received. LCP compression options include Stacker or Predictor.

➤ The error-detection options within LCP activate processes to detect errors. The Quality and Magic Number protocols help ensure reliable connections.

➤ The multilink PPP configuration option supports load balancing over PPP links. This option is supported in Cisco IOS 11.1 and later.

Table 12.1 summarizes the different configuration options within LCP.

Table 12.1	LCP configuration options.		
Option	**Function**	**Protocol**	**Command**
Authentication	Requires a password	PAP	**ppp authentication pap**
	Performs a challenge handshake	CHAP	**ppp authentication chap**
Compression	Compresses data at the source	Stacker	**ppp compress stacker**
	Reproduces data at the destination	Predictor	**ppp compress predictor**
Error Detection	Monitors the data dropped on the link, avoids frame looping	Quality Magic Number	**ppp quality <number 1 - 100>**
Multilink	Performs load balancing across multiple links	MP	**ppp multilink**

Note: RFC 1548 describes the different PPP LCP configuration options in detail.

Configuring PPP

Configuring PPP on a Cisco router requires that both global and interface configuration commands be executed on both the local and remote routers. Figure 12.2 presents an example of two routers needing to establish a PPP link.

A username and password must be set, so the following global configuration command must be executed:

```
Username name password secret-password
```

In this command, *name* and *secret-password* indicate the name of the remote host and password to use for authentication. The password must be the same on both the local and remote routers. Table 12.2 lists the interface commands that must be executed to configure PPP. Figure 12.3 presents the global and interface configuration commands for router A and router B.

Monitoring PPP

You can monitor PPP activity with the **show interface** and **debug ppp chap** commands. The **show interface** command enables you to view PPP LCP and NCP information. Listing 12.1 shows an example of PPP activity on an interface.

Table 12.2 PPP interface commands.	
Command	**Description**
encapsulation ppp	Encapsulates data on this interface as PPP.
ppp authentication pap	Enables password checking for incoming calls.
ppp authentication chap	Forces incoming calls to answer password challenges.

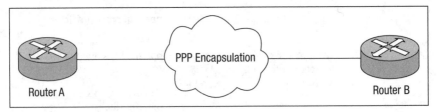

Figure 12.2   PPP.

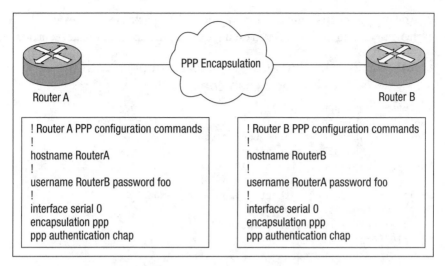

Figure 12.3   PPP configuration.

Listing 12.1   The PPP activity with the **show interface** command.

```
RouterA#sh int s0
Serial0 is up, line protocol is up
  Hardware is HD64570
  Internet address is 172.16.1.1/16
  MTU 1500 bytes, BW 1544 Kbit, DLY 20000 usec,
    rely 255/255, load 1/255
  Encapsulation PPP, loopback not set, keepalive set (10 sec)
  LCP Open
  Open: IPCP, CDPCP
  Last input 00:00:06, output 00:00:06, output hang never
  Last clearing of "show interface" counters never
  Input queue: 0/75/0 (size/max/drops); Total output drops: 0
  Queueing strategy: weighted fair
  Output queue: 0/1000/64/0 (size/max total/threshold/drops)
    Conversations  0/2/256 (active/max active/max total)
    Reserved Conversations 0/0 (allocated/max allocated)
  5 minute input rate 0 bits/sec, 0 packets/sec
  5 minute output rate 0 bits/sec, 0 packets/sec
    34 packets input, 1303 bytes, 0 no buffer
    Received 34 broadcasts, 0 runts, 0 giants, 0 throttles
    0 input errors, 0 CRC, 0 frame, 0 overrun, 0 ignored, 0 abort
    72 packets output, 2819 bytes, 0 underruns
    0 output errors, 0 collisions, 14 interface resets
    0 output buffer failures, 0 output buffers swapped out
    41 carrier transitions
    DCD=up  DSR=up  DTR=up  RTS=up  CTS=up
RouterA#
```

The **debug ppp chap** command displays the CHAP packet exchanges and PAP exchanges. Listing 12.2 displays an example authentication handshake sequence.

Listing 12.2 The PPP authentication sequence with the **debug ppp chap** command.

```
RouterA# debug ppp chap
Serial0: Unable to authenticate. No name received from peer
Serial0: Unable to validate CHAP response.
        USERNAME pioneer not found.
Serial0: Unable to validate CHAP response.
        No password defined for USERNAME pioneer
Serial0: Failed CHAP authentication with remote.
Remote message is Unknown name
Serial0: remote passed CHAP authentication.
Serial0: Passed CHAP authentication with remote.
Serial0: CHAP input code = 4 id = 3 len = 48
```

Note: *The* **debug ppp chap** *command displays the reason why the CHAP request failed.*

ISDN Overview

Integrated services digital network (*ISDN*) refers to the call processing system that enables voice, data, graphics, music, and video to be transmitted over our existing telephone system. ISDN offers several advantages over existing analog modem lines. For example, ISDN connection speeds begin at 64Kbps, whereas typical modem speeds hover between 14.4Kbps and 28.8Kbps. The call setup time for an ISDN call is also much quicker. ISDN can transmit data packets, voice, or video. ISDN is a viable solution for remote connectivity (telecommuting) and access to the Internet. ISDN also supports any of the network-layer protocols supported by Cisco IOS and encapsulates other WAN services, such as PPP.

ISDN can be used to:

➤ Add bandwidth for telecommuting.

➤ Improve Internet response times.

➤ Carry multiple network-layer protocols.

➤ Encapsulate other WAN services.

Basic Rate Interface And Primary Rate Interface

ISDN can be ordered as either *basic rate interface* (*BRI*) or *primary rate interface* (*PRI*). An ISDN BRI service contains two bearer channels (or B channels) of 64Kbps and one data channel (or D channel) of 16Kbps. The B channel carries user data and the D channel carries signaling and control information. The maximum throughput for BRI is 128Kbps (2 B channels * 64Kbps). In North America and Japan, an ISDN PRI service contains 23 B channels and a D channel that enables a maximum throughput of 1.472Mbps. In Europe, PRI service contains 30 B channels, enabling a throughput of 1.920Mbps.

ISDN Protocols

The International Telecommunication Union Telecommunication (ITU-T) standardization sector is an international body that develops worldwide standards for telecommunications technologies. In 1984, ITU-T published a comprehensive list of standard ISDN protocols organizing into groups that address certain topics. Table 12.3 presents some of the ISDN protocols.

Functions And Reference Points

ISDN functions and reference points are the items that describe ISDN service provider standards. Functions and reference points enable you to clearly articulate your needs as you work with service providers to engineer, implement, and maintain ISDN services. *Functions* represent devices or hardware functions within ISDN. Table 12.4 presents basic ISDN devices and their functions.

Reference points describe the logical interfaces between ISDN functions like TAs or NT1s. Table 12.5 lists common ISDN reference points.

You can connect up to eight ISDN-capable devices on a single ISDN line, enabling them to share the ISDN bandwidth. These devices may be things such as ISDN-capable phones, faxes, routers, and/or terminal adapters. Figure 12.4 shows an example of two routers connected to ISDN services.

In Figure 12.4, router A is a TE1 device that already has a built-in BRI connection. Conversely, router B does not have a built-in BRI connection; it has a serial connection and is considered a TE2 device. It requires a TA to convert

Table 12.3 ITU-T standard ISDN protocols.		
Topic	Protocol	Example
Telephone network and ISDN	E-series	E.164—International ISDN addressing.
ISDN concepts, aspects, and interfaces	I-series	I.100—Concepts, structures, and terminology.
Switching and signaling	Q-series	Q.931—ISDN network-layer between terminal and switch.

Table 12.4 ISDN devices and functions.

Device Name	Abbreviation	Function
Terminal Adapter	TA	Converts RS-232, V.35, etc. into BRI signals.
Terminal End-Point 1	TE1	Indicates a router or other device that has a native ISDN interface.
Terminal End-Point 2	TE2	Indicates a router or other device that requires a TA for its BRI signals.
Network Termination 1	NT1	Converts BRI signals for use by the ISDN line.
Network Termination 2	NT2	Indicates a device that supports on-premises ISDN concentration, such as a PBX. A more complex NT1 that also performs layer 2 and 3 functions.
Local Termination	LT	The part of the local exchange that terminates the local loop.
Exchange Termination	ET	The part of the exchange that communicates with other ISDN components.

Table 12.5 ISDN reference points.

Abbreviation	Logical Interface Between
R	TE2 and TA
S	TE1 and NT2
T	NT1 and NT2
U	NT1 and LT

the serial signals into BRI signals. Both router A and router B (with a TA device) can connect to the NT1 device.

 If your router has a BRI interface, you will only need to attach a NT1 device to connect to ISDN services. If your router does not have a BRI interface, you will need to attach a TA and an NT1 to connect to ISDN services. In North America, ISDN BRIs are provisioned without an NT1. It is the responsibility of the customer to provide the NT1 and power for the NT1. Unlike analog telephone lines, if you want a BRI to stay up during a power outage, you must supply uninterrupted power to the NT1. In Europe, ISDN BRIs are provisioned with the NT1 included.

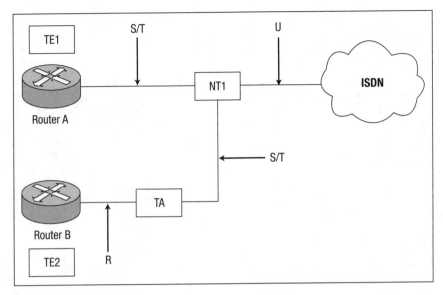

Figure 12.4 ISDN example.

Note: *An ISDN BRI usually interfaces with an NT1 device, and an ISDN PRI usually interfaces with a CSU/DSU.*

Dial-On-Demand Routing

Dial-on-demand routing (DDR) works with ISDN to establish and terminate network connections as traffic dictates. DDR configuration commands define host and ISDN connection information. An access list and DDR dialer group define what type of traffic should initiate an ISDN call. You can configure multiple access lists to look for different types of "interesting" traffic. "Interesting" traffic is simply network traffic that (when it arrives at the router) will trigger the router to initiate the ISDN connection. Figure 12.5 illustrates the DDR process when router A calls router B.

When the router notices some "interesting" traffic, it refers to its ISDN information and initiates setup of the ISDN call through its BRI or PRI and NT1 device. Once the connection is established, normal routing occurs between the two end devices. After "interesting" traffic stops being transmitted over the ISDN connection, the connection idle timer begins—when the idle timer expires, the connection is terminated.

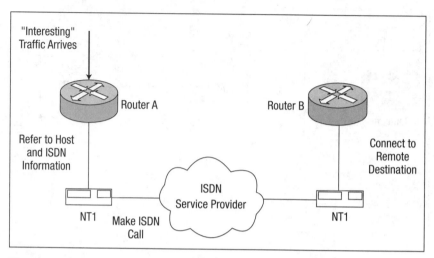

Figure 12.5 DDR routing with ISDN.

Configuring ISDN

You must perform both global and interface configuration tasks when configuring a router for ISDN. Global configuration tasks include specifying the type of ISDN switch your router will connect to at the provider's CO, and defining what type of traffic is "interesting." Table 12.6 lists the ISDN global configuration commands.

Table 12.7 shows the ISDN commands that must be configured on an interface.

Figure 12.6 presents a simple ISDN DDR configuration for router A and router B.

Monitoring ISDN

The commands listed in this section enable you to monitor the activity and operation of ISDN and DDR configurations.

Table 12.6 ISDN global configuration commands.	
Command	**Description**
ISDN switch-type switch-type	Defines an ISDN switch type.
dialer-list dialer-group protocol protocol permit	Defines or restricts (permits or denies) any specific protocol traffic as interesting for a particular dialer group.

Table 12.7   ISDN interface configuration commands.

Command	Description
Interface bri interface number	Chooses the router interface acting as a TE1 device.
encapsulation ppp	Chooses ppp framing.
dialer-group number	Assigns an interface to a specific dialer-group.
dialer map protocol next hop address name hostname speed number dial-string	Maps a layer 3 protocol to a next hop address with a specific name; defines the connection speed; defines the telephone number to dial.
dialer idle-timeout number	Defines the number of seconds of idle time before the ISDN connection is terminated.

You can monitor ISDN and DDR configurations with the following commands:

➤ **show controller bri**

➤ **show interface bri**

➤ **show dialer**

Use the **show controller bri** command to display detailed information about the B and D channels. Listing 12.3 displays an example of the **show controller** command.

Listing 12.3   The **show controller bri** command.

```
RouterA# show controller bri 0
BRI unit 0
D Chan Info:
Layer 1 is ACTIVATED
idb 0x32089C, ds 0x3267D8, reset_mask 0x2
buffer size 1524
RX ring with 2 entries at 0x2101600 : Rxhead 0
00 pak=0x4122E8 ds=0x412444 status=D000 pak_size=0
01 pak=0x410C20 ds=0x410D7C status=F000 pak_size=0
TX ring with 1 entries at 0x2101640: tx_count = 0,
   tx_head = 0, tx_tail = 0
00 pak=0x000000 ds=0x000000 status=7C00 pak_size=0
0 missed datagrams, 0 overruns, 0 bad frame addresses
0 bad datagram encapsulations, 0 memory errors
0 transmitter underruns
B1 Chan Info:
Layer 1 is ACTIVATED
idb 0x3224E8, ds 0x3268C8, reset_mask 0x0
```

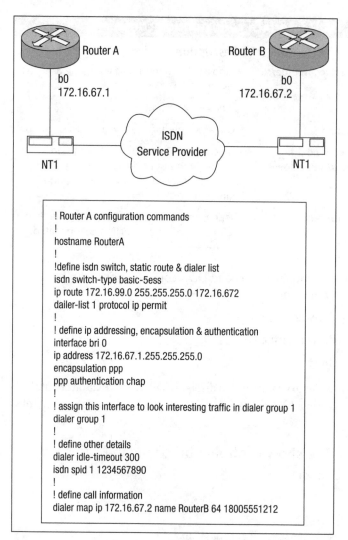

Figure 12.6 DDR configuration example.

```
buffer size 1524
RX ring with 8 entries at 0x2101400 : Rxhead 0
00 pak=0x421FC0 ds=0x42211C status=D000 pak_size=0
01 pak=0x4085E8 ds=0x408744 status=D000 pak_size=0
02 pak=0x422EF0 ds=0x42304C status=D000 pak_size=0
03 pak=0x4148E0 ds=0x414A3C status=D000 pak_size=0
04 pak=0x424D50 ds=0x424EAC status=D000 pak_size=0
05 pak=0x423688 ds=0x4237E4 status=D000 pak_size=0
06 pak=0x41AB98 ds=0x41ACF4 status=D000 pak_size=0
07 pak=0x41A400 ds=0x41A55C status=F000 pak_size=0
TX ring with 4 entries at 0x2101440: tx_count = 0,
```

```
    tx_head = 0, tx_tail = 0
00 pak=0x000000 ds=0x000000 status=5C00 pak_size=0
01 pak=0x000000 ds=0x000000 status=5C00 pak_size=0
02 pak=0x000000 ds=0x000000 status=5C00 pak_size=0
03 pak=0x000000 ds=0x000000 status=7C00 pak_size=0
0 missed datagrams, 0 overruns, 0 bad frame addresses
0 bad datagram encapsulations, 0 memory errors
0 transmitter underruns
B2 Chan Info:
Layer 1 is ACTIVATED
idb 0x324520, ds 0x3269B8, reset_mask 0x2
buffer size 1524
RX ring with 8 entries at 0x2101500 : Rxhead 0
00 pak=0x40FCF0 ds=0x40FE4C status=D000 pak_size=0
01 pak=0x40E628 ds=0x40E784 status=D000 pak_size=0
02 pak=0x40F558 ds=0x40F6B4 status=D000 pak_size=0
03 pak=0x413218 ds=0x413374 status=D000 pak_size=0
04 pak=0x40EDC0 ds=0x40EF1C status=D000 pak_size=0
05 pak=0x4113B8 ds=0x411514 status=D000 pak_size=0
06 pak=0x416ED8 ds=0x417034 status=D000 pak_size=0
07 pak=0x416740 ds=0x41689C status=F000 pak_size=0
TX ring with 4 entries at 0x2101540: tx_count = 0,
    tx_head = 0, tx_tail = 0
00 pak=0x000000 ds=0x000000 status=5C00 pak_size=0
01 pak=0x000000 ds=0x000000 status=5C00 pak_size=0
02 pak=0x000000 ds=0x000000 status=5C00 pak_size=0
03 pak=0x000000 ds=0x000000 status=7C00 pak_size=0
0 missed datagrams, 0 overruns, 0 bad frame addresses
0 bad datagram encapsulations, 0 memory errors
0 transmitter underruns
```

Note: *Both B channels and the D channel are active.*

Use the **show interface** command to display BRI status, encapsulation, and counter information. Listing 12.4 displays an example of the **show interface** command.

Listing 12.4   The **show interface bri** command.

```
RouterA# show interface bri 0
BRI0 is up, line protocol is up (spoofing)
Hardware is BRI
Internet address is 172.16.67.1, subnet mask is 255.255.255.0
MTU 1500 bytes, BW 64 Kbit, DLY 20000 usec,
rely 255/255, load 1/255
Encapsulation PPP, loopback not set, keepalive set (10 sec)
Last input 0:00:07, output 0:00:00, output hang never
Output queue 0/40, 0 drops; input queue 0/75, 0 drops
```

```
Five minute input rate 0 bits/sec, 0 packets/sec
Five minute output rate 0 bits/sec, 0 packets/sec
16263 packets input, 1347238 bytes, 0 no buffer
Received 13983 broadcasts, 0 runts, 0 giants
2 input errors, 0 CRC, 0 frame, 0 overrun, 0 ignored, 2 abort
22146 packets output, 2383680 bytes, 0 underruns
0 output errors, 0 collisions, 2 interface resets, 0 restarts
1 carrier transitions
```

Note: *The encapsulation type is PPP, and two errors were received on the BRI interface.*

Use the **show dialer** command to display general diagnostic information for serial interfaces configured to support DDR. Listing 12.5 displays an example of the **show dialer** command.

Listing 12.5   The **show dialer** command.

```
RouterA# show dialer interface bri 0
BRIO - dialer type = IN-BAND NO-PARITY
Idle timer (900 secs), Fast idle timer (20 secs)
Wait for carrier (30 secs), Re-enable (15 secs)
Time until disconnect 838 secs
Current call connected 0:02:16
Connected to 8986

Dial String Successes Failures  Last called  Last status
8986            0        0       never                    Default
8986            8        3       0:02:16      Success      Default
```

Note: *"IN-BAND" indicates that DDR is enabled and the router is currently connected. The "Dial String" table provides a history of logged calls.*

Practice Questions

Question 1

> Which of the following commands allows you to monitor a PPP authentication sequence on interface serial 0?
>
> ○ a. **sh ppp**
>
> ○ b. **sh ppp s0**
>
> ○ c. **debug ppp authentication s0**
>
> ○ d. **debug ppp authentication**

Answer d is correct. **debug ppp authentication** displays authentication handshake sequence as it is occurring. Answers a, b, and c are incorrect because they all are invalid commands.

Question 2

> If your router does not have a built-in BRI, which device will you need in order to connect to ISDN services? [Choose the two best answers]
>
> ❏ a. NT1
>
> ❏ b. TA
>
> ❏ c. TE1
>
> ❏ d. TE2

Answers a and b are correct. You need a TA to convert the serial signal from your router into a BRI signal and an NT1 to convert the BRI signal for use by the ISDN digital line. A TE1 is a device that *has* a built-in BRI and already transmits BRI signals, so answer c is incorrect. Answer d is incorrect because a device that does *not* have a built-in BRI is considered a TE2.

Question 3

Which protocol is responsible for establishing, configuring, testing, maintaining, and terminating PPP connections?

○ a. BRI

○ b. PRI

○ c. LCP

○ d. NCP

Answer c is correct. LCP has the primary responsibility for a PPP connection. Answer d is incorrect, because NCP is responsible for the configuration supporting network-layer protocols. Answers a and b are incorrect because BRI and PRI are not components within PPP.

Question 4

How can you use ISDN? [Choose all that apply]

❑ a. To improve Internet response times.

❑ b. To encapsulate other WAN services.

❑ c. To add bandwidth for telecommuting.

❑ d. To carry multiple network-layer protocols.

Answers a, b, c, and d are correct.

Question 5

What commands should you use to monitor ISDN or DDR activity? [Choose the three best answers]

❑ a. **show interfaces**

❑ b. **show controllers**

❑ c. **show dialer**

❑ d. **show bri**

Answers a, b, and c are correct. The **show interfaces** command displays status and statistics for each interface on the router, including BRI. The **show controllers** command displays detailed information about BRI channels. The **show dialer** command presents information about current dialer activity and simple call history. Answer d is incorrect because the **show bri** command is invalid.

Question 6

According to ITU-T standards for ISDN protocols, which series of standards deals with switching and signaling?

- ○ a. A-series
- ○ b. E-series
- ○ c. R-series
- ○ d. Q-series

Answer d is correct. The Q-series standards address switching and signaling topics. Answers a and c are incorrect, because A-series and R-series do not exist for ISDN. Although E-series is a valid grouping of standards, it addresses telephone network and ISDN topics; therefore, answer b is also incorrect.

Question 7

Which of the following phases of the PPP connection process is *optional*?

- ○ a. Link establishment
- ○ b. Link quality determination
- ○ c. Network-layer protocol negotiation
- ○ d. Link termination

Answer b is correct. Link quality determination is optional—even though authentication occurs during this phase. Link establishment, network-layer protocol negotiation, and link termination are all required phases during a PPP connection, so answers a, c, and d are incorrect.

Question 8

What is the correct command to define all IPX traffic as "uninteresting" for dialer group 7?

- ○ a. **dialer-group 7 no ipx**
- ○ b. **dialer-group 7 no ipx all**
- ○ c. **dialer-group 7 protocol no ipx**
- ○ d. **dialer-group 7 protocol ipx deny**

Answer d is correct. The syntax for the **dialer-group** command requires a dialer-group, the keyword protocol, the protocol you want to define (IP, IPX, AppleTalk, and so on), and the keyword permit or deny to indicate whether the protocol should be permitted or denied. Answers a, b, and c are all incorrect because they each generate syntax error messages.

Question 9

Which PPP authentication protocol uses a three-way handshake?

- ○ a. PAP
- ○ b. CHAP
- ○ c. LCP
- ○ d. NCP1

Answer b is correct. The CHAP three-way handshake includes the local host requesting authentication, the remote hosts sending an encrypted response, and the local host comparing the received information then accepting or rejecting the connection. PAP only uses a two-way handshake, so answer a is incorrect. LCP and NCP1 are not authentication protocols, so answers c and d are also incorrect.

Question 10

Which of the following is not a component within PPP?

○ a. NCP

○ b. HSSI

○ c. LCP

○ d. HDLC

Answer b is correct. HSSI is a physical interface that supports many layer 2 protocols, including PPP. It is separate from PPP. Answers a, c, and d are all incorrect responses. PPP uses NCP, LCP, and HDLC to perform its function of encapsulating network-layer protocol information.

Need To Know More?

 Downes, Kevin, Merilee Ford, H. Kim Lew, Steve Spanier, and Tim Stevenson: *Internetworking Technologies Handbook, 2ⁿᵈ Edition*, MacMillan Publishing Company, Indianapolis, IN, 1998. ISBN 1-57870-102-3. Chapters 12 and 13 present more information on PPP and ISDN.

 Reed, Kenneth: *Data Network Handbook.* Van Nostrand Reinhold Publishing, 1996. ISBN 0-442-02299-9. Chapter 11 provides more information on voice and data telecommunications.

 Syngress Media, with Richard D. Hornbaker, CCIE: *Cisco Certified Network Associate Study Guide.* Osborne/McGraw-Hill, Berkeley, CA, 1998. ISBN 0-07-882487-7. Chapter 10 addresses wide area networking.

 The official Cisco Web site, **www.cisco.com**, contains several Cisco white papers on topics such as PPP and ISDN configuration and troubleshooting.

 The Computer and Information Science Web site at Ohio State University, **www.cis.ohio-state.edu/hypertext/information/rfc.html**, provides information on Internet RFC documents. You can review detailed information on the RFCs related to PPP and ISDN.

 Using Cisco's documentation CD, you can immediately access Cisco's entire library of end user documentation, selected product news, bug databases, and related information. The documentation CD-ROM is produced monthly.

LAN Switching

Terms you'll need to understand:

√ Bridge

√ Switch

√ Spanning tree protocol

√ Cut-through switching

√ Store-and-forward switching

√ Inter-switch link (ISL)

√ Frame tagging

√ Virtual local area network (VLAN)

√ Half-duplex

√ Full-duplex

Techniques you'll need to master:

√ Describing the advantages of LAN segmentation

√ Describing network congestion problem in Ethernet networks

√ Describing LAN segmentation using bridges

√ Describing the benefits of network segmentation with bridges

√ Describing the operation of spanning tree protocol and its benefits

√ Describing LAN segmentation using switches

√ Distinguishing between cut-through and store-and-forward switching

√ Describing the benefits of network segmentation with switches

√ Describing the benefits of virtual LANs

√ Describing the features and benefits of Fast Ethernet

√ Describing the guidelines and distance limitations of Fast Ethernet

Bridging and switching are solutions to demands from network computing users. As applications such as email, client/server applications, and now voice and video continue to demand more bandwidth, it has become necessary to segment networks for performance purposes. Recently, computer users were connected with only a few other users on the same network. During this time, the distance limitation and bandwidth capacity of the layer 2 technology and media limited the number of users per network. However, computer users expressed the need to add more users to the same network or to connect to other networks. The solutions to these wishes were bridging, switching, and routing. Each of these technologies provides a unique method of increasing bandwidth, functionality, capacity, and performance.

Life Without Bridges, Switches, And Routers

Before bridges, switches, and routers were introduced, computer users wanting to network all attached to the same layer 2 physical media to communicate with each other. We are going to focus on Ethernet as our layer 2 media access technology in this chapter because of its dominance in the market. Ethernet employs a shared media: All devices contend for access to the media to send messages. However, because they all share the same media, as more users are added to the Ethernet segment, the likelihood of another device sending a message at that moment in time increases. Eventually, the network becomes so congested that it becomes difficult to send messages.

Additional networks had to be added to increase the bandwidth available to each device. However, before bridges and switches, devices on different networks could not communicate with each other. The two major requests LAN users had were to increase the physical distance of the LAN network and to increase the number of devices that could be put on each LAN. The invention of the repeater and the bridge addressed these needs.

Repeater

The network in Figure 13.1 illustrates the purpose of a repeater. We will expand upon this network throughout this chapter to illustrate the purpose of bridges, switches, and routers as well. In Figure 13.1 a LAN is illustrated with a repeater connecting one physical and logical LAN. It is important to designate the difference between a physical and a logical LAN. A *physical LAN* is a network that shares access to the same physical media. A *logical LAN* is a network that does not share the same physical media, but logically is on the same layer 2 LAN. A *repeater* does not physically or logically divide a LAN, but simply extends the physical network.

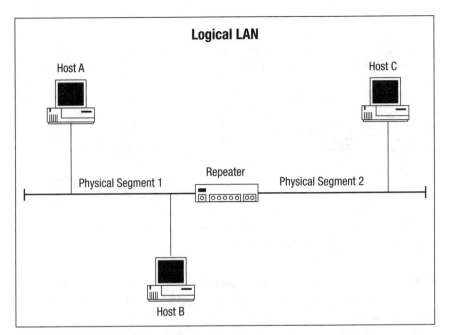

Figure 13.1   LAN with repeater.

A repeater is used to amplify the electrical signal across a physical distance. It does not create two different networks, but only extends the layer 2 network over an increased physical distance. A repeater gives computer users the ability to extend the physical distance of the LAN.

For example, if host A in Figure 13.1 sends a message to host B, the frame will be sent to all users on both sides of the repeater. Therefore, hosts A, B, and C will receive the frame and determine whether it was destined for them or not.

In addition to wanting to extend the physical media, computer users wanted the ability to increase the number of devices on each LAN segment. However, they only had a limited bandwidth (10 Mbps for Ethernet) for the LAN. The invention of the bridge provided a method to filter traffic based on its destination, thereby achieving more bandwidth per logical Ethernet segment. This increase in overall bandwidth allowed more devices to be placed on each logical LAN.

Bridging

A *bridge* is used to physically segment a LAN network into multiple segments. Figure 13.2 illustrates a network with two bridges in it. Note that each host on physical segments a, b, and c is on the same logical layer 2 LAN. However, they are on physically different segments. A bridge reduces the amount of traffic that has to cross the logical LAN as well as each physical segment.

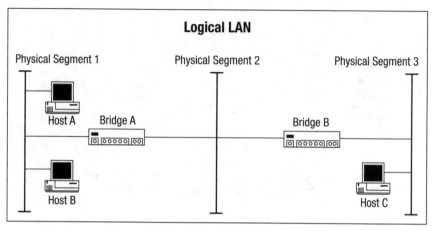

Figure 13.2 LAN with a bridge.

For example, if host A sends a message to host B, the frame will be sent to all users on physical segment 1 only. Bridge A isolates traffic sent from any host on physical segment 1 to another host on physical segment 1 from physical segments 2 and 3. Therefore, none of the bandwidth available on physical segment 2 or 3 is consumed when traffic originating from a host on physical segment 1 is destined for another device on physical segment 1. Therefore, bridges isolate local traffic to one physical segment; they use a forwarding table to do so. Figure 13.3 illustrates the forwarding tables for the two bridges in our network.

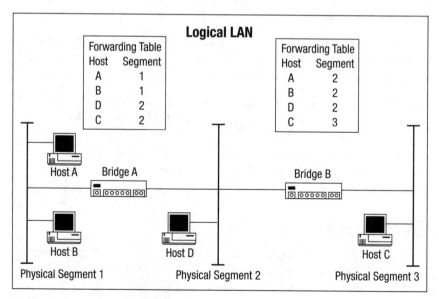

Figure 13.3 Forwarding tables.

A *forwarding table* maintains an entry for every host that identifies the next physical segment to forward a frame en route to the host. A bridge learns the location of every host by looking at the source MAC address in the Ethernet frame when it receives a frame. After a bridge learns the interface that a host exists out of, it caches the entry in its forwarding table.

Therefore, in our example, bridge A is concerned only with the two physical segments that it is connected to. If it receives a frame for someone on physical segment 3, it only "knows" that this frame can reach its destination by sending it to physical segment 2. If host A sends a frame to host C, it would travel across physical segment 1 to bridge A. Bridge A would forward the frame to physical segment 2, where bridge B would determine that it must forward the frame to physical segment 3. Whereas this example illustrated a frame crossing all three physical segments, this is only the case if the sending and destination hosts reside on different physical segments. For example, if host A wants to send a frame to host B, the frame would never have to leave physical segment 1, thereby conserving bandwidth on physical segments 2 and 3. It is important to note that broadcast traffic would still be forwarded to all physical segments. In summary, bridges isolate local traffic to one physical segment, but non-local and broadcast traffic are forwarded. In addition, a bridge also performs the function of a repeater by amplifying the electrical signal.

In summary, the advantages of bridging are as follows:

➤ They increase the amount of bandwidth available by segmenting local traffic from non-local and broadcast traffic.

➤ They increase the physical distance of the physical media by amplifying the electrical signal.

The disadvantages of bridging are as follows:

➤ They increase the latency period to forward frames by 20 percent.

➤ They introduce the possibility of bridging loops.

The most important message to understand about bridges is the way they deal with different types of traffic. Bridges simply forward non-local and broadcast traffic. They drop local traffic because an Ethernet bridge assumes the frame has already reached its destination.

The disadvantages of bridging have been addressed to increase the overall performance of bridging. For example, the latency of bridges continues to be reduced with technological advances in hardware and software that allow for faster frame forwarding rates. Bridging loops are addressed with the *spanning tree protocol* (which we'll discuss shortly). Bridges introduce the possibility of creating a bridged network with multiple paths to a single destination. Typically, this type of redundancy is seen as favorable, but for bridges it can cause problems in the form of *bridging loops*. These occur when circular connections exist in a bridged network. Figure 13.4 illustrates a bridged network with bridging loops.

Figure 13.4 shows that a loop can exist in a network. For example, if someone sends a broadcast message from segment 2, it would be forwarded to physical segment 3 by bridges B and C. Bridge A would then receive two broadcasts and forward both these broadcasts to physical segment 1. Bridge D would have forwarded this broadcast to physical segment 1 as well. Subsequently, bridge D will receive the two broadcasts forwarded by bridge A and forward these packets to physical segment 2. This continuous forwarding of broadcast packets wastes bandwidth. With more complex bridged networks, the broadcast packets can be forwarded exponentially, leading to what is termed a *broadcast storm*. This occurs when so many broadcasts are being continuously forwarded that they consume all the available bandwidth. The elimination of bridging loops is dealt with using the Spanning Tree Protocol, which implements an algorithm that removes all circular connections in a bridged network.

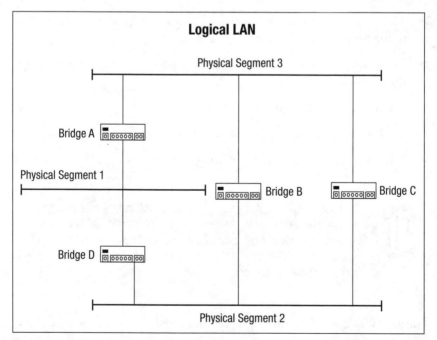

Figure 13.4   Bridged network with bridging loops.

Spanning Tree Protocol

The spanning tree protocol creates a loop-free network topology by placing connections that create loops in a blocking state. It is important to note that this protocol does not eliminate loops, but only blocks the connections that create the loops. The importance of this is that often having loops in a network provides needed redundancy in case of a physical connection being disconnected. Therefore, spanning tree protocol maintains the benefits of redundancy, while eliminating the disadvantages of looping. To illustrate how spanning tree protocol functions, we will use our bridged network in Figure 13.4.

Spanning tree protocol selects a root bridge in the network; in this case, it is bridge A. Next, every other bridge selects one of its ports that gives it the least *path cost* to the root bridge. The least path cost is the sum of the cost to traverse every network between the indicated bridge and the root bridge. The root path cost can be determined in multiple ways; in this case, we have arbitrarily assigned costs to each path. Next, *designated bridges* are determined. These consist of the bridge on each LAN with the lowest aggregate root path cost. The designated bridge is the only bridge on a LAN allowed to forward frames. Table 13.1 details the bridge identifier and its root path cost to reach the root bridge. Figure 13.5 illustrates our network with the root path cost assigned to each bridge interface.

By applying the spanning tree protocol, we block the connection between bridge C and physical segments 2 and 3 because bridge D and bridge B both have lower aggregate root path costs to the root bridge (bridge A). We also block the connection between bridge D and physical segment 2, because bridge B has a lower root path cost than bridge D. In Figure 13.6 we illustrate our bridged network after the spanning tree protocol has been applied. Note that the connections between bridge C and physical segments 2 and 3 are blocked, as well as the connection between bridge D and physical segment 2.

We now have no circular routes in our network, but we maintain redundancy, because the spanning tree protocol is applied whenever a bridge is powered up or a topology change occurs. Therefore, if the connection between bridge B

Table 13.1 Spanning tree protocol.	
Bridge Number	**Aggregate Root Path Cost**
Bridge A	0
Bridge B	10
Bridge C	30
Bridge D	20

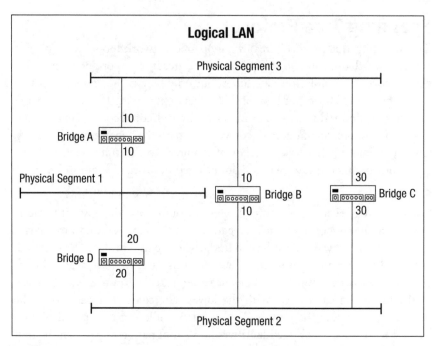

Figure 13.5 Spanning tree protocol root path cost illustration.

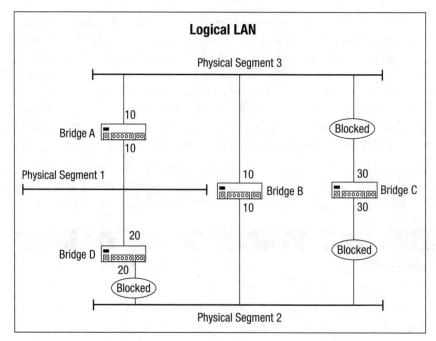

Figure 13.6 Bridged network after spanning tree protocol calculation.

and physical segment B were broken, the spanning tree protocol would run and the connection between bridge D and physical segment 2 would no longer be blocked.

We have seen that a repeater and bridges allowed the LAN to evolve to support greater physical distances, as well as support more users per logical LAN. In the evolution of networking, the next wish of computer users was the ability to communicate with other computer users over an even greater physical distance and across complex networks. Routing was the answer.

Routing

We have discussed routing and routers at length in this book. This section duplicates some of that information; its main purpose, however, is to highlight the advantages of routing versus bridging and switching. Routing provides a method to isolate traffic into logically and physically distinct LANs; bridging and switching physically segments LANs. Routing, however, takes it one step further by isolating logical LANs from other logical LANs. Why do we want to do this? Logically separating LANs allows for different types of LAN technologies (token ring, FDDI, Ethernet, etc.) to communicate with one another without being concerned about the LAN technology being used. We have seen that bridges can provide some options for connecting dissimilar LANs; however, the functionality bridges provide is dwarfed in comparison to that provided by routers. Routers provide the intelligence necessary for complex networks to be interconnected.

Routers provide the logic for implementing security, fragmenting packets, converting between technologies, and a variety of other functions. Routers don't concern themselves with individual hosts on a network, but rather focus on the best path to take to get to the network of a host. Routers only have to determine the best way to forward a packet to a destination network. Furthermore, routers effectively terminate LAN broadcast domains. As we have seen with bridges, all broadcasts from any given device are forwarded to all other devices on the logical LAN. Routers can maintain multiple routes to a destination because they don't forward broadcasts. However, routers still must provide a loop-free routing environment. As we discussed in Chapter 6, routing protocols provide the intelligence to maintain a loop-free environment. This ability adds redundancy and resiliency to a network.

Routers also provide a method for companies to interconnect with other companies without breaching the security of their network. However, routers alone do not provide sufficient security for all networks. Therefore, a plethora of tools and technologies have been developed to heighten the security levels provided between different networks. The growth of the Internet continues to fuel the need for increased security. While routers provide one tool for performing security, organizations require an entire tool set to provide adequate security in today's world. The additional functionality included in routers does not come without costs. The amount of latency for sending packets across routers is estimated at 30 to 40 percent more than that of a LAN media. These numbers have been drastically reduced with the introduction of new technologies into routers. However, the amount of time required to make layer 3 decisions continues to be higher than layer 2 decisions. In summary, the advantages of routing are that they:

➤ Connect dissimilar LANs.

➤ Provide multiple paths to a destination network.

➤ Allow for a more rich set of functionality than that of bridges and switches.

➤ Allow for the interconnection of large and complex networks.

The disadvantages of routers in comparison to bridges and switches are that they:

➤ Increase latency to forward packets.

➤ Increase maintenance complexity.

Switching

Switching is a major enhancement to bridging. It offers increased throughput performance, port density, and greater flexibility in comparison to bridges. In review, bridges—as well as switches—function at the data link layer of the OSI model. However, switches provide higher port densities than bridges, so network administrators typically place fewer users on each switch port, than that of bridges. The term port density refers to the number of ports on one physical device, in this case a switch. Minimizing the number of users per port increases the total bandwidth available per user. In most cases, each user computer or server is given its own port and thereby has dedicated access to the physical media. In the case of Ethernet technology, servers or users realize 10Mb, 100Mb, or even 1,000Mb of bandwidth. Furthermore, most switches are capable of providing full-duplex media access. (An overview of full-duplex technology is provided at the end of this chapter.) It is the architecture of the switch that allows the tremendous rates and high port densities.

Employing hardware-based switching and utilizing intelligent forwarding methods allow switches to achieve these tremendous throughput rates. Switches read the destination address on incoming frames and use this address to determine the proper interface to forward the frame out. Cisco switches perform two primary forwarding methods: *cut-through switching* and *store-and-forward switching*.

Cisco Switching Methods

Both cut-through switching and store-and-forward switching provide increased throughput in comparison to bridges. The hardware-based architectures of switches allows them to make decisions at wire speed. The primary difference between the two methods is the process each uses to switch frames.

> *Note: We have consistently used frames to represent layer 2 data messages in this chapter. The term cell can also be used to identify layer 2 data messages. This term is used when referring to data traffic using the Asynchronous Transfer Mode (ATM) technology. The CCNA exam does not cover this technology, so we have only presented frames in this chapter to simplify the concepts.*

Cut-Through Switching

Cut-through switches introduce a lower level of latency during the switching process than do store-and-forward switches. They achieve increased performance by eliminating the error checking and making forwarding decisions based on only the first six bytes of the incoming frame. (These first six bytes contain the destination MAC address of the frame.) Cut-through switches read the destination address of the incoming and frame and immediately check the forwarding table to determine the proper destination ports. However, this increased performance does allow erred frames to be forwarded more often than store-and-forward switches.

In addition to higher throughput and port densities, switches utilize the concept of a *Virtual LAN (VLAN)* to provide increased functionality in layer 2 switching. VLANs have been adopted by most organizations as an efficient method of segmenting LANs.

Store-And-Forward Switching

Store-and-forward switches have a higher latency than cut-through switches. This switch reads the entire incoming frame and copies the frame into its buffers. After the frame has been completely read, the switch performs the layer 2 cyclical redundancy check to determine if an error occurred during transmission. If the frame has an error, the switch drops the frame. If no error is identified, the switch checks its forwarding table to determine the proper port (in the case of a unicast) or ports (in the case of a multicast) that the frame must be forwarded to. Store-and-forward switches introduce higher latency than cut-through switches because they read the entire frame before making a forwarding decision. However, the added error checking of store-and-forward reduces the number of erred frames that are forwarded.

Virtual Local Area Networks (VLANs)

A VLAN performs the same functions as a normal LAN. However, VLANs extend the flexibility of LANs by allowing users to be assigned to specific LANs on a port-by-port basis versus a device basis. Users on the same VLAN do not have to be connected to the same device. Therefore, LANs no longer are tied to the physical location of users, but can be assigned based on department, functional area, or security levels. By isolating users by department or functional area, network administrators can keep the majority of data traffic within one VLAN, thereby maximizing the amount of traffic switched at hardware speeds versus what is routed at slower software speeds.

The ability to assign a user to a VLAN on a port-by-port basis makes adding, moving, or deleting a user from VLAN simple. For example, let's say a user changes from the accounting to the marketing department. If the network administrator designed the network and VLANs by functional department, this user would have changed VLANs. To accommodate this change, the administrator only has to make a software configuration change in the switch by assigning that user's port to the new VLAN. In addition, VLANs provide the flexibility necessary to group users by security level. As we saw in Chapter 11, this can greatly simplify applying a security policy to a network. In summary, the benefits of VLANs are that they:

➤ Simplify security administration.

➤ Allow users to be grouped by functional area versus physical location.

➤ Simplify moving and adding users.

How are VLANs maintained across multiple switches? Switches use the process of *frame tagging* and the *inter-switch link* (*ISL*) technology to allow VLANs to span multiple switches. ISL and frame tagging are used to connect multiple switches and maintain VLAN identification for traffic passing between the switches. Any time a frame needs to leave one switch for another, it uses frame tagging and ISL. For example, when a frame leaves the one switch destined for another, the first switch encapsulates the frame with an ISL header that "tags" the frame with a user-defined VLAN ID. When the frame arrives at the second switch, it will "know" which VLAN it belongs to. This process is illustrated in Figure 13.7 using the VLAN IDs 10, 20, and 30.

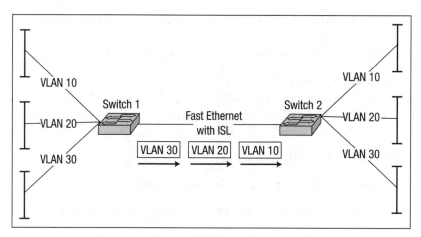

Figure 13.7   ISL and frame tagging.

 Be sure to understand the function of frame tagging, which "tags" a frame with a user-defined VLAN ID.

Fast Ethernet

Ethernet continues to be the layer 2 media of choice for network computer users. The simplicity and flexibility of Ethernet has allowed it to evolve faster than other competing technologies, such as token ring. Many people did not believe that Ethernet was capable of scaling to meet the increasing bandwidth demand of network users. However, organizations and standard bodies have proven these doubters wrong with the introduction of faster and faster Ethernet technology. Ethernet has scaled from 10Mb to *Fast Ethernet* (100Mb) and recently to speeds of *Gigabit Ethernet* (1,000Mb). This section focuses on the Fast Ethernet technology and the advantages gained by implementing it.

When Fast Ethernet was in the nascent stages, two competing theories developed regarding the proper architecture to implement to achieve the higher speeds. The first theory maintained that the current CSMA/CD network access method would scale to the desired higher speeds. The second theory developed a new access method that could be implemented with token ring as well as Ethernet technologies. These two methods are as follows:

➤ **100BaseT** Ethernet using *unshielded twisted pair* (*UTP*) or *shielded twisted pair* (*STP*) cabling. This method is compatible with the IEEE Ethernet specification 802.3.

➤ **100VG-AnyLAN** Provides for 100Mb token ring and Ethernet over 4-pair UTP. This technology has not been adopted very quickly due to its non-compliance with existing IEEE standards, such as IEEE 802.3.

The 100BaseT technology has been adopted and termed as Fast Ethernet. However, Fast Ethernet has many different flavors. Although the media access standard specified by IEEE 802.3 does not change, a few options of physical hardware implementation exist. The different hardware offerings are as follows:

➤ **100BaseTX** Fast Ethernet with category 5 cabling

➤ **100BaseFX** Fast Ethernet with fiber optic cabling

➤ **100BaseX** Fast Ethernet with either fiber or category 5 cabling

The distance limitations of Fast Ethernet are dependent on the physical media chosen as the transport. As we mentioned earlier, fiber optics and category 5 cabling are the predominant transport media in use today. Table 13.2 details the distance limitations with fiber optic and category 5 cabling.

The distance limitations can be extended with the use of repeaters to amplify the signal. In addition, many breakthroughs in fiber optic cable are being developed that are allowing distance limitations to be increased to 5 to 10 kilometers.

Full-Duplex And Half-Duplex Ethernet

Ethernet traditionally operated in *half-duplex mode* because of the technological limitation of shared access to the physical media. Half-duplex allows a device to either send or receive transmissions at any time but not both at the same time. Half-duplex designates that one wire in the twisted pair transmits while the other wire listens for collisions. Because Ethernet is built upon the CSMA/CD media access technology, any time a device in half-duplex mode sends a frame, it must listen to determine if the frame collided with another frame. If a

Table 13.2	Distance limitations of Fast Ethernet with fiber optics and category 5 cabling.	
Media Type	**Media Description**	**Distance Limitation**
Category 5 cable	2 pairs of STP or UTP	100 meters
Fiber optic cable	62.5 micron multimode fiber	400 meters
Fiber optic cable	Single mode fiber	10Km

collision occurs, the device must again send the frame to ensure that it reaches it destination. In the traditional hub environment, all devices shared the physical media, and so the possibility for a collision was present. Thus, it was necessary to implement half-duplex Ethernet.

With the introduction of switches, it was possible to give a device a dedicated physical piece of the logical LAN. The device no longer has to worry about listening to determine if a frame collides. Collisions are no longer possible, because each device has access to its own physical network. So manufacturers included the capability of running Ethernet in full-duplex mode with their Ethernet interfaces. Devices could now simultaneously send and receive messages on both wires, because the second wire no longer is used to listen for collisions. This is why Fast Ethernet (100Mb) sometimes is listed as having the capability of transmitting at 200Mb. In this scenario, a device is receiving and transmitting at 100Mb speeds with a combined throughput of 200Mb.

Practice Questions

Question 1

Which of the following is an advantage of using a repeater for LAN segmentation?

- O a. A repeater logically separates LANs and therefore isolates broadcast traffic.
- O b. A repeater amplifies the electrical signal and therefore extends the physical distance of LANs.
- O c. A repeater physically separates LANs and filters non-local and broadcast traffic from local traffic.
- O d. A repeater performs a rich set of functionality, allowing security and multi-protocol environments.

Answer b is correct. A repeater physically extends a LAN. It also amplifies the electrical signal of LANs and allows greater physical distances between two devices on the LAN. Answer a is incorrect because a repeater does not physically or logically segment a LAN. Answer c is incorrect because a repeater does not perform any filtering of LAN traffic. Answer d is incorrect because repeaters do not have security or protocol conversion functionality.

Question 2

Which of the following are advantages of using a bridge to segment a LAN? [Choose the two best answers]

- ❑ a. A bridge isolates local traffic to only one physical segment of the LAN.
- ❑ b. A bridge logically segments a LAN and therefore isolates non-local and broadcast traffic from local traffic.
- ❑ c. A bridge can extend the physical distance of a LAN by amplifying the electrical signal of the physical media.
- ❑ d. A bridge provides security and a high level of protocol conversion capabilities.

Answers a and c are correct. A bridge isolates local traffic to its originating physical segment; it also can extend the physical media by amplifying the electrical signal between two physically segmented LANs. Answer b is incorrect because a bridge does not logically separate LANs. Therefore, broadcast traffic is forwarded to all nodes on the logical LAN. In addition, non-local LAN traffic must be forwarded between the physical LAN of the originating and destination nodes at a minimum. Answer d is incorrect because bridges do not provide security or a high level of protocol conversion capabilities. Bridges do provide limited protocol conversion capabilities between token ring and Ethernet LANs.

Question 3

What is maintained in a bridge's forwarding table?

- O a. A device's IP address and the IP network that the device resides on.
- O b. A device's MAC address and the physical segment that device resides on.
- O c. A bridge's forwarding table maintains Mac addresses and the best interfaces to use to forward a frame to a destination Mac address.
- O d. The IP network and MAC address of devices.

Answer c is correct. Forwarding tables maintain Mac addresses. In addition, forwarding tables maintain the best interfaces to use to forward a frame to a destination Mac address. Answer a is incorrect because a bridge does not maintain IP addressing in its forwarding table. IP is a layer 3 protocol and is used by routers, not bridges. Answer b is a trick answer because it is partially correct. However, bridges do not maintain the physical segment that a device resides on. Bridges only maintain the next physical segment to forward a frame en route to the device's physical segment. In some cases, the device will exist on this physical segment, however, not in all cases. Answer d is incorrect because bridges do not maintain IP network information.

Question 4

What is the name of the protocol used to eliminate bridging loops?

- O a. Switching
- O b. ISL
- O c. Frame tagging
- O d. Spanning tree

Answer d is correct. The spanning tree protocol is used to remove circular routes in bridged and switched networks. Answer a is incorrect because switching is a layer 2 technology, not a protocol. Answer b is incorrect because ISL is used to allow VLANs to span multiple physical switches. Answer c is incorrect because frame tagging is a process to identify the VLAN of a frame between switches.

Question 5

How many of the following are advantages of routing in comparison to bridging and switching? [Choose the two best answers]

❑ a. Routing provides the functionality to allow complex networks with dissimilar technologies to be connected.

❑ b. Reduced latency.

❑ c. Routing provides a higher level of security.

❑ d. Routing allows faster throughput than bridges and switches because it does not have to consider layer 3 addressing.

Answers a and c are correct. Routing provides a rich set of functionality in comparison to bridges and switches. The ability of routers to identify the best path between two networks using different technologies and layer 3 addressing schemes allows routers to interconnect complex and dissimilar networks. Routers also increase the level of security on networks. Answer b is incorrect because routers typically have higher latency in comparison to bridges and switches. Answer d is incorrect because switches and bridges typically have a higher throughput than routers.

Question 6

Which technology provides faster forwarding rates?

○ a. Routing

○ b. Bridging

○ c. Switching

Answer c is correct. Switching provides the highest forwarding rates in comparison to bridging and routing.

Question 7

> Switches provide higher port densities than bridges.
>
> ○ a. True
>
> ○ b. False

Answer a is correct, True. Switches provide higher port densities than bridges. The increased port density is one of the main factors that allow switches to provide a higher throughput than bridges.

Question 8

> Which of the following switching methods provides the greatest frame throughput?
>
> ○ a. Store-and-forward switching
>
> ○ b. Frame tag switching
>
> ○ c. Cut-through switching
>
> ○ d. ISL switching

Answer c is correct. Cut-through switching provides high throughput frame switching because it only reads a portion of the frame before making the forwarding decision. Cut-through switching does not provide error checking. Answer a is incorrect because store-and-forward switching has slower frame throughput rates than cut-through switching because of its error checking capabilities and because it reads the entire frame before making a forwarding decision. Answer b is incorrect because frame tag switching does not exist; frame tagging is a process used to identify a frame's VLAN between switches. Answer d is incorrect because it is used to allow VLANs to span multiple switches as well.

Question 9

Which of the following are advantages of VLANs? [Choose the two best answers]

- ❑ a. Reduces switching overhead.
- ❑ b. Increases switching throughput.
- ❑ c. Simplifies adds, moves, and changes of users.
- ❑ d. Allows users to be grouped by functional area, not physical location.

Answers c and d are correct. VLANs increase the flexibility of assigning users to LANs. This increase simplicity allows users to be grouped by function rather than physical location, because VLANs can span multiple switches. Answer a is incorrect because VLANs do not reduce the amount of overhead required to switch a frame. Answer b is incorrect because VLANs do not provide any increase switching throughput.

Question 10

Which of the following statements regarding Ethernet technology is true?

- ○ a. Fast Ethernet provides 1,000Mb of throughput performance.
- ○ b. Ethernet technology must be employed using category 5 cabling.
- ○ c. Half-duplex Ethernet provides greater throughput than full-duplex Ethernet.
- ○ d. Full-duplex Ethernet technology doubles the amount of throughput in comparison to half-duplex technology.

Answer d is correct. Full-duplex Ethernet technology allows users to double the amount of throughput. This is accomplished by allowing devices to utilize both wires for transmitting or receiving frames. Answer a is incorrect because Fast Ethernet provides 100Mb of throughput, not 1,000Mb. Answer b is incorrect because Ethernet technology can be implemented on a variety of physical media, not just category 5 cable. However, category 5 cable is the most predominant physical media in use today with Ethernet. Answer c is incorrect because half-duplex provides a lower throughput than does full-duplex.

Need To Know More?

 Chappell, Laura: *Introduction to Cisco Router Configuration*. Cisco Systems Inc., Macmillan Publishing Company, 1998. ISBN 0-7645-3186-7. This book provides a great overview of the concepts tested on the CCNA exam.

 Ford, Merilee, H. Kim Lew, Steve Spanier, and Kevin Downes *Internetworking Technologies Handbook 2nd Edition*. Macmillan Publishing Company, 1998. ISBN 1-56205-102-3. This book is full of resourceful information on Internetworking Technologies.

 Lammle, Todd, Donald Porter, and James Chellis: *CCNA Cisco Certified Network Associate*. Sybex Network Press, Alameda, CA, 1999. ISBN 0-7821-2381-3. This book is a great supplement for learning the technologies tested on the CCNA exam.

 Syngress Media, with Richard D. Hornbaker, CCIE: *Cisco Certified Network Associate Study Guide*. Osborne/McGraw-Hill, Berkeley, CA, 1998. ISBN 0-07882-487-7. Another great book for review, before taking the CCNA exam.

 Visit **www.cisco.com/univercd/cc/td/doc/product/software/ ios113ed/113ed_cr/switch_c/xcisl.htm** for a great article titled *Configuring Routing between VLANs with ISL Encapsulation*.

Sample Test

This chapter provides pointers to help you develop a successful test-taking strategy, including how to choose proper answers, how to decode ambiguity, how to work within the Cisco testing framework, how to decide what you need to memorize, and how to prepare for the test. In this chapter, we also include 70 questions on subject matter pertinent to Cisco Exam 640-407, "CCNA Routing and Switching." After this chapter, you'll find the answer key to this test. Good luck!

Questions, Questions, Questions

Have no doubt that you are facing a test full of specific and pointed questions. The version of the CCNA Routing and Switching exam that you will take is a fixed-length: It will include 70 questions; and you will be allotted 90 minutes to complete the exam. You will be required to achieve a score of 70 percent or better to pass.

For this exam, questions belong to one of two basic types:

➤ Multiple-choice with a single answer

➤ Multiple-choice with multiple answers

Always take the time to read a question at least twice before selecting an answer. Not every question has only one answer; many questions require multiple answers. Therefore, it's important to read each question carefully, to determine how many answers are necessary or possible, and to look for additional hints or instructions when selecting answers. Such instructions often occur in brackets immediately following the question itself (as they do for all multiple-choice, multiple-answer questions). Unfortunately, some questions do not have any right answers and you are forced to find the "most correct" choice.

Picking Proper Answers

Obviously, the only way to pass any exam is to select enough of the right answers to obtain a passing score. However, Cisco's exams are not standardized like the SAT and GRE exams; they are far more diabolical and convoluted. In some cases, questions are strangely worded, and deciphering them can be a real challenge. In those cases, you may need to rely on answer-elimination skills. Almost always, you can immediately eliminate at least one answer out of the possible choices because it matches one of these conditions:

➤ The answer does not apply to the situation.

➤ The answer describes a nonexistent issue, an invalid option, or an imaginary state.

➤ The answer may be eliminated because of the question itself.

After you eliminate all answers that are obviously wrong, you can apply your retained knowledge to eliminate further answers. Look for items that sound correct, but refer to actions, commands, or features that are not present or not available in the situation that the question describes.

If you're still faced with a blind guess among two or more potentially correct answers, reread the question. Try to picture how each of the possible remaining answers would alter the situation. Be especially sensitive to terminology; sometimes the choice of words ("remove" instead of "disable") can make the difference between a right answer and a wrong one.

Only when you've exhausted your ability to eliminate answers, but remain unclear about which of the remaining possibilities is correct, should you guess at an answer. An unanswered question offers you no points, but guessing gives you at least some chance of getting a question right; just don't be too hasty when making a blind guess.

 Because you're taking a fixed-length test, you can wait until the last round of reviewing marked questions (just as you're about to run out of time, or out of unanswered questions) before you start making guesses. Guessing should be your technique of last resort!

Decoding Ambiguity

Cisco exams have a reputation for including questions that can be difficult to interpret, confusing, or ambiguous. In our experience with numerous exams, we consider this reputation to be completely justified. The Cisco exams are tough and deliberately made that way.

The only way to beat Cisco at its own game is to be prepared. You'll discover that many exam questions test your knowledge of things that are not directly related to the issue raised by a question. This means that the answers you must choose from, even incorrect ones, are just as much a part of the skill assessment as the question itself. If you don't know some information about most aspects of CCNA Routing and Switching, you may not be able to eliminate obviously wrong answers because these answers relate to a different area of CCNA Routing and Switching. In other words, the more you know about the question's topic, the easier it will be for you to tell right from wrong.

Questions often give away their answers, but you have to be Sherlock Holmes to see the clues. Often, subtle hints appear in the question text in such a way that they seem almost irrelevant to the situation. You must realize that each question is a test unto itself and that you need to inspect and successfully navigate each question to pass the exam. Look for small clues, such as the mention of times, group permissions and names, and configuration settings. Little things like these can point at the right answer if properly understood; if missed, they can leave you facing a blind guess.

Another common difficulty with certification exams is vocabulary. Cisco has an uncanny knack for naming some utilities and features entirely obviously in some cases, and completely inanely in other instances. Be sure to brush up on the key terms presented at the beginning of each chapter. You may also want to read through the Glossary at the end of this book the day before you take the test.

Working Within The Framework

The test questions appear in random order, and many elements or issues that receive mention in one question may also crop up in other questions. It's not uncommon to find that an incorrect answer to one question is the correct answer to another question, or vice versa. Take the time to read every answer to each question, even if you recognize the correct answer to a question immediately. That extra reading may spark a memory or remind you about a Cisco router IOS feature or function that helps you on another question elsewhere in the exam.

Since you're taking a fixed-length test, you can revisit any question as many times as you like. If you're uncertain of the answer to a question, check the box that's provided to mark it for easy return later on. You should also mark questions you think may offer information that you can use to answer other questions. On fixed-length tests, we usually mark somewhere between 25 and 50 percent of the questions on exams we've taken. The testing software is designed to let you mark every question if you choose; use this framework to your advantage. Everything you will want to see again should be marked; the testing software can then help you return to marked questions quickly and easily.

 For fixed-length tests, we strongly recommend that you first read through the entire test quickly, before getting caught up in answering individual questions. This will help to jog your memory as you review the potential answers and can help identify questions that you want to mark for easy access to their contents. It will also let you identify and mark the really tricky questions for easy return as well. The key is to make a quick pass over the territory to begin with, so that you know what you're up against, and then to survey that territory more thoroughly on a second pass, when you can begin to answer all questions systematically and consistently.

Deciding What To Memorize

The amount of memorization you must undertake for an exam depends on how well you remember what you've read and how well you know the material by heart. If you are a visual thinker, and you can see the configuration commands in your head, you won't need to memorize as much as someone who's less visually oriented. The tests will stretch your recollection of commands, protocols, and functions of the router.

At a minimum, you'll want to memorize the following kinds of information:

➤ The basics of IP addressing and subnetting

➤ The functions of each layer of the OSI model

➤ The pertinent commands for configuring frame relay

➤ The various "show" commands that will allow you to see the status of the subjects mentioned above and throughout the book

If you work your way through this book while sitting at a Cisco router, and try to manipulate this environment's features and functions as they're discussed throughout, you should have little or no difficulty mastering this material. Also, don't forget that The Cram Sheet at the front of the book is designed to capture the material that is most important to memorize; use this to guide your studies as well.

Preparing For The Test

The best way to prepare for the test—after you've studied—is to take at least one practice exam. We've included one here in this chapter for that reason; the test questions are located in the pages that follow (and unlike the preceding chapters in this book, the answers don't follow the questions immediately; you'll have to flip to Chapter 15 to review the answers separately).

Give yourself 90 minutes to take the exam, keep yourself on the honor system, and don't look at earlier text in the book or jump ahead to the answer key. When your time is up, or you've finished the questions, you can check your work in Chapter 15. Pay special attention to the explanations for the incorrect answers; these can also help to reinforce your knowledge of the material. Knowing how to recognize correct answers is good, but understanding why incorrect answers are wrong can be equally valuable.

Taking The Test

Relax. Once you're sitting in front of the testing computer, there's nothing more you can do to increase your knowledge or preparation. Take a deep breath, stretch, and start reading that first question.

Don't rush; you have plenty of time to complete each question and to return to those questions that you skip or mark for return. If you read a question twice and remain clueless, you can mark it. Both easy and difficult questions are intermixed throughout the test in random order. Because you're taking a fixed-length test, don't cheat yourself by spending too much time on a hard question early on in the test, thereby depriving yourself of the time you need to answer the questions at the end of the test.

On a fixed-length test, you can read through the entire test, and before returning to marked questions for a second visit, figure out how much time you've got per question. As you answer each question, remove its mark. Continue to review the remaining marked questions until you run out of time or you complete the test.

Sample Test

Question 1

What are the primary purposes of the OSI model network layer? [Choose the two best answers]

❑ a. Path determination

❑ b. Code formatting

❑ c. Flow control

❑ d. Packet switching

❑ e. Error notification

Question 2

Which of the following are routed protocols? [Choose the two best answers]

❑ a. IGRP

❑ b. EIGRP

❑ c. IP

❑ d. OSPF

❑ e. IPX

Question 3

Which of the following are performed at the data link layer of the OSI model? [Choose the three best answers]

❑ a. Error notification

❑ b. Packet switching

❑ c. Physical addressing

❑ d. Establishing, maintaining, and terminating sessions

❑ e. Frame sequencing

Question 4

Which of the following are examples of LAN protocols? [Choose the three best answers]

❑ a. Frame Relay

❑ b. Token Ring

❑ c. Ethernet

❑ d. FDDI

❑ e. ISDN

Question 5

Given the following physical address, what is the vendor code of this address?

BBD1.4822.53AA

○ a. BBD148

○ b. 2253AA

○ c. BBD1

○ d. 53AA

○ e. 4822

Question 6

Which two answers are characteristics of connection-oriented communication? [Choose the two best answers]

❑ a. Setup and maintenance procedures are performed to ensure delivery of messages.

❑ b. A physical circuit exists between the two communicating devices.

❑ c. It is a best effort type of communication.

❑ d. A virtual connection exists between the two devices.

Question 7

Which of the following are examples of layer 3 addressing? [Choose the two best answers]

❑ a. 172.29.5.12

❑ b. CB255467.3000.B433.A232

❑ c. 0000.B333.A232

❑ d. A4XX

Question 8

If you wanted to view the currently executing configuration file, which of the following commands would you use?

○ a. **show startup-config**

○ b. **show running-config**

○ c. **configure terminal**

○ d. **configure memory**

Question 9

What command would be used to back up a running configuration file?

○ a. **router#copy tftp running-config**

○ b. **router>copy tftp running-config**

○ c. **router#copy running-config tftp**

○ d. **router>copy tftp running**

Question 10

Which of the following commands would set a "enable secret" password on a Cisco router?

○ a. **router#enable secret** *password*

○ b. **router(config-line)#password phoenix**

○ c. **router(config)#enable secret** *password*

○ d. **router(config)#enable password**

Question 11

Which of the following commands would create a text description on an interface of a router?

○ a. **router#description** I am going to pass the CCNA exam

○ b. **router(config)#description** I am going to pass the CCNA exam

○ c. **router(config-line)description** I am going to pass the CCNA exam

○ d. **router(config-if)#description** I am going to pass the CCNA exam

Question 12

Which of the following commands indicates that you want the router to load the software from flash?

○ a. **router(config)# boot system flash**

○ b. **router(config)#boot system ROM**

○ c. **router(config-line)boot system flash**

○ d. **router#boot system flash**

Question 13

Which of the following answers correctly matches a TCP/IP application layer service with its port number?

○ a. SMTP - 44

○ b. FTP - 22

○ c. ICMP - 10

○ d. ARP - 14

○ e. TFTP - 69

Question 14

Which of the following services is used to copy files between Cisco routers?

○ a. SMTP

○ b. SNMP

○ c. TFTP

○ d. RARP

○ e. HTTP

Question 15

Which of the following are characteristics of TCP? [Choose the three best answers]

❑ a. Performs error and duplication checking.

❑ b. Performs acknowledgment windowing to increase efficiency of bandwidth use.

❑ c. Initiates a three-way handshake.

❑ d. Provides logical addressing.

Question 16

What is the function performed by Address Resolution Protocol?

○ a. Maps a known physical address to a logical address.

○ b. Maps a known logical address to a physical address.

○ c. Communicates error messages and control messages between devices.

○ d. A protocol used to get physical and logical addresses from a TFTP server.

Question 17

Which of the following protocols is used to copy a file from one host to another host, regardless of the physical hardware or operating system of the device?

- ○ a. SNMP
- ○ b. FTP
- ○ c. IP
- ○ d. UDP
- ○ e. DNS

Question 18

Which of the following functions do both UDP and TCP perform? [Choose the two best answers]

- ❑ a. Provide destination and source port numbers
- ❑ b. Three-way handshake
- ❑ c. Dynamic datagram size allocation
- ❑ d. Checksum
- ❑ e. Acknowledgments of datagram receipt

Question 19

An IP address is listed below in decimal format. Please indicate the corresponding binary value of this IP address?

172.16.8.8

- ○ a. 10101100.00010000.00001000.00001000
- ○ b. 10101100.00100000.11100000.00000100
- ○ c. 10101100.00010000.00000010.00000111
- ○ d. 11001100.00001111.00011001.00001000

Question 20

An IP address is listed below in binary format. Please indicate the corresponding decimal value of this IP address?

01110000.00001110.00001100.00001000

○ a. 112.14.12.81

○ b. 11.12.12.10

○ c. 112.14.12.8

○ d. 112.14.13.80

Question 21

Which of the following addresses are class C addresses? [Choose the two best answers]

❑ a. 221.15.130.254

❑ b. 10100000.11000000.11111111.11110000

❑ c. 11010001.11001100.10101010.00001111

❑ d. 127.0.0.0

Question 22

Which of the following commands can be used to monitor IP routing protocols? [Choose the three best answers]

❑ a. **show ip route**

❑ b. **show ip interface**

❑ c. **show ip tables**

❑ d. **show ip route protocols**

❑ e. **show ip protocol**

Question 23

With an IP address and subnet mask of 172.10.10.4 255.255.255.128, what is the full range of IP addresses in this subnet?

○ a. 172.10.10.1 through 172.10.10.254

○ b. 172.10.10.129 through 172.10.10.254

○ c. 172.10.10.0 through 172.10.10.127

○ d. 172.10.10.1 through 172.10.10.12

Question 24

With an IP address and subnet mask of 172.10.10.4 255.255.255.128, what is the number of possible subnets?

○ a. 510

○ b. 254

○ c. 1,024

○ d. 14

○ e. 4,094

Question 25

Which of the following commands identifies an IP standard access list?

○ a. **ip access-group 400 out**

○ b. **ip access-group 11 out**

○ c. **ip access-group 145 out**

○ d. **ip access-group 105 out**

○ e. **ipx access-group 805 in**

Question 26

Which of the following commands identifies an IP extended access list?

○ a. **ip access-group 304 in**

○ b. **ip access-group 110 out**

○ c. **ip access-group 215 out**

○ d. **ip access-group 495 out**

○ e. **ipx access-group 805 in**

Question 27

Which of the following cannot be used to permit or deny traffic with IP extended access lists?

○ a. TCP port number

○ b. Destination IP address

○ c. IP sequence number

○ d. Source IP addresses

Question 28

What is the valid range for an IPX extended access list?

○ a. 0 through 99

○ b. 100 through 199

○ c. 800 through 899

○ d. 900 through 999

Question 29

Which of the following commands can be used to show access lists? [Choose the three best answers]

- ❏ a. **show ip interfaces**
- ❏ b. **show ipx interfaces**
- ❏ c. **show access-lists**
- ❏ d. **show access lists**

Question 30

Which of the following are disadvantages of using a bridge to segment a LAN? [Choose the two best answers]

- ❏ a. Increases the latency period to forward frames by 20 percent.
- ❏ b. A bridge logically segments a LAN and therefore isolates non-local devices from local traffic.
- ❏ c. A bridge can extend the physical distance of a LAN by amplifying the electrical signal of the physical media.
- ❏ d. Introduces the possibility of bridging loops.

Question 31

What is maintained in a bridge's forwarding table?

- ○ a. A device's IP address and the IP network that the device resides on.
- ○ b. A device's MAC address and the physical segment that device resides on.
- ○ c. A device's MAC address and the next physical segment to forward a frame to while in route to the physical segment that the device resides on.
- ○ d. The IP network and MAC address of devices.

Question 32

What is the name of the protocol used to pass VLAN information between switches?

○ a. Switching

○ b. ISL

○ c. Frame tagging

○ d. Spanning tree

Question 33

How many of the following are disadvantages of routing in comparison to bridging and switching? [Choose the two best answers]

❑ a. Routing provides the functionality to allow complex networks with dissimilar technologies to be connected

❑ b. Increased latency

❑ c. Reduced security

❑ d. Increased complexity

Question 34

Frame tagging is used to tag a frame with a unique VLAN ID between switches.

○ a. True

○ b. False

Question 35

Which of the following switching methods provides error-checking capabilities?

○ a. Store-and-forward switching

○ b. Frame tag switching

○ c. Cut-through switching

○ d. ISL switching

Question 36

Which of the following is a component within PPP? [Choose the three best answers]

- ❑ a. NCP
- ❑ b. HSSI
- ❑ c. LCP
- ❑ d. HDLC

Question 37

Which of the following are not services provided by the transport layer? [Choose the three best answers]

- ❑ a. Establishing a session
- ❑ b. Ensuring that the segment sent is error free
- ❑ c. Ending a session
- ❑ d. Keeping the sending and receiving station from sending segments at the same time

Question 38

What commands should you use to monitor PPP activity?

- ○ a. **show interfaces**
- ○ b. **show protocol**
- ○ c. **show ppp**
- ○ d. **show bri**

Question 39

Which PPP authentication protocol uses a two-way handshake?

- ○ a. PAP
- ○ b. CHAP
- ○ c. LCP
- ○ d. NCP

Question 40

Which of the following functions *can* be performed with ISDN? [Choose the three best answers]

❑ a. Improve Internet response times.

❑ b. Encapsulate other WAN services.

❑ c. Add bandwidth for telecommuting.

❑ d. Authenticate remote hosts.

Question 41

Which of the following commands will display Frame Relay information about serial interface 1?

○ a. **sh frame-relay s1**

○ b. **sh frame-relay interface s1**

○ c. **sh interface s1**

○ d. **sh ip interface brief**

Question 42

Cisco does not support which of the following Frame Relay LMI protocol variations?

○ a. IETF

○ b. ANSI

○ c. Q933A

○ d. Cisco

Question 43

Frame Relay operates primarily at which layers of the OSI model?

○ a. Transport and network

○ b. Network and data link

○ c. Data link and physical

Question 44

Which of the following devices can serve as a DCE? [Choose the three best answers]

❑ a. Router

❑ b. Terminal

❑ c. Modem

❑ d. CSU

Question 45

Which of the following common WAN services is not supported by Cisco?

○ a. ISDN

○ b. Frame Relay

○ c. PPP

○ d. BGP

○ e. HDLC

○ f. SDLC

Question 46

Which of the following is a valid IPX address for network 4d?

○ a. 4d80.c747.b122

○ b. 4d.0080.c747.b122

○ c. 4d.172.16.101.123

○ d. 4d

Question 47

Which of the following routing protocols will not support an IPX network?

○ a. RIP

○ b. NLSP

○ c. EIGRP

○ d. IGRP

Question 48

To enable IPX, what is the first IPX configuration command that must be executed on a router?

○ a. **ipx routing**

○ b. **ipx protocol**

○ c. **ipx interface**

○ d. **ipx network**

Question 49

Which router command displays the contents of the IPX route table?

○ a. **show ipx traffic**

○ b. **show ipx route**

○ c. **show ipx server**

○ d. **show ipx table**

Question 50

Which of the following protocols is used within the network layer of the NetWare protocol suite?

○ a. Ethernet

○ b. UDP

○ c. IPX

○ d. ARP

Question 51

Which router commands, if executed from the global configuration prompt, will enable IGRP routing for autonomous system 77 and network 172.25.0.0?

○ a. **router igrp 77** then **network 172.25.0.0**

○ b. **router igrp 172.25.0.0**

○ c. **router igrp** then **network 172.25.0.0**

○ d. **network 172.25.0.0**

Question 52

Which of the following is not a solution to problems experienced by distance vector routing protocols?

- ○ a. Split horizon
- ○ b. Route poison
- ○ c. Counting to infinity
- ○ d. Maximum hop count
- ○ e. Hold-down timers

Question 53

Which of the following routing protocols sends link state packets to all routers in its area?

- ○ a. BGP
- ○ b. RIP
- ○ c. IGRP
- ○ d. OSPF

Question 54

Which of the following prompts indicates that the router is in user mode?

- ○ a. Router>
- ○ b. Router#
- ○ c. Router(config)#
- ○ d. Router:

Question 55

The command **show cdp neighbors** displays which of the following? [Choose the four best answers]

- ❑ a. Neighbor's device ID
- ❑ b. Neighbor's hardware platform
- ❑ c. Neighbor's IOS version
- ❑ d. Neighbor's port type and number
- ❑ e. Local port type and number

Question 56

Which of the following router commands displays a list of keywords needed for the command **"show"**?

- ○ a. **"sh?"**
- ○ b. **"sh ?"**
- ○ c. **"show?"**

Question 57

When you first log in to a Cisco router under normal circumstances, what router mode are you in?

- ○ a. RXBOOT
- ○ b. Privileged
- ○ c. Global configuration
- ○ d. User

Question 58

If you needed to disable the enhanced editing feature of a Cisco router, which command would you enter?

- ○ a. **no editing**
- ○ b. **no terminal editing**
- ○ c. **terminal no editing**
- ○ d. **disable editing**

Question 59

In order to display a brief description of the help system in privileged mode, which of the following sequence of keystrokes must be typed at the prompt? [Choose the two best answers]

- ☐ a. "help"
- ☐ b. "h"
- ☐ c. "CTRL+H"
- ☐ d. "?"

Question 60

Which of the following layers is most concerned with the representation of data?

- ○ a. Application
- ○ b. Presentation
- ○ c. Session
- ○ d. Transport

Question 61

If your router has a built-in BRI, which function will you need to connect to ISDN services?

- ○ a. NT1
- ○ b. TA
- ○ c. TE1
- ○ d. TE2

Question 62

With what is the application layer primarily concerned?

- ○ a. Providing services for user applications
- ○ b. Data representation
- ○ c. Dialog management
- ○ d. Data transport

Question 63

A packet, frame, and bits conversion process includes which layers (in order)?

○ a. Session, transport, network

○ b. Network, data link, physical

○ c. Presentation, session, transport

○ d. Network, transport, data link

Question 64

Which of the following is a reason why the industry uses a layered model? [Choose best answers that apply]

❑ a. Network operations and troubleshooting can be simplified.

❑ b. Standard interfaces can be defined for vendor compatibility.

❑ c. Enhancements for one layer can be isolated from the other layers.

❑ d. Designs and development efforts can be made in a modular fashion.

❑ e. Complex internetworking components can be divided into discrete subsets.

Question 65

Which of the following layers is most concerned with end-to-end communication?

○ a. Application

○ b. Presentation

○ c. Session

○ d. Transport

Question 66

The presentation layer provides which of the following services? [Choose the three best answers]

❑ a. Data representation

❑ b. Data compression

❑ c. Dialog management

❑ d. Data transmission

❑ e. Data encryption

Question 67

Which command, when executed successfully, verifies that two routers are routing packets between them successfully? [Choose the three best answers]

❑ a. **ping**

❑ b. **show interface**

❑ c. **trace**

❑ d. **telnet**

Question 68

Which of the following is an interior routing protocol? [Choose the three best answers]

❑ a. RIP

❑ b. IGRP

❑ c. OSPF

❑ d. BGP

Question 69

Which router commands, if executed from the global configuration prompt, will enable RIP routing for network 172.23.0.0?

- ○ a. **router rip 13** and **network 172.23.0.0**
- ○ b. **router rip all**
- ○ c. **router rip** and **network 172.23.0.0**
- ○ d. **network 172.23.0.0**

Question 70

If you are extremely security conscious, which PPP authentication protocol should you implement?

- ○ a. CHAP
- ○ b. DDR
- ○ c. PAP

Answer Key

1. a, d	19. a	37. a, c, d	55. a, b, d, e
2. c, e	20. c	38. a	56. b
3. a, c, e	21. a, c	39. a	57. d
4. b, c, d	22. a, b, e	40. a, b, c	58. c
5. a	23. c	41. c	59. a, b
6. a, d	24. a	42. a	60. b
7. a, b	25. b	43. c	61. a
8. b	26. b	44. a, c, d	62. a
9. c	27. c	45. d	63. b
10. c	28. d	46. b	64. a, b, c, d, e
11. d	29. a, b, c	47. d	65. d
12. a	30. a, d	48. a	66. a, b, e
13. e	31. c	49. b	67. a, c, d
14. c	32. b	50. c	68. a, b, c
15. a, b, c	33. b, d	51. a	69. c
16. b	34. a	52. c	70. a
17. b	35. a	53. d	
18. a, d	36. a, c, d	54. a	

Question 1

Answers a and d are correct. The network layer of the OSI model performs both path determination and packet switching. Path determination is the process of identifying the best path to a destination across an internetwork. Packet switching is the process of moving a packet from one network interface to another. Answer b is incorrect because code formatting occurs at the presentation layer of the OSI model, not the network layer. Answer c is incorrect because flow control occurs at the data link or transport layer. Answer e is incorrect because the network layer does not perform any error notification.

Question 2

Answers c and e are correct. Both IP and IPX are layer 3 routed protocols. Open Shortest Path First (OSPF), Interior Gateway Routing Protocol (IGRP) and Enhanced Interior Gateway Routing Protocol (EIGRP) are routing protocols; therefore, answers a, b, and d are incorrect.

Question 3

Answers a, c, and e are correct. The data link layer performs error notification, physical addressing, and frame sequencing, among other things. Answer b is incorrect because packet switching is performed at the network layer. Answer d is incorrect because establishing, maintaining, and terminating sessions occurs at the session layer.

Question 4

Answers b, c, and d are correct. Token Ring, Ethernet, and FDDI are all layer 2 LAN protocols. Answers a and e are incorrect because Frame Relay and ISDN are WAN protocols; however, they both do function at layer 2 of the OSI model.

Question 5

Answer a is correct. The first six digits of the physical address represent the vendor code. Answer b is incorrect because the last six numbers of the physical address represent the serial number, not the vendor code. Answers c, d, and e have no meaning on their own and therefore are incorrect.

Question 6

Answers a and d are correct. Both a virtual connection and setup and maintenance functions are performed during connection-oriented communication. Answer b is incorrect because a physical circuit is not necessary for connection-oriented communication. Answer c is a characteristic of connectionless communication, not of connection-oriented communication, and therefore is incorrect.

Question 7

Answers a and b are correct. Answer a is an example of an IP logical address or a network layer address. Answer b is an example of an IPX logical address or a network layer address. Answer c is incorrect because it is an example of a physical or layer 2 address, not a network or layer 3 address. Answer d has no meaning and therefore is incorrect.

Question 8

Answer b is correct. The command to display the executing configuration/running configuration file to a console terminal is **show running-config**. Answer a is incorrect because this command displays the backup configuration/startup configuration file. Answers c and d are incorrect because these are used to modify configuration files, not to show configuration files.

Question 9

Answer c is correct. When backing up a running configuration file, the file needs to be copied from the router to a TFTP server. Answer a is incorrect because it would copy a file from a TFTP server to the router, when we really want the opposite. Answer b is incorrect because the command is being executed from user EXEC mode. Answer d is incorrect because the command is executed from user EXEC mode and it is in the wrong format.

Question 10

Answer c is correct. The command **enable secret** is the correct command. Answer b is incorrect because the word "password" is not used for setting an "enable secret" password. Answer a is incorrect because the enable secret password is set while in configuration mode, not privileged EXEC mode. Answer d is incorrect because this command is used to set the "enable" password, not the "enable secret" password.

Question 11

Answer d is correct. The command description is executed from the interface configuration mode and is the correct command to create a text description on an interface of a router. Answer a is incorrect because the command is executed from privileged EXEC mode. Answer b is incorrect because the command is executed from global configuration mode. Answer c is incorrect because the syntax of "router(config-line)" is incorrect.

Question 12

Answer a is correct. The command **boot system flash** is used to load software from flash. Answer b is incorrect because the command **boot system ROM** is used to load software from ROM. Answer c is incorrect because the command **boot system flash** is not executed in configuration line mode. Answer d is incorrect because the command **boot system flash** is not executed from privileged EXEC mode.

Question 13

Answer e is correct. TFTP uses the TCP port number 69. Answers a and b are incorrect because the correct port number is not matched with the application layer service. Answers c and d are not application layer services, and therefore are incorrect.

Question 14

Answer c is correct. TFTP is a scaled down version of FTP used to copy files between Cisco routers or to TFTP servers. Answer a is incorrect because SMTP is a mail protocol, not a file transfer protocol. SNMP is network management protocol, not a file transfer protocol, and therefore b is incorrect. RARP is a protocol used to map an unknown logical address to a known physical address, and therefore d is incorrect. HTTP is used for Web browsing, and therefore e is incorrect.

Question 15

Answers a, b, and c are correct. Error and duplication checking, acknowledgment windowing, and the three-way handshake are some of the characteristics of TCP. However, TCP is not responsible for logical addressing. IP performs logical addressing in the TCP/IP suite, and therefore answer d is incorrect.

Question 16

Answer b is correct. ARP maps a known logical address to an unknown physical address. Answer a is incorrect because it describes RARP, not ARP. Answer c is incorrect because it has nothing to do with ARP. Answer d is incorrect because ARP does not retrieve logical addresses, nor does a TFTP server have to be in the picture.

Question 17

Answer b is correct. FTP is used to copy files between hosts and is not dependent on the operating system or physical hardware of each device. Answers a, c, d, and e are not file transfer protocols and therefore are incorrect.

Question 18

Answers a and d are correct. Answer a is correct because the destination and source port numbers are provided in both the UDP and TCP headers. In addition, answer d is correct because both TCP and UDP provide for a checksum in the header to verify accurate delivery. However, answer b is incorrect because only TCP performs the three-way handshake. Answer c is incorrect because UDP does not dynamically set datagram sizes, but assigns each datagram the same size. Finally, only TCP provides reliability in its data transport. Therefore, answer e is incorrect because UDP does not generate acknowledgments for the receipt of datagrams.

Question 19

Answer a is correct, because the dotted decimal value 172.16.8.8 is equivalent to the binary value 10101100.0001000.00001000.00001000. Answers b, c, and d are incorrect because these binary values are not equivalent to 172.16.8.8.

Question 20

Answer c is correct, because the conversion of these binary bits yields a decimal value of 112.14.12.8. Answer a can be quickly identified as incorrect by noting that the fourth octet begins with a 1, but its value is not greater than 128. Answers b and d can immediately be eliminated, because converting them to binary does not yield the correct results.

Question 21

Answers a and c are correct. Answer a can be identified as correct because it has a decimal value between 192 and 223. Answer c can be identified as correct because the first 3 binary digits are 110. Answer b can be eliminated because the first 3 binary digits are 101, not 110. Answer d can be eliminated because the dotted decimal value is not between 192 and 223.

Question 22

Answers a, b, and e are correct. The three commands **show ip route, show ip interface,** and **show ip protocol** all can be used to monitor routing protocols. Each command shows unique information regarding routing protocols. Answers c and d can be eliminated because they are not Cisco IOS commands.

Question 23

Answer c is correct. An IP address of 172.10.10.4 255.255.255.128 indicates a class B address with a nine-bit subnet mask. The valid range in dotted decimal notation for this IP address is 172.10.10.0 through 172.10.10.127. Answers a, b, and e can be eliminated because they do not fall within this range of IP addresses.

Question 24

Answer a is correct. The number of subnets can be derived by using the formula 2n-2. A class B address of 172.10.10.4 with a nine-bit subnet mask indicates that nine-bits are used for identifying networks. Therefore, we can take 2 to the power of 9 and subtract 2 to yield the number of networks. Answers b, c, d, and e are not the correct result of our formula, and therefore can be eliminated.

Question 25

Answer b is correct. The command in answer b identifies an IP standard access list by the access list number 11, which is the proper numeric range for identifying an IP standard access list. Answer a is incorrect because it uses the access list number 400. The access list number 400 is not reserved for IP standard access lists, and therefore is incorrect. Answer c is incorrect because the access list number 145 is reserved for IP extended access lists, not IP standard access lists. Answer d is incorrect because the number 105 is reserved for IP extended access lists not IP standard access lists. Answer e is incorrect because it is an IPX access list, not an IP access list.

Question 26

Answer b is correct. The correct numeric range for an IP extended access list is 100-199. Answers a, c, d, and e all fall outside of the correct IP extended access list range and therefore are incorrect.

Question 27

Answer c is correct. The IP sequence number cannot be used to permit or deny traffic with IP extended access lists. IP extended access lists can permit or deny traffic using TCP port number, source IP address, and destination IP address, and therefore, answers a, b, and d are all incorrect.

Question 28

Answer d is correct. IPX extended access lists are identified by a numeric range between 900 and 999. Answers a, b, and c are incorrect because they do not fall within the correct numeric range for IPX extended access lists.

Question 29

Answers a, b, and c are correct. The commands **show ip interfaces, show ipx interfaces**, and **show access-lists** all can be used to show access lists. Answer d is incorrect because the command **show access lists** is not in the correct format.

Question 30

Answers a and d are correct. Bridges have approximately a 20 percent increase in frame forwarding rates in comparison to repeaters or physical media. In addition, implementing bridges to segment a layer 2 network introduces the possibility of bridging loops in a network. Answers b and c are incorrect because these are actually advantages of bridges.

Question 31

Answer c is correct. A bridge only maintains a device's physical MAC address and the next physical segment to forward a frame to while in route to the destination device. Answer a is incorrect because bridges do not maintain IP addresses. Answer b is incorrect because bridges don't maintain the physical segment that a device resides on, but only maintain the next physical segment to forward a frame to while in route to the destination device. Answer d is incorrect because bridges do not maintain IP networks.

Question 32

Answer b is correct. ISL is a communication protocol used between switches to communicate common VLANs between devices. Answer a is incorrect because a switch is a physical device, not a protocol. Answer c is incorrect because frame tagging is a process employed by switches, not a protocol. Answer d is incorrect because the spanning tree protocol is used to eliminate loops in bridged networks.

Question 33

Answers b and d are correct. Routers increase the latency of forwarding packets/frames between networks. In addition, the increased functionality provided by routers often increases the complexity of networks. Answers a and c are incorrect because these are actually advantages of routing in comparison to bridging and switching.

Question 34

Answer a is correct, True. Frame tagging is used to tag a frame with a unique VLAN ID between switches, and therefore, answer b is incorrect.

Question 35

Answer a is correct. Store-and-forward switching is a method of forwarding frames by copying the entire frame into the buffer of the switch and making a forwarding decision. Answer a is correct because store-and-forward switching provides error checking that is not provided by cut-through switching. Answers b and d are not switching methods and therefore are incorrect. Answer c is incorrect because cut-through switching does not provide error-checking capabilities.

Question 36

Answers a, c, and d are correct. PPP uses NCP, LCP, and HDLC to perform its function of encapsulating network-layer protocol information. Answer b is incorrect. Although HSSI is a physical interface that supports many layer 2 protocols including PPP, it is separate from PPP.

Question 37

Answers a, c, and d are correct. The session layer provides services to establish sessions, end sessions, and manage the dialogue between the sending and receiving stations. Ensuring that the segment sent is error free *is* handled within the transport layer; therefore, answer b is incorrect.

Question 38

Answer a is correct. The **show interfaces** command displays status and statistics for each interface on the router—including those encapsulated with PPP. Answer b is incorrect because the **show protocol** command displays detailed information of the routed protocols on the router. Answers c and d are incorrect because the **show ppp** and **show bri** commands are invalid.

Question 39

Answer a is correct. PAP only uses a two-way handshake to allow the remote host to identify itself to the local host. Answer b is incorrect because CHAP uses a three-way handshake in its procedure. LCP and NCP are not authentication protocols. Therefore, answers c and d are also incorrect.

Question 40

Answers a, b, and c are correct. ISDN can be used to improve Internet response times, encapsulate other WAN services, add bandwidth for telecommuting, and carry multiple network-layer protocols. Answer d is incorrect because authenticating remote hosts can be performed using PPP (PAP or CHAP), not ISDN.

Question 41

Answer c is correct. The command **sh interface s1** displays the configuration and statistics for serial 1 interface on the router. Answers a and b are incorrect because the **sh frame-relay s1** and **sh frame-relay s1** interface commands are invalid. Answer d is also incorrect because the **sh ip interface brief** command displays ip addressing and status information for all interfaces, not Frame Relay information.

Question 42

Answer a is correct. IETF is a type of frame encapsulation supported by Cisco that enables Cisco devices to communicate with non-Cisco devices across a Frame Relay network. Answers b, c, and d are incorrect because Cisco supports LMI extensions from American National Standards Institute (ANSI), International Telecommunication Union–Telecommunication Standardization Sector (Q933A), and the "Gang of Four" (Cisco). In other words, ANSI, Q933A, and Cisco LMI variations are supported by Cisco.

Question 43

Answer c is correct. Frame Relay operates within the data link layer and over the physical layer. Answers a and b are incorrect because Frame Relay does not contain any layer 3 (network) or layer 4 (transport) information.

Question 44

Answers a, c, and d are correct. Modems, CSUs, and some routers can be configured to serve as DCE devices. Terminals cannot be configured to act as DCEs, but they can be configured as DTEs; therefore, answer b is incorrect.

Question 45

Answer d is correct. BGP is not a WAN service supported by Cisco; it's a routing protocol supported by Cisco. ISDN, Frame Relay, PPP, HDLC, and SDLC are all WAN services supported by Cisco equipment, so answers a, b, c, e, and f are all incorrect.

Question 46

Answer b is correct. It is a complete IPX logical address for network 4d and node 0080.c747.b122. Answer a is incorrect because it is a node address and does not contain network information. Answer c is incorrect because it contains an IPX network number (4d), but also includes an IP address. Answer d is incorrect because it is only the IPX network number and is not a valid IPX logical address.

Question 47

Answer d is correct. IGRP will not support an IPX network. Answer a is incorrect because RIP is the default routing protocol within an IPX network.

Answers b and c are also incorrect because NLSP and EIGRP can be used as the routing protocol for IPX.

Question 48

Answer a is correct. The **ipx routing** command enables IPX routing within the router; the other commands can be executed after IPX has been enabled. Answer d is incorrect because the **ipx network** command assigns a network number to a router interface. Answers b and c are also incorrect because the **ipx protocol** and **ipx interface** commands are not valid commands.

Question 49

Answer b is correct. The **show ipx route** command displays the contents of the IPX routing table. Answer c is incorrect because the **show ipx server** command displays the information learned through SAP advertisements. Answer a is incorrect because the **show ipx traffic** command displays the number and type of IPX packets transmitted and received by the router. The **show ipx table** is not a valid command; therefore, answer d is incorrect.

Question 50

Answer c is correct. IPX is the network-layer protocol used within NetWare's protocol suite. Answer a is incorrect because Ethernet is a data link layer protocol that supports NetWare. UDP is a transport layer protocol, but it is used within the TCP/IP suite, so answer b is incorrect. Answer d is incorrect because ARP resides at the network layer within the TCP/IP suite.

Question 51

Answer a is correct. The **router igrp 77** command enables IGRP routing for autonomous system 1 and the **network 172.25.0.0** command enables the router to advertise that network to other routers. Answers b and c are incorrect because the **router igrp** command requires an autonomous system to be specified. Answer d is incorrect because you must first specify a routing protocol and enter routing protocol configuration mode before configuring a network to be advertised.

Question 52

Answer c is correct. Counting to infinity can result from the slow convergence inherent with distance vector protocols. Answers a, b, d, and e are incorrect.

Split horizon, route poison, maximum hop count, and hold-down timers are techniques to reduce the occurrence and impact of the counting to infinity situation.

Question 53

Answer d is correct. OSPF is a link state routing protocol that uses link state packets to pass the state of its links to all routers within its area Answer a is incorrect because BGP is an exterior routing protocol that communicates reachability information between domains. RIP and IGRP are distance vector protocols that send all or part of their route tables to their neighbors; therefore, answers b and c are incorrect.

Question 54

Answer a is correct. A greater than sign (>) after the host name (in this case "Router") indicates the router is in user mode. Answer b is incorrect because a pound sign (#) immediately following the hostname indicates that the router is in privileged mode. The text "(config)#" after the hostname indicates that the router is in global configuration mode. Therefore, answer c is incorrect. A colon (:) after the hostname is not a valid router mode indicator, so answer d is incorrect.

Question 55

Answers a, b, d, and e are correct. The neighbor's device ID, hardware platform, port type and number, and the local port type and number are all displayed by the **show cdp neighbors** command. The neighbor's IOS version is displayed by the **show cdp entry** command, so answer c is incorrect.

Question 56

Answer b is correct. The "**sh ?**" displays the keyword needed to complete the **show** command. The "**sh?**" and "**show?**" keystrokes display the commands beginning with the text "sh" and "show," respectively. Therefore, answers a and c are incorrect.

Question 57

Answer d is correct. Upon login, the router is placed in user mode. Answer a is incorrect because RXBOOT mode is for router recovery. Answer b is incorrect because you must first enter user mode before entering privileged mode. Answer c is also incorrect because you enable global configuration mode after you are in privileged mode.

Question 58

Answer c is correct. The command **terminal no editing** disables the enhanced editing mode on a router. Answers a, b, and d are incorrect because **no editing**, **no terminal editing**, and **disable editing** are not valid commands.

Question 59

Answers a and b are correct. The **help** and **h** commands display a brief description of the help system for any command mode. Answer d is incorrect because the question mark "?" displays the list of possible commands when it is typed at the prompt, regardless of the router's current mode. The Ctrl+H keystroke displays nothing. Therefore, answer c is incorrect.

Question 60

Answer b is correct. The presentation layer's chief concern is data representation. The application layer provides services for user applications, so answer a is incorrect. The session layer mainly performs session management; therefore, answer c is incorrect. Answer d is incorrect because the transport layer handles different aspects of data transport that include end-to-end communication, sending segments from one host to another, and reliable transport.

Question 61

Answer a is correct. You will still need an NT1 to convert the BRI signal for use by the ISDN digital line. Answer b is incorrect because a BRI functions as a TA. Answer c is incorrect because a TE1 is a device that *has* a built-in BRI and already transmits BRI. Answer d is incorrect because a device that *does not* have a built-in BRI is considered a TE2.

Question 62

Answer a is correct. The application layer provides services for user applications. Answer b is incorrect because the presentation layer's chief concern is data representation. The session layer mainly performs management so answer c is incorrect. The transport layer primarily focuses on aspects of data transport; therefore, answer d is incorrect.

Question 63

Answer b is correct. The network layer converts segments into packets. The data link layer converts packets into frames. The physical layer converts frames into bits. Answer a is incorrect because the session layer sends *data* to the transport layer. Answer c is incorrect because the transport layer converts data into segments. Answer d is incorrect because the layers are out of order; the transport layer communicates with the network layer and the network layer communicates with the data link layer.

Question 64

Answers a, b, c, d, and e are correct.

Question 65

Answer d is correct. The transport layer handles different aspects of data transport, which include end-to-end communication, sending segments from one host to another, and reliable transport. Answer a is incorrect because the application layer provides services for user applications. Because the presentation layer's chief concern is data representation, answer b is incorrect. The session layer mainly performs session management; therefore, answer c is incorrect.

Question 66

Answers a, b, and e are correct. The presentation layer concerns itself with data representation, data compression, and data encryption. Because the session layer handles dialog management, answer c is incorrect. The transport layer handles data transmission, so answer d is incorrect.

Question 67

Answers a, c, and d are correct. The **ping** and **trace** commands verify routing by sending and receiving packets across the network. In order for the **telnet** command to be successful, packets must be sent and received properly, so it also verifies that packets are being routed. Although the **show interface** command displays the status of the interfaces on a router, it does not indicate whether packets are reaching their destination; therefore, answer b is incorrect.

Question 68

Answers a, b, and c are correct. RIP, IGRP, and OSPF are interior routing protocols used to communicate route information within an autonomous system. Answer d is incorrect because BGP is designed to communicate route information between autonomous systems; therefore, it is an exterior routing protocol.

Question 69

Answer c is correct. The **router rip** command enables RIP routing and the **network 172.23.0.0** command enables the router to advertise that network to other routers. Answers a and b are incorrect because the **router rip** command does not require an autonomous system or additional parameters. Answer d is incorrect because you must first enter routing protocol configuration mode before configuring a network to be advertised.

Question 70

Answer a is correct. CHAP uses a three-way handshake and transmits encrypted data between the remote and local hosts. Answer b is incorrect because DDR is not a PPP authentication protocol. Answer c is incorrect because PAP transmits authentication data in clear text from the remote host to the local host.

Glossary

Advanced distance vector protocol—A routing protocol that combines the strengths of distance vector and link state routing protocols. Cisco's EIGRP is considered an advanced distance vector protocol.

Application layer—The highest layer of the OSI model (layer 7). It is closest to the end user and selects appropriate network services to support end user applications such as email or FTP.

Area—See *autonomous system*.

ARP (Address Resolution Protocol)—ARP is used to map a known logical address to an unknown physical address. A device performs an ARP broadcast to identify the physical address of a destination device. This physical address is then stored in cache for later transmissions.

Autonomous system—A group of networks under common administration and sharing a routing strategy. Sometimes referred to as a *domain* or *area*.

Bandwidth—The available capacity of a network link over a physical medium.

BGP (Border Gateway Protocol)—An exterior routing protocol that exchanges route information between autonomous systems.

Boot field—The lowest four binary digits of a configuration register. The value of the boot field determines the order in which a router searches for Cisco IOS software.

BRI (basic rate interface)—An ISDN interface that contains two B channels and one D channel for circuit-switched communication for data, voice, and video.

Bridge—A device used to physically segment a LAN into multiple physical segments. A bridge uses a forwarding table to determine which frames need to be forwarded to specific segments. Bridges isolate local traffic to the originating physical segment, but forward all non-local and broadcast traffic.

Buffering—A method of flow control used by the transport layer that involves the memory buffers on the receiving hosts. The transport layer of the receiving system ensures that sufficient buffers are available and that data is not transmitted at a rate that exceeds the rate at which the receiving system can process it.

Carrier detect signal—A signal received on a router interface that indicates whether the physical layer connectivity is operating properly.

CDP (Cisco Discovery Protocol)—A Cisco proprietary protocol that operates at the data link layer. CDP enables network administrators to view a summary protocol and address information about other directly connected Cisco routers (and some Cisco switches).

Channel—A single communication path on a system. In some situations, channels can be multiplexed over a single connection.

CHAP (Challenge Handshake Authentication Protocol)—An authentication protocol for PPP that uses a three-way, encrypted handshake to force a remote host to identify itself to a local host.

CIDR (Classless Interdomain Routing)—Implemented as a solution to the rapid depletion of IP address space in the Internet and to minimize the number of routes on the Internet. CIDR provides a more efficient method of allocating IP address space by removing the concept of classes in IP addressing. CIDR enables routes to be summarized on powers-of-two boundaries, thus reducing multiple routes into a single prefix.

Classful addressing—Categorizes IP addresses into ranges that are used to create a hierarchy in the IP addressing scheme. The most common classes are A, B, and C, which can be identified by looking at the first three binary digits of an IP address.

CO (central office)—The local telephone company office where all local loops in an area connect.

Configuration register—A numeric value (typically displayed as hexadecimal) used to specify certain actions on a router.

Congestion—A situation that can occur during data transfer if one or more computers generate network traffic faster than it can be transmitted through the network.

Connectionless network services—A type of connection where devices do not maintain any type of acknowledgment services between them. Therefore, connectionless network services are not said to maintain a "virtual connection" between the sending and receiving devices.

Connection-oriented network services—A type of connection where devices provide acknowledgments to indicate the reception of data. Therefore, connection-oriented network services are said to maintain a "virtual connection" between the sending and receiving devices.

Console—A terminal attached directly to the router for configuring and monitoring the router.

Convergence—The process where all routers within an internetwork exchange route information and eventually agree on optimal routes through the internetwork.

Counting to infinity—A routing problem where the distance metric for a destination network is continually incremented because the internetwork has not fully converged.

CPE (Customer Premises Equipment)—Terminating equipment such as telephones or modems supplied by the service provider, installed at the customer site, and connected to the network.

CRC (Cyclic Redundancy Check)—An error-checking mechanism where the receiving node calculates a value based on the data it received and compares it to the value stored within the frame from the sending node.

CSMA/CD (carrier sense multi-access/collision detection)—A physical specification used by the Ethernet to provide contention-based frame transmission. CSMA/CD specifies that a sending device shares a physical transmission media and must listen to determine if a collision occurs after transmitting.

Cut-through switching—A method of forwarding frames based on the first six bytes contained in the frame. It provides higher throughput than store-and-forward switching because it requires only six bytes of data to make the forwarding decision. However, cut-through switching does not provide error checking like its counterpart store-and-forward switching.

DARPA (Defense Advanced Research Projects Agency)—A government agency designed to develop advanced defense capabilities. It is now known as simply ARPA.

DCE (data communications equipment)—The device at the network end of a user-to-network connection that provides a physical connection to the network, forwards traffic, and provides a clocking signal used to synchronize data transmission between the DCE and DTE devices.

DDR (dial-on-demand routing)—A technique where a router can initiate and terminate a circuit-switched connection over ISDN or telephone lines to meet network traffic demands.

De-encapsulation—The process by which a destination peer layer removes and reads the control information sent by the source peer layer in another network host.

Default mask—A binary or decimal representation of the number of bits used to identify an IP network. The Class of the IP address defines the default mask. A default mask is represented by four octets of binary digits. The mask can also be presented in dotted decimal notation.

Default route—A network route established (that usually points to another router) to receive and attempt to process all packets for which no route appears in the routing table.

Delay—The amount of time necessary to move a packet through the internetwork from source to destination.

Demarc—A point of demarcation between the carrier's equipment and the CPE.

Discard eligibility bit—A bit that can be set to indicate that a frame may be dropped, should congestion occur within the frame relay network.

Distance vector protocol—An interior routing protocol that relies upon distance and vector or direction to choose optimal paths. A distance vector protocol requires each router to periodically send all or a large part of its route table to its neighboring routers.

DLCI (data link connection identifier)—A value that specifies a PVC or SVC in a frame relay network.

DNS (Domain Name System)—A system used to translate fully qualified host names or computer names into IP addresses and vice versa.

Domain—See *autonomous system*.

Dotted decimal notation—A method of representing binary IP addresses in a decimal format. Dotted decimal notation represents the four octets of an IP address in four decimal values separated by decimal points.

DTE (data terminal equipment)—The device at the user end of the user-to-network connection that connects to a data network through a DCE device.

Dynamic route—A network route that adjusts automatically to changes within the internetwork.

EGP (Exterior Gateway Protocol)—An exterior routing protocol that exchanges route information between autonomous systems. EGP has become obsolete and is being replaced by BGP.

EIGRP (enhanced interior gateway routing protocol)—A Cisco-proprietary routing protocol that includes features of both distance vector and link state routing protocols. It is considered to be an advanced distance vector protocol.

Encapsulation—Generally speaking, the process of wrapping data in a particular protocol header. In the context of the OSI model, the process by which a source peer layer includes header and/or trailer control information with a PDU destined for its peer layer in another network host. The information encapsulated instructs the destination peer layer how to process the information.

EXEC—The user interface for executing Cisco router commands.

Exterior routing protocol—A routing protocol that conveys information between autonomous systems; it is widely used within the Internet. BGP is an example of an exterior routing protocol.

Flash—Router memory that stores the Cisco Internetwork Operating System image and associated microcode. Flash is erasable, reprogrammable ROM that retains its content when the router is powered down or restarts.

Flat routing protocol—A routing environment where all routers are considered peers and can communicate with any other router in the network as directly as possible. A flat routing protocol functions well in simple and predictable network environments.

Flow control—A mechanism that throttles back data transmission to ensure that a sending system does not overwhelm the receiving system with data.

Frame check sequence— Extra characters added to a frame for error control purposes. It is the result of a CRC.

Frame relay—A switched, data link layer protocol that supports multiple virtual circuits using HDLC encapsulation between connected devices.

Frame tagging—A method of "tagging" a frame with a unique user-defined VLAN. The process of tagging a frame allows VLANs to span multiple switches.

FTP (File Transfer Protocol)—A protocol used to copy a file from one host to another host, regardless of the physical hardware or operating system of each device. FTP identifies a client and server during the file transfer process. In addition, it provides a guaranteed transfer by using the services of TCP.

Full-duplex—A physical transmission process on a network device where one pair of wires transmits data, while another pair of wires receives data. Full-duplex transmission is achieved by eliminating the possibility of collisions on an Ethernet segment, thereby eliminating the need for a device to sense collisions.

Function—A term that refers to the different devices and hardware tasks they perform within ISDN.

Global configuration mode—A router mode that enables simple router configuration commands to be executed such as router names, banners, and passwords. Global configuration commands affect the whole router, rather than a single interface or component.

GNS (Get Nearest Server)—A request sent by an IPX client to locate the closest active server of a particular service. Depending on where the service can be located, either a server or a router can respond to the request.

Half-duplex—A physical transmission process whereby one pair is used to transmit information and the other pair is used to receive information or to sense collisions on a physical media. Half-duplex transmission is required on Ethernet segments with multiple devices.

Handshake—The process of one system making a request to another system prior to a connection being established. Handshakes occur during the establishment of a connection between two systems and address matters such as synchronization and connection parameters.

HDLC (high-level data link control)—A bit-oriented, synchronous data link layer protocol that specifies data encapsulation methods on serial links.

Header—Control information placed before the data during the encapsulation process.

Hierarchical routing protocol—A routing environment that relies upon several routers to comprise a backbone. Most traffic from non-backbone routers traverses the backbone routers (or at least travels to the backbone) in order to reach another non-backbone router. This is accomplished by breaking a network into a hierarchy of networks where each level is responsible for its own routing.

Hold-down—The state into which a route is placed so that routers will not advertise or accept updates for that route until a timer expires.

Hop count—The number of routers a packet passes through on its way to the destination network.

Host name—A logical name given to a router.

HSSI (high-speed serial interface)—A physical standard designed for serial connections that require high data transmission rates. The HSSI standard allows for high-speed communication that runs at speeds up to 52Mbps.

ICMP (Internet Control Message Protocol)—A protocol that communicates error messages and controls messages between devices. Thirteen different types of ICMP messages are defined. ICMP allows devices to check the status of other devices, to query the current time, and to perform other functions such as ping and traceroute.

IGRP (Interior Gateway Routing Protocol)—A Cisco-proprietary distance vector routing protocol that uses hop count as its metric.

Initial configuration dialog—The dialog used to configure a router the first time it is booted or when no configuration file exists. The initial configuration dialog is an optional process used to simplify the configuration process.

Integrated routing—A technique where a router routing multiple routed protocols shares resources. Rather than using several routing protocols to support multiple routed protocols, a network administrator can use a single routing protocol to support multiple routed protocols. EIGRP is an example of a routing protocol that supports integrated routing.

Interdomain router—A router using an exterior routing protocol such as BGP to exchange route information between autonomous systems.

Interfaces—Router components that provide the network connections where data packets move in and out of the router. Depending on the model of router, interfaces exist either on the motherboard or on separate, modular interface cards.

Interior routing protocol—A routing protocol that exchanges information within an autonomous system. RIP, IGRP, and OSPF are examples of interior routing protocols.

Intradomain router—A router using an interior routing protocol such as IGRP to convey route information with an autonomous system.

IP (Internet Protocol)—One of the many protocols maintained in the TCP/IP suite of protocols. IP is the transport mechanism for TCP, UDP, and ICMP data; it also provides the logical addressing necessary for complex routing activity.

IP extended access list—A way of filtering IP traffic on a router interface based on source and destination IP address or port, IP precedence field, TOS field, ICMP-type, ICMP-code, ICMP-message, IGMP-type, and TCP established connections.

IP standard access list—A way of filtering IP traffic on a router interface based on the source IP address or address range.

IPX (Internet Packet Exchange)—The layer 3 protocol used within NetWare to transmit data between servers and workstations.

IPX extended access list—A way of filtering IPX traffic on a router interface based on the source and destination IPX address or address range, IPX protocol, and source and destination sockets.

IPX SAP filter—A way of filtering SAP traffic on a router interface. SAP filters are used to filter SAP traffic origination or traffic destined for specific IPX addresses or address ranges.

IPX standard access list—A way of filtering IPX traffic on a router interface based on the source IPX address or address range.

ISDN (Integrated Services Digital Network)—A communication protocol offered by telephone companies that permits telephone networks to carry data, voice, and other traffic.

ISL (inter-switch link)—A protocol used to allow VLANs to span multiple switches. It is used between switches to communicate common VLANs between devices.

Keepalive frames—PDUs transmitted at the data link layer that indicate whether the proper frame type is configured.

LAN protocols—Protocols that identify layer 2 protocols used for the transmission of data within a LAN. The three most popular LAN protocols used today are Ethernet, token ring, and FDDI.

LCP (Link Control Protocol)—A protocol that configures, tests, maintains, and terminates PPP connections.

Link state packet—A broadcast packet that contains the status of a router's links or network interfaces.

Link state protocol—An interior routing protocol where each router sends only the state of its own network links across the network, but sends this information to every router within its autonomous system or area. This process enables routers to learn and maintain full knowledge of the network's exact topology and how it is interconnected.

LLC (logical link sub-layer)—A sub-layer of the data link layer. The LLC sub-layer provides the software functions of the data link layer.

LMI (Link Management Interface)—A set of enhancements to the Frame Relay protocol specifications.

Load—An indication of how busy a network resource is. CPU utilization and packets processed per second are two indicators of load.

Local loop—The line from the customer premises to the telephone company's CO.

Logical addressing—Network layer addressing is most commonly referred to as logical addressing versus the physical addressing of the data link layer. A logical address consists of two parts: the network part and the node part. Routers use the network part of the logical address to determine the best path to the network of a remote device. The node part of the logical address is used to identify the specific node to forward the packet on the destination network.

Logical AND—A process of comparing two sets of binary numbers to result in one value representing an IP address network. The logical AND is used to compare an IP address against its subnet mask to yield the IP subnet on which the IP address resides.

MAC (media access control layer)—A sub-layer of the data link layer that provides the hardware functions of the data link layer.

MAC address—A physical address used to uniquely define a device.

Metric—The relative cost of sending packets to a destination network over a specific network route. Examples of metrics include bandwidth, delay, and reliability.

MIB (Management Information Database)—A database that maintains statistics on certain data items. The protocol SNMP uses MIBs to query information about devices.

Multicasting—A process of using one IP address to represent a group of IP addresses. Multicasting is used to send messages to a subset of IP addresses in a network or networks.

Multipath routing protocol—A routing protocol that loads balances over multiple optimal paths to a destination network when the cost of the paths are equal.

Multiplexing—A method of flow control used by the transport layer in which it combines application conversations over a single channel by interleaving packets from different segments and transmitting them.

NBMA (nonbroadcast multiaccess)—A multiaccess network that either does not support broadcasts or for which sending broadcasts is not feasible.

NCP (Network Control Program)—A collection of protocols that establish and configure different network layer protocols for use over a PPP connection.

NCP (NetWare Core Protocol)—A collection of upper-layer server routines that satisfy requests from other applications.

NetBIOS (Network Basic Input/Output System)—A common session-layer interface specification from IBM and Microsoft that enables applications to request lower-level network services.

NetWare—A popular local area network (LAN) operating system developed by Novell Corporation that runs on a variety of different types of LANs.

NetWare shell—An upper-layer NetWare service that determines whether application calls require additional network services.

Network discovery—When a router starts up, this is the process by which it learns of its internetwork environment and begins to communicate with other routers.

NIC (network interface card)—A board that provides network communication capabilities to and from a network host.

NLSP (NetWare Link State Protocol)—A link state routing protocol used for routing IPX.

NOS (Network Operating System)—A term used to describe distributed file systems that support file sharing, printing, database access, and other similar applications.

NVRAM (non-volatile random access memory)—A memory area of the router that stores permanent information, such as the router's backup configuration file. The contents of NVRAM are retained when the router is powered down or restarts.

OSI (Open Systems Interconnect) model—A layered networking framework developed by the International Organization for Standardization. The OSI model describes seven layers that correspond to specific networking functions.

OSPF (open shortest path first)—A hierarchical link state routing protocol that was developed as a successor to RIP.

Packet switching—A process by which a router moves a packet from one interface to another.

PAP (Password Authentication Protocol)—An authentication protocol for PPP that uses a two-way, unencrypted handshake to enable a remote host to identify itself to a local host.

Parallelization—A method of flow control used by the transport layer in which it combines multiple channels and increases the effective bandwidth for the upper layers.

Path length—The sum of the costs of each link traversed up to the destination network. Some routing protocols refer to path length as *hop count*.

PDU (protocol data unit)—A unit of measure that refers to data that is transmitted between two peer layers within different network devices. Segments, packets, and frames are examples of PDUs.

Peer-to-peer communication—A form of communication that occurs between the same layers of two different network hosts.

Physical connection—A direct physical connection between two devices.

Ping—A tool for testing IP connectivity between two devices. A ping sends multiple IP packets between a sending and a destination device. The destination device responds with an ICMP packet to notify the sending device of its existence.

POP (Point of Presence)—A physical location where a carrier has installed equipment to interconnect with a local exchange carrier.

PPP (Point-to-Point Protocol)—A standard protocol the enables router-to-router and host-to-network connectivity over synchronous and asynchronous circuits such as telephone lines.

Presentation layer—Layer 6 of the OSI model. The presentation layer is concerned with how data is represented to the application layer.

PRI (primary rate interface)—An ISDN interface that contains 23 B channels and one D channel for circuit-switched communication for data, voice, and video. In North American and Japan, a PRI contains 23 B and one D channel. In Europe, it contains 30 B channels and one D channel.

Privileged mode—An extensive administrative and management mode on a Cisco router. This router mode permits testing, debugging, and commands to modify the router's configuration.

Protocol—A formal description of a set of rules and conventions that defines how devices on a network must exchange information.

PSTN (Public Switched Telephone Network)—A term used to identify the circuit-switching facilities maintained for voice analog communication.

PVC (Permanent Virtual Circuit)—A virtual circuit that is permanently established and ready for use.

RAM (random access memory)—A memory area of a router that serves as a working storage area. RAM contains data such as routing tables, various types of cache and buffers, as well as input and output queues and the router's active configuration file. The contents of RAM are lost when the router is powered down or restarts.

RARP (Reverse Address Resolution Protocol)—RARP provides the exact opposite mapping from ARP. RARP maps a known physical address to a logical address. Diskless machines that do not have a configured IP address when started typically use RARP. RARP requires the existence of a server that maintains a physical to logical address mapping.

Reference point—An identifier of the logical interfaces between functions within ISDN.

Reliability—A metric that allows the network administrator to arbitrarily assign a numeric value to indicate a reliability factor for the link. The reliability metric is simply a method to capture an administrator's experience with a given network link.

RIP (Routing Information Protocol)—A widely-used distance vector routing protocol that uses hop count as its metric.

ROM (read-only memory)—An area of router memory that contains a version of the Cisco Internetwork Operating System image—usually an older version with minimal functionality. ROM also stores the bootstrap program and power-on diagnostic programs.

ROM monitor—A mode on a Cisco router where the software executing is maintained in ROM.

ROM monitor mode (RXBOOT)—A router maintenance mode that enables router recovery functions when the IOS file in Flash has been erased or is corrupt.

Route aggregation—A process of combining multiple IP address networks into one superset of IP address networks. Route aggregation is implemented to reduce the number of routing table entries required to accurately forward IP packets in an internetwork.

Route poisoning—A routing technique where a router immediately marks a network as unreachable as soon as it detects the network is down. The router broadcasts the update throughout the network and maintains this poisoned route in its route table for a specified period of time.

Route table—An area of a router's memory that stores the network topology information used to determine optimal routes. Route tables contain information such as destination network, next hop, and an associated metric.

Routed protocol—A routed protocol provides the information required for the routing protocol to determine the topology of the internetwork and the best path to a destination. The routed protocol provides this information in the form of a logical address and other fields within a packet. The information contained in the packet allows the router to direct user traffic. The most common routed protocols include IP and IPX.

Router modes—Modes that enable the execution of specific router commands and functions. User, privileged, and setup are examples of router modes that allow you to perform certain tasks.

Routing algorithm—Well-defined rules that aid routers in the collection of route information and determination of the optimal path.

Routing loop—An event where two or more routers have not yet converged and are propagating their inaccurate route tables. In addition, they most likely are still switching packets based on their inaccurate route tables.

Routing protocols—Routing protocols use algorithms to generate a list of paths to a particular destination and the cost associated with that path. Routers use routing protocols to communicate among each other the best route to use to reach a particular destination.

Routing tables—A routing table is maintained by a router and identifies a destination network and the next hop that a packet should take to reach that destination network.

RS-232—RS-232 is a physical standard used to identify cabling types for serial data transmission for speeds of 19.2Kbps or less. RS-232 connects two devices communicating over a serial link with either a 25-pin (DB-25) or 9-pin (DB-9) serial interface. RS-232 is now known as EIA/TIA-232.

Running configuration file—The executing configuration file on a router.

SAP (Service Advertisement Protocol)—An IPX protocol that serves as a means to inform network clients of available network resources and services.

SDLC (synchronous data link control)—SDLC is primarily used for terminal to mainframe communication. SDLC requires that one device is labeled as the primary station and all other devices are labeled as secondary stations. Communication can only occur between the primary station and the secondary station.

Session—A dialogue between presentation layers on two or more different systems.

Session layer—Layer 5 of the OSI model. It is concerned with establishing, managing, and terminating sessions between applications on different network devices.

Setup mode—The router mode triggered on startup if no configuration file resides in NVRAM.

Shortest path first—See *link state protocol*.

Single path routing protocol—A routing protocol that only uses one optimal path to a destination.

Sliding windows—A method by which TCP dynamically sets the window size during a connection, allowing either device involved in the communication to slow down the sending data rate based on the other device's capacity.

SMTP (Simple Mail Transfer Protocol)—SMTP is used to pass mail messages between devices. It uses TCP connections to pass the email between hosts.

Socket—The combination of the sending and destination TCP port numbers and the sending and destination IP addresses defines a socket. Therefore, a socket can be used to uniquely define any UDP or TCP connection.

Spanning tree protocol—The spanning tree protocol is used to eliminate all circular routes in a bridged or switched environment while maintaining redundancy. Circular routes are not desirable in layer 2 networks because of the forwarding mechanism employed at this layer.

Split horizon—A routing mechanism that prevents a router from sending information it received about a network back to its neighbor that originally sent the information. This mechanism is very useful in preventing routing loops.

SPX (Sequenced Packet Exchange)—The layer 4 protocol used within NetWare to ensure reliable, connection-oriented services.

Startup configuration file—The backup configuration file on a router.

Static route—A network route that is manually entered into the route table. Static routes function well in very simple and predictable network environments.

Store-and-forward switching—A method of forwarding frames by copying the entire frame into the buffer of the switch and making a forwarding decision. Store-and-forward switching does not achieve the same throughput as its counterpart, cut-through switching, because it copies the entire frame into the buffer, versus only the first six bytes. However, store-and-forward switching provides error checking that is not provided by cut-through switching.

Subinterface—One of possibly many virtual interfaces on a single physical interface.

Subnetting—A process of splitting a classful range of IP addresses into multiple IP networks to allow more flexibility in IP addressing schemes. Subnetting overcame the limitation of address classes and allowed network administrators the flexibility to assign multiple networks with one class of IP addresses.

Switch—A switch provides increase port density and forwarding capabilities when compared to bridges. The increased port densities of switches allow LANs to be micro-segmented, thereby increasing the amount of bandwidth delivered to each device.

TCP (Transmission Control Protocol)—One of the many protocols maintained in the TCP/IP suite of protocols. TCP provides a connection-oriented and reliable service to the applications that use its services.

TCP three-way handshake—The three-way handshake is a process by which TCP connections send acknowledgments between each other when setting up a TCP connection.

TCP windowing—A method of increasing or reducing the number of acknowledgments required between data transmissions. This allows devices to throttle the rate at which data is transmitted.

Telnet—A standard protocol that provides a virtual terminal. Telnet enables a network administrator to remotely connect to a router.

TFTP (Trivial File Transfer Protocol)—A protocol used to copy files from one device to another. TFTP is a stripped down version of the FTP.

Tick—A measure of network delay time—about $1/18^{th}$ of a second. In RIP version 2, ticks serve as the primary value used in determining best path.

Traceroute—An IP service that allows a user to utilize the services of UDP and ICMP to identify the number of hops between sending and receiving devices and the paths taken from the sending to the receiving devices. Traceroute also provides the IP address and DNS name of each hop. Typically, traceroute is used to troubleshoot IP connectivity between two devices.

Trailer—Control information placed after the data during the encapsulation process.

Transport layer—Layer 4 of the OSI model is positioned between the upper and lower layers of the model. It is concerned with segmenting upper-layer applications, establishing end-to-end connectivity through the network, sending segments from one host to another, and ensuring the reliable transport of data.

UDP (User Datagram Protocol)—One of the many protocols maintained in the TCP/IP suite of protocols. UDP is a layer 4 best effort delivery protocol and therefore maintains connectionless network services.

User mode—A display-only mode on a Cisco router. Only limited information about the router can be viewed within this router mode; no configuration changes are permitted.

V.35—V.35 is a physical standard used to identify cabling types for serial data transmission for speeds up to 4Mbps. The V.35 standard was created by the International Telecommunication Union-Telecommunication Standardization Sector (ITU-T).

Virtual connection—A logical connection between two devices created through the use of acknowledgments.

VLAN (virtual local area network)—A VLAN is a method of assigning devices to specific LANs based on the port they attach to on a switch, not by physical location. VLANs extend the flexibility of LANs by allowing devices to be assigned to specific LANs on a port-by-port basis versus a device basis.

VLSM (Variable Length Subnet Masking)—VLSM provides more flexibility in assigning IP address space. (A common problem with routing protocols was the necessity of all devices in a given routing protocol domain to use the same subnet mask.) Routing protocols that support VLSM allow administrators to assign IP networks with different subnet masks. This increased flexibility saves IP address space because administrators can assign IP networks based on the number of hosts on each network.

WAN protocols—WAN protocols identify layer 2 protocols used for the transmission of data within a WAN.

Well-known ports—A set of ports between 1 and 1,023 that are reserved for specific TCP/IP protocols and services.

Index

CORIOLIS HELP CENTER

Here at The Coriolis Group, we strive to provide the finest customer service in the technical education industry. We're committed to helping you reach your certification goals by assisting you in the following areas.

Talk to the Authors

We'd like to hear from you! Please refer to the "How to Use This Book" section in the "Introduction" of every Exam Cram guide for our authors' individual email addresses.

Web Page Information

The Certification Insider Press Web page provides a host of valuable information that's only a click away. For information in the following areas, please visit us at:

www.coriolis.com/cip/default.cfm

- Titles and other products
- Book content updates
- Roadmap to Certification Success guide
- New Adaptive Testing changes
- New Exam Cram Live! seminars
- New Certified Crammer Society details
- Sample chapters and tables of contents
- Manuscript solicitation
- Special programs and events

Contact Us by Email

Important addresses you may use to reach us at The Coriolis Group.

eci@coriolis.com

To subscribe to our FREE, bi-monthly online newsletter, *Exam Cram Insider*. Keep up to date with the certification scene. Included in each *Insider* are certification articles, program updates, new exam information, hints and tips, sample chapters, and more.

techsupport@coriolis.com

For technical questions and problems with CD-ROMs. Products broken, battered, or blown-up? Just need some installation advice? Contact us here.

ccs@coriolis.com

To obtain membership information for the *Certified Crammer Society*, an exclusive club for the certified professional. Get in on members-only discounts, special information, expert advice, contests, cool prizes, and free stuff for the certified professional. Membership is FREE. Contact us and get enrolled today!

cipq@coriolis.com

For book content questions and feedback about our titles, drop us a line. This is the good, the bad, and the questions address. Our customers are the best judges of our products. Let us know what you like, what we could do better, or what question you may have about any content. Testimonials are always welcome here, and if you send us a story about how an Exam Cram guide has helped you ace a test, we'll give you an official Certification Insider Press T-shirt.

custserv@coriolis.com

For solutions to problems concerning an order for any of our products. Our staff will promptly and courteously address the problem. Taking the exams is difficult enough. We want to make acquiring our study guides as easy as possible.

Book Orders & Shipping Information

orders@coriolis.com

To place an order by email or to check on the status of an order already placed.

coriolis.com/bookstore/default.cfm

To place an order through our online bookstore.

1.800.410.0192

To place an order by phone or to check on an order already placed.

CERTIFIED CRAMMER SOCI[ETY]

PHI SLAMMA CRAMMA

A breed apart, a cut above the rest—a true professional. Highly skilled and superbly trained, certified IT professionals are unquestionably the world's most elite computer experts. In an effort to appropriately recognize this privileged crowd, The Coriolis Group is proud to introduce the Certified Crammer Society. If you are a certified IT professional, it is our pleasure to invite you to become a Certified Crammer Society member.

Membership is free to all certified professionals and benefits include a membership kit that contains your official membership card and official Certified Crammer Society denim ball cap em[bla]zoned with the Cert[ified] Crammer Society cres[t] proudly displaying [the] Crammer motto "P[hi] Slamma Cramma"—an[d] featuring a genuine leather bill. The kit also includes your password to the Certified Crammers-Only Web site containing monthly discreet messages designed to provide you with advance notification about certification testing information, special book excerpts, and inside industry news not found anywhere else; monthly Crammers-Only discounts on selected Coriolis titles; *Ask the Series Editor* Q and A column; cool contests with great prizes; and more.

GUIDELINES FOR MEMBERSHIP

Registration is free to professionals certified in Microsoft, A+, or Oracle DBA. Coming soon: Sun Java, Novell, and Cisco. Send or email your contact information and proof of your certification (test scores, membership card, or official letter) to:

Certified Crammer Society Membership Chairperson
THE CORIOLIS GROUP, LLC
14455 North Hayden Road, Suite 220, Scottsdale, Arizona 85260-6949
Fax: 480.483.0193 • Email: ccs@coriolis.com

APPLICATION

Name:

Society Alias:

Choose a secret code name to correspond with us and other Crammer Society members. Please use no more than eight characters.

Address:

Email: